Faith and the Future of the Countryside

Faith and the Future of the Countryside

Pastoral and theological perspectives on rural sustainability

Edited by
Alan Smith
and
Jill Hopkinson

CANTERBURY
PRESS
Norwich

© The contributors 2012

First published in 2012 by the Canterbury Press Norwich
Editorial office
13–17 Long Lane,
London, EC1A 9PN, UK

Canterbury Press is an imprint of Hymns Ancient & Modern Ltd
(a registered charity)
13A Hellesdon Park Road, Norwich,
Norfolk, NR6 5DR, UK

www.canterburypress.co.uk

British Library Cataloguing in Publication data

A catalogue record for this book is available
from the British Library

978 1 84825 117 5

Originated by The ManilaTypesetting Company
Printed and bound in Great Britain by
CPI Group (UK) Ltd., Croydon, CR0 4YY

Contents

CONTENTS

About the contributors

Professor Elizabeth Dowler is part of the Social Policy Group in the Department of Sociology of the University of Warwick. She is a Registered Public Health Nutritionist who works on the social and policy aspects of the food system. She was a Senior Marie Curie Research Fellow at University College Dublin and is a Director member of the Food Ethics Council UK. She is a member of several research steering groups and committees for the Food Standards Agency and Defra. Elizabeth is a member of the Iona Community. She is writing in a personal capacity.

Dr Edward P. Echlin is an ecological theologian who has lectured in universities and theological colleges. He is author of numerous articles and seven books, including *Climate and Christ: A Prophetic Alternative* (Columba Press, 2010). Edward is an organic fruit and vegetable grower with a special interest in theology and food security. He is currently Honorary Research Fellow at Leeds Trinity University College, and Visiting Scholar at Sarum College, Salisbury.

Dr Tim Gibson is the author of *Church and Countryside: Insights from Rural Theology* (SCM Press, 2010). He is a writer, journalist and lecturer, based in rural Somerset. His work has appeared in a variety of publications, such as *The Daily Telegraph, The Independent* and *The Western Morning News*, and he is a frequent contributor to a number of magazines. He currently teaches at the South West Ministry Training Course and the Southern Theological Education and Training Scheme, where he is also Director of the MA programme.

Revd Dr Albert Jewell is a Methodist minister of nearly 50 years' standing who in his last post served as pastoral director of Methodist Homes for the Aged. After retirement to Leeds he completed his PhD on the sources of well-being in a sample of 500 older Methodists. He has spoken and published widely on the spirituality of ageing and is currently editing a book on Spirituality, Personhood and Dementia. He is vice-chair of the Christian Council on Ageing and editor of its biannual *Dementia Newsletter*.

Revd Canon Jeremy Martineau OBE, has been Agricultural Chaplain and Diocesan Rural Officer in Carlisle Diocese, Rural Adviser in the Bristol Diocese and was National Rural Officer for the Church of England during 1990–2003. He was joint secretary of the Archbishops' Commission on Rural Areas and an author of *Faith in the Countryside*. He is author/editor of several books on rural ministry and mission. He helped establish the National Churches Tourism Group, now the Churches Tourism Association. He is currently Director of the Centre for Studies in Rural Ministry and Chair of the Tourism Group of St David's Diocese.

Revd Lorna Murray is a Methodist minister who for almost 20 years was employed as a Mental Health Chaplain within the NHS. For the past four years she has been involved specifically in rural mental health. She is faith groups representative on Choose Life's [suicide prevention strategy] Remote and Rural Working Group, and mental health representative in the Church of Scotland's Rural Strategy Team. She also works in South India, teaching counselling skills and learning about rural issues, including the benefits of partnership between health and community development workers.

Dr Anne Richards is National Adviser for mission theology, new religious movements and alternative spirituality for the Archbishops' Council of the Church of England. She is the convenor of the ecumenical Mission Theology Advisory Group producing resources for the Church on spirituality, theology, reconciliation, evangelism and mission. She is a prolific writer and speaker, with a particular interest in rural issues. Author of *The Grass is Always Greener* (Church House Publishing, 2002) and contributor to *Re-Shaping*

Rural Ministry (Canterbury Press, 2009), she also writes regularly for *Country Way*.

Professor Mark Shucksmith OBE is Professor of Planning at Newcastle University and is a board member of the Commission for Rural Communities. Previously he was Co-Director of the Arkleton Centre for Rural Development Research and of the Scottish Centre for Research on Social Justice, University of Aberdeen. He chaired the Committee of Inquiry into Crofting and was a member of the Affordable Rural Housing Commission. He has directed numerous research projects and is a prolific author. His main areas of research include rural development, social exclusion in rural areas, agricultural change and pluriactivity, and rural policy. In 2010 he was elected to the Academy of Social Sciences.

Revd Canon Graham Usher is the Rector of Hexham Abbey in Northumberland and Area Dean of Hexham Deanery. He was an ecologist before training for ordination and is a Secretary of State appointee to the Northumberland National Park Authority and Chairman of the Forestry Commission's North East Regional Advisory Committee.

Professor Neil Ward is Dean of the Faculty of Social Sciences, University of East Anglia. He began his academic career at University College London, has held chairs at Newcastle and Leeds Universities, and was Director of Newcastle University's Centre for Rural Economy during 2004–08. He has also worked for periods on secondment to the Cabinet Office and as an adviser to the Economic and Social Research Council. His research interests have been in rural economies, agricultural, environmental and regional policy and the governance of environmental controversies. He is currently working on experimental participatory approaches to flood-risk modelling and management.

Revd Canon Dr Dagmar Winter is the Rural Affairs Officer for the Diocese of Newcastle, alongside being Priest-in-Charge of Kirkwhelpington with Kirkharle, Kirkheaton and Cambo, and Area Dean. She is Vice-Chair of the Northumberland Uplands LEADER Local Action Group, Chaplain to Farm Crisis Network

Northumberland, and a member of General Synod of the Church of England and of its Rural Affairs Group. In her spare time she attempts to pursue her academic interest in New Testament studies.

Canon Professor Michael Winter OBE is Director of the Centre for Rural Policy at the University of Exeter. He has researched and written widely on issues of land and environmental policy and management, and rural sociology and politics, holding numerous research grants from research councils and government. He is a member of Defra's Science Advisory Council and was one of the founding Commissioners of the Commission of Rural Communities. He is an Anglican Reader and a lay Canon of Exeter Cathedral.

Acknowledgements

The editors are extremely grateful to the contributors to this volume, who have worked creatively within a long-term editorial process. Our thanks are particularly due to Dagmar Winter, Nick Read and Jeremy Martineau for the extensive work they did on editing some of the final texts.

There were 34 papers contributed to the *Faith and the Future of the Countryside* conference in November 2010. The papers here were selected to reflect the breadth of issues important at the time. No implication should be drawn from omission from this collection.

Many things have changed in the years since the publication of *Faith in the Countryside* in 1990. This collection is offered as a further contribution to the debate. It is not the first set of thoughts on the future of the countryside nor will it be the last.

Introduction

Christian Churches in the UK have always played a significant role in the countryside. This was highlighted in the seminal report, *Faith in the Countryside*, published in 1990. The report was the result of more than two years of work by the Archbishops' Commission on Rural Areas (ACORA), chaired by Lord Prior. Members were drawn from industry, rural development and agriculture, the emerging environmental lobby and from four Christian denominations.

The Commissioners spent much time listening to the realities of rural community life and church life. Their report had a major impact on the life of the Church at the time and was taken seriously by Government, academic institutions and civil society organizations. Their work opened doors and enabled partnerships to be formed by the Church with key organizations such as the county Rural Community Councils, the National Farmers Union and other agricultural bodies, and with government both local and national.

To mark the twentieth anniversary of the publication of *Faith in the Countryside* a major ecumenical conference was held at The Hayes, Swanwick, Derbyshire in November 2010. It drew together more than 200 academics, church leaders, rural officers and agricultural chaplains, local church clergy and lay people to reflect on the future for rural communities through the lens of sustainability. Its purpose was to strengthen rural churches and the relationships between the church and those organizations also working in the countryside. It aimed to reinforce the commitment of churches to a meaningful and engaged presence in rural communities in a way which undergirded mission and ministry. This was based on the conviction that rural communities have great potential for the future and churches are a vital part of this.

There are at least 15,000 churches in rural areas of England, belonging to at least seven denominations (of these 9639 are Anglican, approximately 3000 Methodist, and around 400 Baptist churches).[1] With a presence in almost every rural community, churches are a living part of the countryside. Generally a much higher proportion of people in the countryside are actively involved in their local church than in urban areas. But rural churches have their problems and challenges. Sustaining buildings and finding officers can be difficult, especially for smaller congregations. Ministry in rural areas has its joys, and the close relationship between church and community in many places brings with it opportunities for new contacts, service and mission that are not present elsewhere. However, the complexities of engaging in ministry with multiple congregations and buildings should not be underestimated and there must be better support and training to enable people to respond to the new ways of doing things required by the modern rural church.

Rural communities are popular and good places to live. Many people have a long cherished dream of escaping to live in the countryside. Statistically, if you live in a rural area you are less likely to be unemployed, have a low income, be in receipt of benefits, be without qualifications or skills, have a baby before the age of 16, die prematurely, be anxious, homeless or live in fear of crime. Escalating house prices in villages and hamlets over the last 20 years confirms this desire for many to live in the countryside. The question is whether they want to truly be a part of a rural community or just use it as a dormitory.

State of the countryside

We have come a long way in 20 years. Rural populations continue to grow by around 80,000 each year. The population of rural England is now around 9.8 million, roughly 19% of the population of England as a whole (Commission for Rural Communities, 2010, p. 16). However, there is a significant loss of younger generations from rural communities, who leave to continue education, find work and housing.

Rural communities contain ageing populations who can make a big contribution to the life and vibrancy of a place. Older people, however, also need more health care, social care and other public services which cost more to deliver in rural areas.

Rural England can be described as having economies rather than a single economy due to the complicated interrelationships between urban and rural areas. Roughly five million employees live in rural England – 20% of England's workforce (Commission for Rural Communities, 2010, p. 106) – many of whom commute to work in larger towns and cities. Those working in urban areas have higher incomes than in equivalent jobs in rural areas. In many rural settlements buying or even renting property is out of the question for even those on moderate incomes and especially for those reliant on local jobs often paid at the minimum wage.

One quarter of all VAT-registered businesses are in rural areas (roughly 500,000 enterprises), some of whom trade nationally and internationally, relying on ICT (information and communication technology) to do business (Commission for Rural Communities, 2010, p. 124). In 2007 businesses in rural areas contributed £144 billion to national Gross Value Added (GVA) productivity – around 14% of the total (Commission for Rural Communities, 2010, p. 103).

Rural areas are particularly reliant on the public sector for jobs, especially in more remote, sparsely populated areas, where up to one third of jobs are in this sector as opposed to one quarter in less sparsely populated rural areas. Large cuts in public sector jobs will have a disproportionately large impact on some of these areas.

Food production

Agriculture is still vitally important. Farming is responsible for the maintenance of millions of hectares of land and for the production of 60% of the UK's food needs overall and 73% for indigenous products (Global Food Security Project, 2010). Food manufacturing is the UK's single largest manufacturing sector. The food and drink supply chain is a major part of the UK economy, accounting for 7% of GDP, employing 3.7 million people (Cabinet Office, 2008, p. iii). The agri-food sector generates £80 billion annually (Defra, 2010). In 2005, UK meat, milk and eggs had a market value of around £8 billion, and were produced from more than 150,000 farm businesses (Global Food Security Project, 2010).

Agriculture already offers significant additional public benefits such as maintenance of landscape, habitat creation and enhancement, and species protection. Farming can offer a wide range of ecosystem services in order to help mitigate the impact of climate change, such as carbon sequestration, water quality and flood alleviation.

The spiritual dimension of landscape and environment should not be forgotten. The natural world is not just the plaything or resource base for humans. Land, landscape and biodiversity all have a spiritual element associated with them, for people of all faiths and none. This supports the view that humans should be seen as much a part of the natural world as plants and animals are, and not set apart. This understanding of the intricate relationship between humans and nature needs to be more strongly reflected in policy and decision making so that they do not happen in isolation from each other. Both are part of an holistic whole.

Disadvantage

Rural areas are diverse places and no one set of statistics or descriptive words can adequately address the great differences between particular places or larger geographic areas. However, one major factor is the difference between household incomes, with great wealth and great poverty existing side by side in many rural communities. Approximately one fifth of rural households live at or below the poverty line. The more sparsely populated areas tend to have higher proportions of households on low incomes, with urban areas still having the highest proportions (Commission for Rural Communities, 2010, pp. 86–9). In rural areas these disadvantaged households are dispersed, and tend not to be easily identifiable. This means that policies to tackle disadvantage in rural areas are difficult to formulate and implement, with the risk that those in greatest need receive the least help. It is these groups of people – some of whom are single, pensioners, or families with young children – that are at the greatest risk. It is these groups that churches need to be even more aware of within their midst.

Existing public transport services, limited as they are in the countryside, have been subject to early spending cuts, and this now means that it is the most vulnerable in society, without access to their own transport, who are further excluded from easy access to services such as health care and unemployment support. The relentless targeting of benefits announced in the 2010 and 2011 budgets and the Comprehensive Spending Review (CSR) in 2010 put pressure on the lowest income households who have less ability to cut their expenditure and limited options for employment, particularly in the remotest rural areas. Time-limited benefits may encourage the few who need it to find work, but will simply put additional pressure on those who are genuinely in need and perhaps are only seeking help for a short period of time.

Affordable housing

Homelessness is not just confined to towns; lack of affordable housing is characteristic of many rural parts of England. The affordability gap between wages and house prices over the past decade has widened in every rural district (National Housing Federation, 2011). The average price of a home in the countryside is over £40,000 more than in towns and cities (Commission for Rural Communities, 2010). Added to this, people living in rural areas spend 9%–19% more on everyday requirements than people in urban areas (Joseph Rowntree Foundation, 2010). Three quarters of a million people are now on waiting lists for an affordable home in rural England, and 7,600 are registered as homeless (National Housing Federation, 2011). For rural communities, the lack of affordable housing not only impacts on individuals but also on the future of whole villages, in terms of their ability to sustain essential local services and generate local employment.

Faith in the Countryside recommended that receipts from the sale of council houses should be kept by local authorities to fund the building of new rented housing. This was not implemented by the then Government and has not been since. The announcement in the 2010 CSR that councils will be able to keep their income from rented property and use it to maintain homes for current and future tenants is a step in the right direction in retaining a good-quality stock of housing for those who need it. However, other policies, such as the 50% cut in the capital investment for the building of new affordable homes, will have a serious impact on the growing numbers of households in rural England on local authority waiting lists. At the proposed new rate of building of an average of 37,500 new affordable homes in England each year, to cover both rural and urban areas, rural households are unlikely to be housed in the next quarter of a century.

Within the localism agenda the requirement for neighbour-hood plans and the opportunity for communities to use the 'right to' powers to challenge to deliver services, to list and buy assets of community value and to build will allow local communities to have more influence over their own future, with the ability to re-flect local needs. However, the need for neighbourhood plans to conform to the local plan prepared by the local authority will inevi-tably limit options in some places. The use of referenda to approve new developments such as affordable housing (provided through, for example neighbourhood development orders) has the poten-tial to be extremely divisive in many settlements and may prevent any development of any kind. It is important that the countryside is economically competitive and socially inclusive. We wait to see whether the proposals for the New Homes Bonus, to give a sum of money to councils related to the council tax for each new house built, will unlock the logjam in building more affordable housing.

Changes to housing benefit rules will make it more difficult for many lower-paid people to live in expensive rural areas. More seri-ously, it may contribute to some parts of the countryside becoming monochrome middle-class areas surrounded by concentrations of people on low income, in towns and urban fringe estates. There is concern that placing a time limit on the duration of a tenancy for those needing council housing, or charging up to 80% of local market rent will also put pressure on the most disadvantaged or vulnerable rural households. With limited tenure and significantly higher rents, families will lose their long-term security and be in danger of losing their social networks and contacts if forced to move. This would, at a stroke, remove from rural communities exactly those longer-standing residents who are likely to be the focus of Big Society initiatives. The long-term sustainability of rural communities is directly related to retaining and encouraging young families and young people to remain there to live and work. Mixed communities are the greatest potential for Big Society-style mutuality and self-help.

Big rural Society

Faith in the Countryside lamented the growth of individualism, even in 1990, and suggested that it was affecting and destroying community life in rural areas. The report stated that some national government policies were eroding community life in rural areas, and that individualism and inappropriate public policy were becoming issues of justice, with the need to offer protection for the disadvantaged. In the years since *Faith in the Countryside* was published, rural society has changed in many ways but this underlying issue remains the same. Isolation remains a challenge; rural churches already do much to tackle issues of isolation and stress, but more may be needed.

The Government's desire to develop a Big Society will have many implications and create many opportunities for churches. The Big Society is about local people taking action for themselves. This represents a change from expecting local and national government to make the first moves to engage with local communities. The onus will be on local communities to initiate local debate and then negotiate with local government on how their aspirations and practical ideas can be delivered.

The Localism Act has been designed to support initiatives within the Big Society. For example, up to 5000 Community organizers will be trained to work in their local areas to deliver the Big Society agenda. The creation of new community groups is being encouraged, with the opportunity to create mutual societies, co-ops and social enterprises in order for communities to take advantage of the right to buy (assets of community value) and the right to challenge (to run public services). The implications of the CSR will mean that for many communities this will be an essential reality not a 'nice' added extra to life. However, the charitable sector may not be able to fill the gap with cuts to grants from local government and a probable reduction in charitable giving. The people served and supported by these organizations will have few if any alternative sources of support. Speaking in October 2010, Dame Suzi Leather, Chair of the Charity Commission, said: 'It's questionable whether the voluntary and charity sector will be able to fill all the gaps left by cuts to public services . . . In many cases, they have already been that public service.' (*The Independent*, 2010).

Baroness Warsi, Conservative Party Chairman, in her address to the Church of England Bishops in September 2010 commented that the 2008 Citizenship Survey stated that those who are religiously observant are more likely to volunteer and give to charity than their non-believing or non-practising counterparts. She went on to say: 'We must foster a new culture of social responsibility – not by legislation but by example and collaboration' (Warsi, 2010). However, the activities that churches provide for the wider community, the creative use of buildings and the informal actions of congregation members are already making a significant contribution to the Big Society in rural areas and elsewhere.

The Big Society concept includes much which commends it to the church. Within the core concept is a move away from the dominant emphasis on the individual to a focus on the importance of the person in community. The emphasis that the Big Society places on neighbourliness and mutual support is a welcome development. Encouraging problem-solving at the most local level may be particularly helpful in addressing difficult issues. It may also ultimately offer encouragement for some people to think of themselves as citizens rather than just consumers.

Implicit within the Big Society is the question: Who is my neighbour? If 'Big' is taken seriously then neighbour is an inclusive concept within any community. A narrow view of neighbour will mean that those who are excluded now will remain excluded, and the ability to respond to new groups and needs will not be grasped by anyone. The challenge is to equip those who have the skills and ability to respond to the Big Society to do so within a broad concept of neighbour encompassing the unfamiliar as well as those who are 'like us'. Churches have a major role to play here – being organizations that already try to support and resource the most excluded in society. It is likely that all churches – wherever they are and whatever their size – will need in future to respond to the needs of the poorest in society more than they are now.

Churches have much that can be contributed to the Big Society:

1 Buildings – with a presence in almost every rural community, the church building can offer a meeting place for the whole community, and with appropriate adaptation could be a place for a shop, Post Office, IT training facility, tourist information centre, older persons' and children's facilities among many other things.
2 Volunteers – members of rural church congregations already volunteer within, organize and lead a wide range of other community organizations. However, as with other rural organizations, many volunteers are already over-committed and are ageing.
3 Partnership working – through the skills and initiatives of their members, rural churches have the potential to work in partnership with other community organizations and with local government to tackle specific issues.
4 Social interaction and care – rural churches organize events and activities that offer a place for social interaction that starts to address issues of isolation and loneliness. Formal and informal pastoral care and visiting are an important part of ensuring that a community supports the most vulnerable.

5 Spirituality and worship – regular opportunities for the community to worship together as a whole.

However, government locally and nationally needs to recognize that churches are part of the fabric of life. Access is needed on an equal basis with others to relevant funding streams to support projects that benefit the wider community. The squeamishness that some funders exhibit in dealing with churches does not assist in addressing issues of concern.

Baroness Warsi also said to the Bishops in 2010: 'Under our plans, you [the Christian churches] will have more power, more responsibility, and more choice over how to get involved in your communities and over how to apply your skills.' The conference, Faith and the Future of the Countryside, was a forum where these challenges were examined and debated by a wide range of people who are working in the countryside.

The themes of this book

The 2010 Faith and the Future of the Countryside Conference examined rural sustainability in the light of four complementary themes: community, economy, environment and church, offering theological reflection and recommendations for the future. The 34 papers offered for discussion predominantly dealt with issues relating to community, environmental concerns including climate change, and the rural church.

The papers selected to appear in this collection address some of the key issues for the future of rural communities and their churches including housing, land use, Big Society and sustainability. In selecting papers there was much good material that regrettably had to be left out and will be published elsewhere.

Chapter 1 reviews the changes in rural policy and economy since 1990 (Neil Ward). Chapters 2 and 3 explore land use (Michael Winter) and food production and consumption (Elizabeth Dowler). Although there is not a chapter that specifically deals with the future for UK agriculture, the important issues of how land is used and what for, food security, consumption and production, are addressed in these two chapters. Both issues will be profoundly important for the future of rural and indeed all communities.

The sustainability of rural communities is examined by Dagmar Winter, and Mark Shucksmith explores in some detail the impact of the lack of affordable housing. Other essential issues for the future of rural communities include climate change (Edward Echlin), older people (Albert Jewell) and mental health (Lorna Murray).

Spirituality through the rural environment and particularly trees is addressed by Graham Usher, and Tim Gibson develops an interesting discussion in relation to spirituality, the Eucharist and the Big Society. Church buildings also have the ability to tell the Christian story, and Jeremy Martineau discusses the contribution of church tourism to the rural economy.

The final chapter is a reflection by Anne Richards on the power of the occasional offices (baptisms, weddings and funerals) for mission and evangelism in rural communities. It is a timely reminder of the ability of ordinary Christian people to make a significant and long-lasting difference to individuals and the wider community.

There are two serious and regrettable omissions from this book: children and young people, and rural schools. Both are essential for the future of rural communities; without them rural communities will not be balanced or have any long-term sustainability. There are particular barriers to accessing services for young people, especially education, recreation, transport, health care, housing, training and employment. Services in rural communities need to be intentionally planned and delivered to take into account the needs of young people (as well as other groups). This rarely happens.

> Children are the group that are most likely to live in a household with an income below the poverty threshold after housing costs in both urban and rural areas. These types of households include both couples and lone parent families. (Defra, 2011, p. 55)

In some rural communities there has been a significant reduction in the numbers of school-age children, with the ultimate prospect of school closures, particularly primary schools, and withdrawal of service provision for children and young people. Young people in many rural communities have to travel long distances to schools, colleges and places of employment, on infrequent and expensive public transport. This limits their access to education provision and employment.

The omission of chapters on young people and rural schools, both vital to the future of the countryside, does not mean that the churches do not take these issues seriously – they do. Churches have been, and continue to be, one of the major voluntary sector providers of youth work in England as well as providing several thousand rural schools (both primary and secondary). Churches have worked in partnership with statutory youth services and a wide range of other agencies at all levels, and particularly through the networks of local churches, to provide opportunities for young people, and will continue to do so.

We commend this book to you as a resource for preaching and reflecting theologically on issues affecting rural congregations and whole rural communities in the twenty-first century. It will allow you to engage with a wide range of rural related issues that all contribute to the future of rural churches and their mission and ministry to surrounding communities.

The book has been prepared from an ecumenical perspective for those leading and working within rural churches and for those living and working in the countryside. It is also of relevance to those who take policy decisions affecting millions of rural residents.

+*Alan Smith, Bishop of St Albans*

Jill Hopkinson, National Rural Officer

October 2011

References

Archbishops' Commission on Rural Areas, 1990, *Faith in the Countryside*, Worthing: Churchman Publishing.

Cabinet Office, 2008, *Food Matters: Towards a strategy for the 21st Century*, London: The Strategy Unit, Cabinet Office.

Commission for Rural Communities, 2010, *State of the Countryside 2010*, Cheltenham: Commission for Rural Communities.

Department for Environment, Food and Rural Affairs, 2011, *Statistical Digest of Rural England 2011*, PB13534, London: Government Statistical Service.

Department for Environment, Food and Rural Affairs, 2010, *Food Statistics Pocketbook*, London: National Statistics, www.defra.gov.uk/statistics/files/defra-stats-foodfarm-food-pocketbook-2010.pdf

Global Food Security Project, 2010, *Facts and Figures*, Biotechnology and Biological Sciences Research Council, www.foodsecurity.ac.uk/issue/facts.html

The Independent, '"Charities will bear brunt of cuts in public sector," says Dame Suzi', 10 June 2010, www.independent.co.uk/news/uk/politics/charities-will-bear-brunt-of-cuts-in-public-sector-says-dame-suzi-1996201.html

Her Majesty's Treasury, 2010, *Spending Review 2010*, London: The Stationery Office.

Joseph Rowntree Foundation, 2010, *A Minimum Income Standard for Rural Households*, p. 35, www.jrf.org.uk/sites/files/jrf/minimum-income-standards-rural-full.pdf

National Housing Federation, 2011, 'Rural Homelessness Rockets by 25% as Downturn hits the Countryside Hard', News, 2 February 2011, www.housing.org.uk/news_and_press.aspx?p=9

Warsi, S., 2010, Address to Church of England Bishops 15 September 2010, www.sayeedawarsi.com/2010/09/baroness-warsi-speaks-to-the-bishops-of-the-church-of-england/

Note

1 Anglican figures based on information from the Research and Statistics Department of the Archbishops' Council. Other figures based on estimates by the Arthur Rank Centre.

England's rural economies: 20 years on from *Faith in the Countryside*

NEIL WARD

Faith in the Countryside 20 years on

Faith in the Countryside, the report of the Archbishops' Commission on Rural Areas, was published in September 1990. The Commission, whose work took two years to complete, was established following the earlier success of the Archbishop of Canterbury's Commission on Urban Priority Areas. Its report, *Faith in the City*, had been published in 1985 to widespread public debate and controversy (Archbishop of Canterbury's Commission on Urban Priority Areas, 1985). The Archbishops' Commission on Rural Areas involved 21 Commissioners and took oral and written evidence from a wide range of organizations and individuals, almost 600 in all. The work included visits to more than 320 localities in 41 dioceses, and the Commission met an estimated 6,000 people (Archbishops' Commission on Rural Areas, p. 331).

The Archbishops' Commission was one of several major reviews of rural society and rural policy in the period 1988–90. The European Commission published a Green Paper, 'The Future of Rural Society', in 1988, proposing to develop a pan-European rural policy (Commission of the European Communities, 1988). Subsequently, the House of Lords Select Committee on the European Communities (1990) conducted a major inquiry, prompted in part by the European Commission's proposals. The then European Community was at that time particularly interested in reform to the Common Agricultural Policy (eventually agreed in 1992), coupled with the development of a stronger support policy for rural communities and businesses beyond the farming sector through the growth of the European Structural Funds following the accession of Spain and Portugal in 1986. The European Community and the House of Lords Select Committee both recognized in their respective reports that there was no longer a single 'rural problem' but different kinds of challenges and opportunities in different kinds of rural places. The European Commission, in its Green Paper on the future of rural society (1998), set out a typology of at least three different kinds of rural problems, each affecting different types of rural area in Europe (more accessible areas, agriculturally dependent areas, and the most marginal areas). The House of Lords Select Committee (1990) argued that rural policy needed to better reflect the diversity of rural conditions within the member states. It was in this context of a move away from the sense of a 'single rural problem' that the Archbishops' Commission on Rural Areas set about its work. Its terms of reference (1990, p. i) were wide-ranging and as follows:

- To examine the effects of economic, environmental and social change on the rural community.
- To describe the changing nature of the Church in the countryside.
- To examine the theological factors which bear upon the mission and ministry of the Church in rural areas.
- In the light of the above, to make recommendations for consideration and action.

This chapter reflects on 20 years of rural change in England since the publication of *Faith in the Countryside* and takes as its particular focus the economic aspects of rural life and public policy measures to support rural economies. It first considers what *Faith in the Countryside* had to say about the economy of rural areas, assessing continuity and change between 1990 and 2010. It goes on to chart the four phases in the treatment of rural economy issues since 1990. These are characterized as:

- Liberalization and integration – coming to terms with the new rural economy (1990–97).

- Modernization and institution-building – resourcing rural renewal (1997–2001).
- The accident of Defra and post-foot and mouth retrenchment (2001–07).
- Responsive-mode reviews to tackle rural disadvantage (2007–10).

The evolution of rural economies and public policy, 1990–2010

Re-reading *Faith in the Countryside* 20 years on, one is struck by how much some things have changed but also by how little others have. In the report's chapter on the economy of rural areas, the discussion of telecommunications looks quaintly dated, for example. There is no mention of the internet, a term that was yet to enter popular usage, although there is a brief case study of a teacher's wife in a Dorset village, working from home for the Atomic Research Council 'relaying her results by telecomputer' (p. 54). Now, of course, broadband infrastructure would be one of the most prominent economic development issues in England's rural areas.

Globalization does not feature in the discussion, and there is little sense of international competition (from China and India, for example) shaping the development of manufacturing and service-sector businesses. Now, few would deny the importance of the international flow of goods, services, people and ideas in shaping economic (and social) life in England's local areas, both urban and rural.

There is also little discussion of environmental issues, especially questions of environmental sustainability, and no mention of climate change. The 'environmental aspects of farming' are cast, what now seems very narrowly, in terms of nature conservation and landscape protection. Yet now, strategic reviews of the future of farming and land management often start from the perspective of resource use and environmental sustainability, and climate change is widely recognized as posing not just a constraint upon, but also a set of opportunities for, businesses in rural areas. Over the report's 40 pages on the rural economy a seemingly disproportionate amount of time is spent on agriculture, including discussion of the perennial issue of agricultural support policies. Notably, concerns were raised about 'surplus land' – an issue that really does feel as if it is from another age – with potential land surplus estimated 20 years ago as 1.3 million hectares by 1999 and between 5.5 and 5.75 million hectares by 2015 (p. 65).

Some issues endure, however. The report highlighted the trend towards the diversification of rural economies away from dependence on primary production and land-based industries, and this trend has continued. Similarly, reading the report one is struck by the lack of clarity about the big strategic choices facing rural areas – a difficulty that persists 20 years later.

The next section briefly charts the evolution of public policy affecting rural economies over the period 1990–2010, dividing the period into four distinct phases (although this carving up of history is intended simply as a heuristic device and is inevitably a simplification of how events have unfolded). The period covers the Government of John Major; which saw the first Rural White Paper for England in over 40 years, and then goes on to trace what can be characterized as 'the rise and fall' of rural policy under New Labour (see Ward and Lowe, 2007). This trot through the recent 'politics of the rural economy' is in order to set the scene for a discussion of the current place of rural economies in the context of the economic downturn, and to identify some key questions about their prospects over the coming years.

Liberalization and integration – coming to terms with the new rural economy (1990–97)

Between 1990 and 1997, rural policy came to take on a new lease of life during the John Major years of the Thatcher–Major Governments. During the period up to 1992 there was a preoccupation with the reform and liberalization of the Common Agricultural Policy (CAP), agreed in 1992, and the development (and significant expansion) of the European Structural Funds for rural development purposes (particularly during the 1994–9 programming period). Following the 1992 General Election, the

Major Government became concerned about the political advance of the Liberal Democrats in the south-west of England and so embarked on drawing up a Rural White Paper to help give new impetus to reform of rural policy. The White Paper was produced under the joint leadership of John Gummer, the then Secretary of State for the Environment and a former Minister of Agriculture, and William Waldegrave, the Minister of Agriculture and a former Minister of State in the Department of Environment (Shaw, 1997). The White Paper (*Rural England: A Nation Committed to a Living Countryside*), published in 1995, lacked specific new resource commitments, but sought to improve the co-ordination of rural policy, especially between the then Department of the Environment and the Ministry of Agriculture, Fisheries and Food (MAFF). There was little emphasis on rural economic issues as an object of analysis, intervention and support, and famously there was no mention at all of rural poverty and deprivation. Nor was there much sense of rural development policy and support becoming increasingly Europeanized through the expansion of the Structural Funds, 'Europe' being a toxic issue for the Major Government. There was, however, recognition of the need to encourage farm diversification and enterprise and a sense that a more holistic and cross-cutting approach was needed to guide the development of diverse rural localities.

Modernization and institution-building – resourcing rural renewal (1997–2001)

When New Labour came to power with its landslide victory in May 1997, the party's manifesto had little to say about rural issues, except for a commitment to allow a free vote on the controversial question of hunting with hounds. However, within a couple of years, a variety of seemingly disparate factors combined to help bring rural policy closer to the forefront of New Labour's reformist vision of national renewal.

Following the 'mad cow disease' affair, MAFF was widely seen as a failing department and in need of reform. At the same time, a series of lean years for farming had led to a farm incomes crisis, with farming unions pleading for extra subsidies to bail out the industry (in 1997, 1998 and 1999). An impending further reform of the CAP to accommodate EU enlargement therefore brought an opportunity for a rethink in the UK of how farming was subsidized over the period 1997 to 1999. A third factor was the creation of the Regional Development Agencies (RDAs) to co-ordinate economic development in the English regions. These were put together by merging existing agencies in the regions, including the then Rural Development Commission (RDC), which left the question of what to do with the RDC's national offices. Combining the central functions of the RDC with the then Countryside Commission to establish a new Countryside Agency was a knock-on consequence that meant a new and relatively powerful quango emerged on the rural policy scene with a sense of drive and ambition to make a mark and establish itself. Finally, the 1997 General Election result had unexpectedly produced a new and relatively large cohort of Labour MPs in rural and semi-rural constituencies who were keen to articulate a New Labour vision for the countryside in response to the increasingly vocal campaign of the Countryside Alliance, which had sought to mobilize a wider rural constituency to defend hunting and which was attracting extensive media attention.

Together these factors created the conditions under which rural issues came to assume far greater prominence under New Labour than had been envisaged. For example, Tony Blair commissioned a Cabinet Office review of rural economies as part of the first tranche of work by his Performance and Innovation Unit (1999), and a new Rural White Paper was published at the end of November 2000 (*Our Countryside: The Future – A Fair Deal for Rural England*) which committed an extra £1 billion of spending on rural programmes. A radical step was taken in 2000 to implement the reformed CAP in England through the use of the modulation measures to redirect spending from direct support (compensation) payments towards agri-environment and rural economic development schemes. This effectively doubled the resources going into agri-environment schemes over the period 2000–6.

The accident of Defra and post-foot and mouth retrenchment (2001–07)

Unfortunately, New Labour's Rural White Paper was rapidly over-taken by events when in February 2001, less than three months after its publication, the UK fell victim to a serious outbreak of foot and mouth disease (FMD), which wrought havoc across large parts of rural England and dominated the rural scene for months to come. Almost 6.5 million animals were slaughtered and the outbreak was estimated to have cost £5 billion to the public sector and £3 billion to the private sector. Notably, at the height of the crisis in March, the Prime Minister had taken charge of the Government's response and decided to delay the 2001 General Election for a month because of the disruption being caused. Following the second Labour landslide, Prime Minister Blair shuffled his Cabinet and, unexpectedly, what had been trailed in the manifesto as a new Department for Rural Affairs emerged as the Department for Environment, Food and Rural Affairs (Defra). The additional inclusion of responsibility for environmental protection, including climate change, in Defra's hastily thrown together portfolio meant that environmental sustainability became the central focus, and with perverse effects.

The initial intention had been to raise the profile of rural issues across government, with rural affairs and rural development envisaged in a central and integrating role in the new department, but Defra had the opposite effect of marginalizing rural affairs. Wider rural economic development lost ground within government to the renewed emphasis on the sustainability of the food chain and a preoccupation with a farming industry that represented an ever diminishing economic force in the countryside. To make matters worse, Lord Haskins was appointed to review the various quangos and agencies working to Defra. The resultant Modernising Rural Delivery review (Haskins, 2003) was driven by a farm-centric view of the world and led to the axing of the Countryside Agency. Its research, advice and advocacy role was handed to the new Commission for Rural Communities (CRC) that was to be a small fraction of its size. Socio-economic programmes for rural areas were taken on by the RDAs and there was a strong sense of Defra having quietly shelved its rural responsibilities as the number of civil servants working on rural affairs was radically pared back to fewer than 20 (see House of Commons Environment, Food and Rural Affairs Committee, 2008).

Alongside this dismantling of the national policy infrastructure for rural economies, Labour politicians and government officials had been grappling with the loss of momentum behind the building up of the English regions as institutional territories for sub-national economic development following the vote to reject proposals for a directly elected regional assembly in the north-east of England in November 2004. A seemingly off-the-peg solution was deemed by some in the then Office of the Deputy Prime Minister to lie in the concept of 'city-regions' to drive economic regeneration and growth in the English regions. These would embrace the major conurbations and their surrounding commuter hinterlands as the main economic development priority areas, but leave rural economies as a neglected backwater in sub-national economic development (see Ward, 2006, for a rural critique). RDAs were obliged to have rural programmes of some sort, but senior RDA figures were generally preoccupied with focusing their energies and resources on larger-scale investments in their cities, where it was the common view that agencies could deliver better value for money in an age where central government-set targets on jobs created and per capita Gross Value Added ruled the day.

Responsive-mode reviews to tackle rural disadvantage (2007–10)

The period following the Modernising Rural Delivery reforms saw the gradual dismantling of the institutions of rural affairs policy for England. In 2007, however, there was a flurry of new reviews. The new Prime Minister, Gordon Brown, signalled a break with the past and in devising his 'Government of all the talents' brought in Matthew Taylor, a Liberal Democrat MP, to review how planning and land-use policy could better support rural business and the provision of affordable rural housing. At the same time, a new outbreak of FMD in Surrey and severe flooding in Yorkshire and Gloucestershire brought a new sense of crisis to many rural areas. As part of the response, Gordon Brown asked Stuart Burgess, the Government's Rural Advocate and Chairman of the CRC, to prepare a report on the ways in which the rural economy could be strengthened. These two exercises coincided with the work of the Commons Environment, Food and Rural Affairs Committee (2008), which had decided to hold an inquiry into the Government's approach to rural economic development in England. Together these reviews and enquiries signalled a heightened sense of interest and concern about the health of the rural economy unprecedented since the last major FMD crisis of 2001.

The Rural Advocate's report sought to emphasize the economic contribution rural areas make to England's national economy and estimated that targeting areas of underperformance in rural economies could potentially double the £325 billion generated each year by rural firms (CRC, 2008). In its early years, CRC had been steered to focus its work more narrowly on tackling rural disadvantage – that is, overcoming the specific social and economic problems that arise as a consequence of sparsity of population and geographical remoteness. The Advocate's report also helped to show that some rural areas had been economically thriving and could make even greater contributions if their potential were better recognized by government and regional bodies. Among other measures, it proposed that the Government should convene national and regional summits to focus attention on realizing the potential of rural economies.

The Taylor Review (Taylor, 2008) was a more detailed review and produced 48 recommendations focused on the planning system and aimed at making more land available for affordable housing in rural areas and promoting new business development, especially through home-based working. The Review was well received, although by this time the 2008 economic crash was rapidly developing into a full-blown economic recession and government became increasingly preoccupied with coping with the national downturn and the deficit as the 2010 election approached.

The economic crisis and rural economies

Instability in the international banking and financial sectors first became apparent with the sub-prime mortgage problems in the USA destabilizing inter-bank credit markets and triggering the Northern Rock collapse in the UK in the summer of 2007. The 'credit crunch' led to the near collapse of the banking system in the autumn of 2008 and prompted hugely expensive government bailouts of banks in several countries, effectively funded by taxpayers. In the UK, national economic growth forecasts for 2009 and 2010 were dramatically reduced and the level of public sector debt increased significantly. At the depths of the recession, UK GDP fell by 2.3% in a single quarter (the first quarter of 2009). The recession has been the longest in the UK since the Second World War, with six consecutive quarters of negative growth, as well as the deepest, with GDP falling by 6.4% – almost two percentage points worse than the previous deepest recession in the 1980s, which saw a fall of 4.6% (Harari, 2010).

All main political parties in the UK approached the 2010 General Election proposing unprecedented programmes of public spending cuts to reduce the deficit, and differed only relatively marginally on the scale and timing of cuts required. As a result, the public had been expecting severe cuts in public spending, and public institutions had been preparing themselves for almost two years ahead of the Comprehensive Spending Review of October 2010, yet without any clear sense of the detail of how the reduction in public spending might be distributed between different sectors and programmes. The new Government's June 2010 emergency budget set out steps to tighten public finances by a total of £113 billion by 2014–15. Of this, approximately £30 billion came from higher taxes, £11 billion from welfare reforms announced in the Budget, £10 billion from lower debt-interest costs and £61 billion from cuts to central government departmental expenditure programmes.

The geographical dimensions, and especially the rural dimensions, of the current economic downturn and reductions in public expenditure remained relatively under-discussed in national public and political debate. (For an international geographical assessment, however, see Harvey, 2010.) As we have seen from the experience since 2001, national politicians and civil servants have generally been slow to grasp the contribution economic activity in rural areas makes to national economic well-being, despite the best efforts of agencies such as the CRC. Ominously for rural interests, the abolition of the CRC was announced soon after the 2010 General Election as an early casualty in the cull of quangos.

England's rural areas contain 9.7 million people, over 5.5 million employees, including over 34% of company directors, and around 1 million businesses. There are generally higher levels of employment and lower levels of unemployment than in urban areas, and marginally higher rates of new firm formation (Lowe and Ward, 2007). Over the 10 years since 1995, annual rates of growth of Gross Value Added have been higher in rural towns and villages and dispersed areas than in the major urban centres, although this fact usually goes unacknowledged amid all the hyperbole about the power and potential of England's city-regions.

In some respects, rural economies can be seen to be at the cutting edge of social and economic changes in the twenty-first century. Combining living and working from home is more prevalent in rural areas, for example, and rural women are much more likely to be entrepreneurial in setting up their own businesses. Rural businesses also have to strive to overcome the disadvantages of distance and sparsity in order to survive and thrive, and this can be a stimulus to innovative practices in business collaboration and in the use of information and communication technologies (ICT). Nevertheless, problems remain. Many rural areas suffer from relatively low wages, which means that even before the economic downturn there were almost two million people below the national poverty line. This is equivalent to a 'lost city' of poverty about the size of the Birmingham conurbation, but because these households are dispersed through rural areas across England, they do not register as a policy problem requiring concerted attention.

Moreover, dependence on public sector jobs is leaving some rural places more vulnerable as public expenditure cuts are implemented. For example, predominantly rural local authority areas in England have a significantly higher proportion of jobs in the public sector compared to other types of area – 33% compared to 27% (Rose Regeneration, 2010). This vulnerability is often compounded by lower wage levels and smaller local workforces in more sparsely populated and geographically peripheral rural areas. The Office of Budgetary Responsibility has forecast that general government employment will fall by around 500,000 between 2010–11 and 2014–15 in the UK (House of Commons Treasury Committee, 2010, p. 14). Because some areas of government spending have been ring-fenced for protection (such as health and overseas aid) and others have been singled out as preferences for being spared the worst of the cuts (such as schools and defence), public sector job losses are likely to fall disproportionately in sectors such as local government, environmental protection, transport and the arts. Public sector employment is important for rural areas (CRC, 2010). Other quasi-public bodies are also facing significant cuts to budgets, such as universities, which provide some 260,000 full-time equivalent jobs in England with a further 300,000 full-time equivalent (FTE) generated by their activities (Universities UK, 2010).

In 2010, Rose Regeneration and the Rural Services Network – a network of the most rural local authorities – developed a Rural Vulnerability Index based on a composite of statistical indicators including average pay, the proportion of jobs in the public sector, the proportion of the population that is economically active and the number of Job Seekers Allowance claimants. The outcome shows a strong geographical patterning, with the most geographically peripheral areas (Isle of Wight, County Durham, Northumberland, Cornwall) ranked as the most vulnerable and the most central and accessible (Oxfordshire, Cambridgeshire, Bedfordshire) ranked as the least (Rose Regeneration, 2010).

To counter concerns about particular rural vulnerabilities, however, there is also evidence of resilience in rural economies as a result of their business structure. Seemingly fragile rural economies are often those with the highest preponderance of small rural micro-businesses, and this business form has proved particularly adaptive and resilient during past crises. For example, a recent re-survey of almost 1,000 rural businesses in north-east England by the Centre for Rural Economy (Atterton and Affleck, 2010) found that some firms saw opportunities in the recession, and the overall picture was a relatively positive and optimistic one, with many business owners planning growth, taking advantage of ICT improvements and innovating to exploit new markets. Other surveys have also revealed how small firms have been performing marginally better during the economic downturn than their urban counterparts. In a survey of 6,300 respondents in England, Scotland and Wales, for example, Anderson *et al.* (2010) found that rural firms appeared less susceptible to external economic changes because of stronger degrees of local embeddedness, more local and stable customer bases and lower levels of dependence on external finance.

The increasing interconnectedness of rural businesses is highlighted by the changing degree of internet usage over the past 10 years. The Centre for Rural Economy survey of rural businesses in north-east England repeated a survey from 10 years earlier. In 1999, some 43% of businesses surveyed did not have access to the internet. By 2009, this proportion had fallen to below 12%. Businesses used the internet not only for gathering information but also (in 43% of cases) for marketing products and (in 56% of cases) purchasing supplies. Across the sample, 83% of respondents had access to broadband in their business premises (Atterton and Affleck, 2010, pp. 43–4).

The depth and severity of the economic downturn of 2008–09 has prompted a new wave of critical analysis about the nature of economic growth and development. Broadly, these might be grouped into structural critiques of the international political economy of capitalism (Harvey, 2010), qualitative critiques of the nature of work and well-being in an increasingly globalized and competitive 'knowledge-economy' (Florida, 2010) and ecological critiques which start from the challenges of climate change and carbon reduction in considering new models of economic organization and governance (Newell and Paterson, 2010).

Harvey (2010) argues that periodic crises in capitalism are not only inevitable but also necessary to its continuity. He highlights the power of international banking and finance to produce new risks and vulnerabilities and notes how the poorest and most economically disadvantaged are likely to have to bear the brunt of the costs. A key feature of the current crisis has been the way in which seemingly geographically particular economic and financial problems – such as the rapid expansion of sub-prime mortgages in the USA between 1998 and 2006 and the rapid increase in the rate of foreclosures in the low-income areas of older cities like Cleveland and Detroit – had such speedy and extensive knock-on effects around the world. The way that the relations between places come to be transformed by capitalism and its crises is a theme that runs strongly through Harvey's critique. Notably, the spatial relations of capitalism are relatively little studied and understood. Indeed, Harvey draws attention to the ways that the economics profession dismally failed to see the current crisis coming. When on a visit to the London School of Economics in November 2008 the Queen asked why this was so, a round-table discussion of senior and eminent economists was convened at the British Academy (see Belsey and Hennessey, 2009). It concluded: 'In summary, Your Majesty, the failure to foresee the timing, extent and severity of the crisis and to head it off, while it had many causes, was principally a failure of the collective imagination of many bright people, both in this country and internationally, to understand the risks to the system as a whole' (p. 10). On the role of financiers and their willingness to seek higher returns through taking on greater risk, they observed that it is 'difficult to recall a greater example of wishful thinking combined with hubris', but acknowledged that they, like many others, had been caught up in a 'psychology of denial' (p. 9).

Florida's critique is both less trenchant and more idealistic than Harvey's, but starts from the argument that each great economic downturn, such as the long depression of the late nineteenth century and the great Depression of the 1930s, eventually comes to be seen as bringing opportunities to remake economies and societies and so produce new paradigms of growth and prosperity (Florida, 2010). Florida's past work has pointed to the role of what he calls 'the creative class' (Florida, 2002), and this remains central to his optimistic vision of socio-economic change that has become fashionable among many economic development professionals in the UK. He suggests that following the current crisis, new patterns of consumption will unfold, bringing new attitudes towards work, leisure and mobility, with innovation coming much more to the heart of a more knowledge- and service-based economy. New forms of infrastructure will speed up the movement of people, goods and ideas, and this will have the effect of transforming the economic geography of the globe. Notably, Florida's vision for what he calls 'the great reset' following the current crisis sees a much denser economic landscape organized around 'mega-regions' such as the eastern seaboard of the USA, or the regions around London, Amsterdam, Tokyo, Shanghai and Mumbai. Taken together, he claims, the world's 40 largest mega-regions account for two-thirds of all global economic activity and 85% of the world's technological innovation, while housing just 18% of its population (Florida, 2010, p. 143). It is these places, he argues, that will drive the development of new industries, new jobs and new ways of living.

Florida's vision can be criticized for its urban-centricity and utopianism but, nevertheless, there is some evidence that the creative classes are a feature of socio-economic change in England's rural areas (Naylor, 2007). Indeed, the Taylor Review (2008, p. 123) reported that the growth in the proportion of knowledge-intensive businesses between 1998 and 2005 had increased by 46% in rural areas compared to just 21% in urban areas. The challenge of attracting economically valuable 'knowledge workers' to rural areas has therefore begun to be considered by local economic development bodies in some of England's regions.

Even before the economic downturn, increasing recognition of climate change and the need to reduce emissions of greenhouse gases had been stimulating national and international measures to encourage the shift to a 'post-carbon economy', and this shift has gathered new impetus in recent years.

Newell and Patterson (2010) use the term climate capitalism to describe the model which squares capitalism's need for continual economic growth with the efforts to decarbonize economic activity. Decoupling emissions growth from economic growth will inevitably pose huge challenges for governments and businesses, but the recent financial crisis, it is argued, opens up unusual room for manoeuvre. Four possible future scenarios are offered for how climate capitalism might play out. In the first, labelled 'climate capitalist utopia', carbon disclosure and reporting becomes routinized and investment is efficiently directed to renewable energy, energy efficiency and conservation, and carbon capture. Regulators of financial markets and national tax systems are structured to incentivize businesses to find alternatives to fossil fuels, and emissions trading systems help to reduce the costs of meeting emissions targets. At the same time, northern investment helps facilitate a wholesale shift in the global south to move away from reliance on fossil fuels and fast-forward to low carbon economies. (In other scenarios, carbon markets and carbon trading either fail to take hold and lose legitimacy, becoming subject to 'carbon scams', or work but serve the interests of richer countries and large corporations at the expense of the world's poor, or are actively managed and intervened in through some form of 'new Marshall Plan' or 'climate Keynesianism'). Newell and Patterson argue that we are only in the early stages of the economic transformation that climate change is stimulating. What is even clearer is that the implications of decarbonization for the nature of economic life in rural England, our patterns of settlement structure and our ways of moving goods and people about, have been given remarkably little thought to date, especially given the scale of the likely challenges ahead (but see Rural Coalition, 2010, pp. 19–21 as an exception).

Key issues for the future and recommendations for discussion, action and reflection

To sum up the discussion so far, the diversity of rural conditions was already being recognized, both in academic research but also by policy-making institutions such as the European Commission, at the time that *Faith in the Countryside* was published. From the vantage point of 2010, there is clearly no single 'rural problem' in England that encapsulates the variety of challenges and difficulties facing people and businesses in different types of rural area – whether these be access to services, affordable housing, employment opportunities, overdependence on declining industries, or problems from development pressures and growth.

Similarly, there is increasing recognition that there is no such thing as 'the rural economy', with its implications of a singular, bounded and separate economic system. (Likewise, the notion of 'the rural community' found in the terms of reference for *Faith in the Countryside* jars today.) Rather, there is economic activity in rural areas (and there are a multiplicity of different types of communities, both geographical and otherwise). The key processes of change in England's rural economies over the past 20 years include the (geographically variable) decline of agriculture as an economic force, especially in terms of providing employment, the net flow of population from larger towns and cities to smaller towns and more rural areas, the process of rural demographic ageing, and the rise of the service economy, including leisure and tourism but also personal and business services.

The particular challenges and difficulties faced by those living and working in rural areas have been of variable concern and interest to different British governments over the past 20 years but, rather unexpectedly perhaps, did come to assume some prominence during the first New Labour Government as part of its modernizing vision of national renewal and reform. Since then, national policy debate about rural economic development has generally lost both prominence and a sense of direction, and been subject to preoccupations with questions of national and regional institutional changes and technocratic issues of Public Service Agreement targets and indicators of rural productivity (see, for example, House of Commons Environment, Food and Rural Affairs Committee, 2007). A notable exception has been the renewed focus on the affordable housing question in recent years. The economic downturn and the public expenditure cuts are likely to have particular and distinctive implications for people and jobs in rural areas compared to larger towns and cities, and it is possible that those most remote and sparsely populated areas may fare worst of all.

Nevertheless, the downturn is also bringing some hope in offering alternative visions of how economic life might best be organized and managed ranging from international banking regulation and carbon trading at one end of the scale to new models of homeworking and social enterprise at the other. It is vital that, in the

English context, a rural perspective is brought to bear on efforts to envision alternative socio-economic futures, and that those interested in rural well-being are active contributors to these sorts of debates (see Lowe and Ward, 2009, for one of many examples of rural futures exercises). By way of concluding, I would offer the following recommendations for discussion, action and reflection.

Working and living: The ICT revolution has probably been the single most important technological change affecting rural businesses in the 20 years since *Faith in the Countryside*, and the implications of greater interconnectedness and speedier communications are increasingly being realized in the development of small rural businesses. Defra's new Structural Reform Plan (published in July 2010) has redefined the Department's strategic priorities, and rural affairs get, disappointingly, very little mention. There is, nevertheless, a commitment to work to improve broadband provision in rural areas and stimulate private investment to develop the best superfast broadband network in Europe by 2015. Key questions remain:

- How can the ICT infrastructure needs of England's rural areas be better represented and met over the next decade, and how can the opportunities improved ICT infrastructure brings be better promoted and realized among rural businesses, public service providers and households?
- How can the barriers and obstacles to enterprise and entrepreneurship through home-based working in rural areas, including those identified in the Taylor Review (2008), be removed as swiftly as possible?

Social change and geographical mobility: Demographic change in England's rural areas is likely to be a key process reshaping ways of living and working in the two decades ahead. Debates about rural change over the past 30 years have been prone to romanticized ideals about stability, changelessness and local rural communities that cast in-migration as a disruptive and threatening force. It is clear that rural in-migration can be a positive process, not least from the perspective of new business formation and improved employment opportunities. At the same time, the loss of young people from rural settlements is frequently seen in negative terms, even when out-migration is driven by enhanced employment and higher education training opportunities. So questions for further consideration are:

- How might the role of people moving into (and out of) rural areas come to be understood in more positive terms, and entrepreneurial in-migration be actively encouraged and supported?
- What might the need for life-long learning mean for the provision of learning and skills to businesses and people of all ages in more remote and sparsely populated rural areas?

England's rural economies in the post-carbon world: The UK is well placed to play a leading role internationally in decarbonization and the evolution of the post-carbon global economy. This is in part because of the role played by successive British governments in international climate-change negotiations, but also because of the prominence of British science and technology in understanding global environmental change and innovating in green technologies. In rural areas to date, attention has focused on the potential role of land-based businesses in the supply of renewable energy and the role of farming practices in reducing greenhouse gas emissions. However, there are a much broader range of opportunities to strengthen the low-carbon economy, including small-scale household and community renewable energy schemes, environmental services, and new modes of rural transport provision. And so a final set of questions are:

- How might national policies better enable local communities, businesses and agencies in rural areas to realize the opportunities of the low-carbon economy?
- How might innovation and experimentation in new and less energy-consuming ways of living and working best be encouraged and learned from?

References

Anderson, A., Osseichuk, E. and Illingworth, L., 2010, 'Rural small businesses in turbulent times: Impacts of the economic downturn', *International Journal of Entrepreneurship and Innovation* 11(1), pp. 45–56.

Archbishops' Commission on Rural Areas, 1990, *Faith in the Countryside*, Worthing: Churchman Publishing.

Archbishop of Canterbury's Commission on Urban Priority Areas, 1985, *Faith in the City: A Call to Action by Church and Nation*, London: Church House Publishing.

Atterton, J. and Affleck, A., 2010, *Rural Businesses in the North East of England: Final Survey Results*, Newcastle: Centre for Rural Economy.

Belsey, T. and Hennessey, P., 2009, 'The Global Financial Crisis: Why Didn't Anyone Notice?' *British Academy Review* (Issue 14, November), pp. 8–10.

Commission for Rural Communities, 2008, *England's Rural Areas: Steps to Release their Economic Potential*, Cheltenham: Commission for Rural Communities.

Commission for Rural Communities, 2010, *State of the Countryside 2010*, Cheltenham: Commission for Rural Communities.

Commission of the European Communities, 1988, *The Future of Rural Society*, Commission Communication, 29 July COM(88) 371 final, Brussels: Commission of the European Communities.

Department of Environment / Ministry of Agriculture, Fisheries and Food, 1995, *Rural England: A Nation Committed to a Living Countryside*, London: Department of Environment.

Department of the Environment, Transport and the Regions, 2000, *Our Countryside: The Future – A Fair Deal for Rural England*, London: Department of the Environment, Transport and the Regions.

Florida, R., 2002, *The Rise of the Creative Class: And How it's Transforming Work, Leisure, Community and Everyday Life*, New York: Perseus Book Group.

Florida, R., 2010, *The Great Reset: How New Ways of Living and Working Drive Post-Crash Prosperity*, New York: Harper Collins.

Harari, D., 2010, *Economic Indicators, August 2010*, House of Commons Research Paper 10/49. London: House of Commons Library.

Harvey, D., 2010, *The Enigma of Capital: And the Crises of Capitalism*, London: Profile Books.

Haskins, C., 2003, *Rural Delivery Review: A Report on the Delivery of Government Policies in Rural England*, London: Department for Environment, Food and Rural Affairs,

House of Commons Environment, Food and Rural Affairs Committee, 2008, *The Potential of England's Rural Economy*, Session 2007–8, Paper HC 544, London: The Stationery Office.

House of Commons Treasury Committee, 2010, *June 2010 Budget*, Session 2010–11, Paper HC 350, London: The Stationery Office.

House of Lords Select Committee on the European Communities, 1990, *The Future of Rural Society*, HL Paper 80–I, London: Stationery Office.

Lowe, P. and Ward, N., 2007, 'Sustainable rural economies: Some lessons from the English experience', *Sustainable Development* 15, pp. 307–17.

Lowe, P. and Ward, N., 2009, 'England's rural futures: A socio-geographical Approach to scenarios analysis', *Regional Studies* 43, pp. 1319–32.

Naylor, R., 2007, 'Creative industries and rural innovation', pp. 43–60, in S. Mahroum (ed.), *Rural Innovation*, London: National Endowment for Science, Technology and the Arts.

Newell, P. and Paterson, M., 2010, *Climate Capitalism: Global Warming and the Transformation of the Global Economy*, Cambridge: Cambridge University Press.

Performance and Innovation Unit, 1999, *Rural Economies*, London: Cabinet Office.

Rose Regeneration, 2010, *Rural Vulnerability Index*, Lincoln: Rose Regeneration.

The Rural Coalition, 2010, *The Rural Challenge: Achieving Sustainable Rural Communities for the 21st Century*, London: The Rural Coalition.

Shaw, R., 1997, 'The Rural White Paper in England: the origins, production and immediate consequences of the White Paper', *Journal of Environmental Planning and Management* 40, pp. 381–85.

Taylor, M., 2008, *Living Working Countryside: The Taylor Review of Rural Economy and Affordable Housing*, London: Department for Communities and Local Government.

Universities UK, 2010, *Making an Economic Impact: Higher Education and the English Regions*, London: Universities UK.

Ward, N., 2006, Memorandum of evidence, pp. 90–2, House of Commons Housing, Planning, Local Government and the Regions Committee, *Is There A Future for Regional Government?* Session 2005–6, HC 977–II, London: Stationery Office.

Ward, N. and Lowe, P., 2007, 'Blairite modernization and countryside policy', *The Political Quarterly* 78 (3), pp. 412–21.

2

The land and human well-being

MICHAEL WINTER

James Lovelock (2009) in his most recent book issues a 'final warning' that the hard-wired desire in humans to continue 'business as usual' will probably 'prevent us from saving ourselves'. Our consumption of finite resources is too high, the impacts we are having on the globe and its climate are too great. We face formidable challenges across a range of fronts, so much so that the Government's Chief Scientific Adviser, John Beddington (2009), has warned of a 'perfect storm' of food shortages, scarce water and insufficient energy resources facing the world by 2030. At the heart of these challenges, both in terms of potential solutions and devastating further loss, lies 'the land'.

This chapter explores the contributions to human well-being and human survival made by land and the challenges posed to society and to policy makers by the many competing uses for it. Later we will consider and assess the recent conception of 'ecosystem services' (ES). The chapter could have focused on 'nature' or 'the environment', or perhaps, given the context, 'creation', but the notion of 'the land' serves to root our thinking in a reality that everyone can relate to as it is always beneath us, the ground of our being – the parallels with theological language are clear and the sacred connotations of the land equally so. By contrast, nature and the environment are often perceived at a distance. Nature is out there, not quite here. Nature is gazed at in the exotic appeal of wildlife programmes on television revealing strange and unknowable creatures and places. A mental distance between people and nature pervades our society and culture, whereas the vast majority of us inhabit land in some form or other: houses, urban waste land, playing fields, gardens, pavements, roads, shopping malls, factories, farms, fields, woods, mountains. Land is literally ubiquitous, the stuff of all our lives. We walk over it every day even if it is just across a room, we look out on it, we eat food grown on it, we drink water that is stored in it or on it, and we are warmed by energy dug out of it. Our leisure, even if entirely vicarious, is often land based as we watch football matches on turf that may have 'sacred' qualities too, or TV period dramas set in rural villages or country estates.

But it is perhaps because land is so integral to human life and experience that it is taken for granted and consequently neglected in our formulations of intellectual problems. We have not tended to use land as a framework for analysis and prescription in the context of climate change, consumerism, health and the many other issues that confront our species. One of the main purposes of this chapter is to confront this neglect and to propose the land as a concept that has huge potential for building creative synergies between ethics and science, between the material and the social, and between theology and policy. But it would be wholly disingenuous to suggest that none of the groundwork for this enterprise has yet been accomplished. Indeed, recent policy and research work has been refreshing in this respect, and so the chapter commences with an overview of a major strand of thinking that seeks not only to understand the material world in its wider social and economic context (the ecosystem services approach), but does so through the policy lens of human well-being.

As will be clear from the second section of the chapter, I have empathy with this approach and some expectation that it may deliver modest gains. However, this is a pragmatic position and should not detract from some of the difficulties that are thrown up by notions of ecosystem services and well-being, and these are discussed in the third section of the chapter. In particular, there is a fundamental problem at the heart of the ecosystem approach which is only partially addressed by bringing well-being into the equation. This problem can be characterized as the absence of a moral or normative imperative, without which radical change is hard to envision. This signals the need, as set out in the fourth section of the chapter, to consider the land in a normative sense. In other words, we need to consider the ways in which land *should* be used and ways in which land *should* contribute not only to human well-being, in the secular terms in which it has been developed, but also to 'goodness'; in other words, to human living that is for the good of self, others, the planet and therefore the glory of God. The aim is to make this argument not primarily through theological or philosophical proposition, although there is some of that, but through engaging with some of the findings of empirical science, both social and natural.

Ecosystem services and well-being: a new paradigm

The ecosystem service approach, recently the subject of a major national assessment exercise (UK NEA, 2010), recognizes the dependency of human kind on planetary life support systems, so called 'natural capital'. It is attractive to some policy makers and scientists because it links nature or the land (ecosystems) with economics (services), thereby offering a way forward for policy through the operation of tools of economic governance. It offers the prospect of engendering respect and care for the natural environment through processes of economic valuation. Services have a value, whether recognized through monetary values in existing markets or, to continue with the economic terminology, as 'positive externalities'. These positive externalities are goods or services that may have no market value but are of human value nonetheless, and there are means of measuring that value. Advocates of an ecosystem services approach seek to identify those values and to suggest ways in which values might be incorporated in policy and market mechanisms. The approach as set out in the Millennium Ecosystem Assessment is shown in Figure 2.1.

A sign of the importance that the ecosystem services approach has assumed in recent years is that a search using one of the main academic search engines (ISI Web of Science) for the 5 years up to September 2010 produced 2,471 published papers with ES in the topic descriptor and 426 with the term in the title. It has been pressed into service in contexts as diverse as shrimp ponds in China (Liu *et al.*, 2010), the role of earthworms in tropical agroforestry (Fonte and Six, 2010), the management of the floodplains of

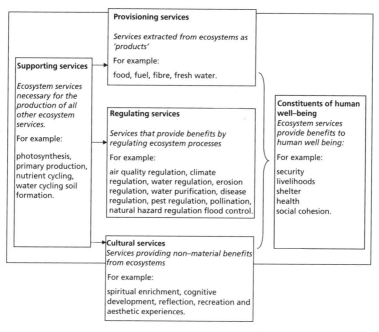

Figure 2.1: Ecosystem services: general framework (after Millennium Assessment, 2005).

England (Posthumus, 2010), and the positive contribution of dung beetles (Nichols *et al.*, 2008).

The national assessment completed in 2011 involved in-depth scientific reviews of the broad habitats to be found in the UK – such as mountains and moorlands, enclosed farmland – as well as reviews of the evidence base for the generic categories of services as set out in Figure 2.1. But the aim is not just to review but also, crucially, to value services and in particular to address the vexed question of valuing those benefits derived from the 'natural' world that would otherwise be considered 'free'. So while food, as a provisioning service, has a direct market price, other regulating services that may flow from agriculture systems, such as flood protection or carbon sequestration, are not so easily valued, hence the need for the construction of new or proxy markets drawing on a range of techniques championed by environmental economists (Pearce,

Connect

With the people around you. With family, friends, colleagues and neighbours. At home, work, school or in your local community. Think of these as the cornerstones of your life and invest time in developing them. Building these connections will support and enrich you every day.

Be active

Go for a walk or run. Step outside. Cycle. Play a game. Garden. Dance. Exercising makes you feel good. Most importantly, discover a physical activity you enjoy and that suits your level of mobility and fitness.

Take notice

Be curious. Catch sight of the beautiful. Remark on the unusual. Notice the changing seasons. Savour the moment, whether you are walking to work, eating lunch or talking to friends. Be aware of the world around you and what you are feeling. Reflecting on your experiences will help you appreciate what matters to you.

Keep learning

Try something new. Rediscover an old interest. Sign up for that course. Take on a different responsibility at work. Fix a bike. Learn to play an instrument or how to cook your favourite food. Set a challenge you will enjoy achieving. Learning new things will make you more confident as well as being fun.

Give

Do something nice for a friend, or a stranger. Thank someone. Smile. Volunteer your time. Join a community group. Look out, as well as in. Seeing yourself, and your happiness, linked to the wider community can be incredibly rewarding and creates connections with the people around you.

Figure 2.2: Five ways to well-being (Aked *et al.*, 2008).

2006). There is a strand within the ecosystem services approach, therefore, and arguably it is the dominant one, that places great emphasis on economic calculations. There would be obvious and important implications for decision making and the allocation of resources if such an approach were to be embedded in the political and economic structures of modern society. Land management decisions based solely on the market value of commodities produced from the land (food, timber, etc.) are likely to be different from those based additionally on existing and potential non-market services (biodiversity, carbon sequestration, public enjoyment, etc.).

By properly valuing all ecosystem services, it is argued, human well-being is likely to be best served. Indeed the relationship between the value of services and the sum total of human well-being is interlinked, certainly in economic theory. Much as the ecosystem service approach has sought to rescue the natural environment from the sidelines of economy and society and place it centre stage, so too the new well-being approach seeks to move the goals of policy away from economics – gross national product or value added – to more broadly conceived notions of human happiness and fulfilment (feeling good and functioning well). The New Economics Foundation (NEF), which has pioneered, inter alia, the 'happy planet index' and 'national accounts of well-being', argues for building five actions into day-to-day lives as the foundation for well-being, as set out in Figure 2.2.

This secular 'rule of life' feeds into the new 'stewardship' of ecosystem services, with walking, running, cycling, gardening and catching sight of the beautiful linked to cultural services in the discourse of ecosystem services.

Problems with the ecosystem approach

Of course, this approach to potentially incorporating the environment in wider decision making and resource allocation is not without its critics. There are broadly three lines of attack, which might loosely be categorized as philosophical, political and scientific (although inevitably there is overlap between these arguments among certain writers critical of the approach). The philosophical critique is based on those who have argued, very persuasively, that there are inherent limits to seeking to place economic value on all things. As Kant argued more than two centuries ago:

> everything has a *price* or a *dignity*. If it has a price, something else can be put in its place as an equivalent; if it is exalted above all price and so admits of no equivalent, and then it has dignity. What is relative to universal human inclinations and needs has a *market price* . . .; but that which constitutes the sole condition under which anything can be an end in itself has not merely a relative value – that is, a price – but has an intrinsic value – that is, *dignity*. (Kant, 1785, p. 77, emphasis in the original, quoted in O'Neill, 2007, p. 6)

Kant clearly had slavery in mind but there are possibilities here for extending 'dignity' beyond the human agent, and certainly Kant was embarking on a course of demanding limits to market logic, which finds echoes in contemporary misgivings over the economistic language that characterizes the ES approach. O'Neil (2007), writing before ecosystem services had attained such common currency but when one of its precursors – the language of natural capital – was in its ascendancy, puts it thus:

> We do not live in capital or stocks or bundles of assets. We live in places that are significant in a variety of different ways for different communities and individuals. And the natural world in which humans have entered and will one day leave is that, a natural world with its own history: it is not 'capital'. . . . Environments, plural, are not merely bundles of resources. They are where human lives go on, places to which humans have a lived relation of work, struggle, wonder and dwelling. (p. 108)

Talking specifically about ecosystem services, Norgaard (2010) puts it even more starkly, claiming that what started as a humble economic metaphor has become integral to how we are addressing the future of humanity:

The metaphor of nature as a stock that provides a flow of services is insufficient for the difficulties we are in or the task ahead. Indeed, combined with the mistaken presumption that we can analyze a global problem within a partial equilibrium economic framework and reach a new economy project-by-project without major institutional change, the simplicity of the stock-flow framework blinds us to the complexity of the human predicament. The ecosystem services approach can be a part of a larger solution, but its dominance in our characterization of our situation and the solution is blinding us to the ecological, economic, and political complexities of the challenges we actually face. (p. 1219)

To sum up the philosophical critique, the claim is that there are logical errors in using economic metaphors to approach what are essentially non-economic problems, and these difficulties ultimately limit the analytic utility of the ES concept.

The political critique centres on the consequences of the policy roll-out of the ES approach which, some have argued, may have perverse, even negative, consequences. Thus McAfee and Shapiro (2010) have shown that the development of markets in biodiversity, carbon and hydrological management through payments for ecosystem services in Mexico has clashed with antipoverty and local development goals. So too Kosoy and Corbera (2010) argue that the process of production, exchange and consumption of ecosystem services may be characterized by power asymmetries which are as likely to reproduce as to address inequalities in access to natural resources and services. Indeed, the emergence of new property rights for newly marketized ecosystem services may lead to increasing inequality.

Finally in this section we turn, briefly, to the scientific critique. Ridder (2008) acknowledges that the focus on ecosystem services offers a justification for the conservation of biodiversity that, on pragmatic grounds, will prove attractive to many ecologists. However, Ridder points out that most services are provided not in fact by a particular whole ecosystem, but by any group of species that fulfil certain basic functional criteria and which is therefore capable of flourishing on a site. For example, food as a provisioning

service from agricultural land may be dependent on certain species, soil microbes, pollinators and so forth but not single species
in an agricultural ecosystem. Indeed, biodiversity, in and of itself,
presents many challenges to the provision of food, due to pests and
diseases. But his critique is more profound than this. He points out
that biodiversity has come to play a pivotal role in the ecosystem
services approach as part of an equilibrium biology in which everything is held to play a part and any perturbation is inherently risky
to the whole. Ridder's counter-argument is that of non-equilibrium
ecology, which holds that ecosystem functioning is largely the result
of opportunistic interactions between fluctuating and unstable species populations (see also O'Neill, 2001). In short, nature's stability may be over-played by advocates of the ecosystem approach as
ecosystem change is ubiquitous:

> Conservationists have been almost unanimous in their failure to
> acknowledge this distinction between resilient and sensitive eco-
> system services. Not only does this threaten the credibility of con-
> servation science, but also increases the likelihood that natural
> area management becomes hijacked by the demand that ecosys-
> tem service provision be made the dominant management criteria.
> (Ridder, 2008, p. 781)

Nicholson et al. (2009) are somewhat more measured in their critique but make some similar points, citing 'the linkage between
biodiversity and ecosystem function' (p. 1142) as not yet well
understood. They highlight too the lack of understanding of 'the
thresholds of scale or levels of disruption that can result in rapid
collapse or change of state of an ecosystem service' (p. 1142). In
this context, feedbacks between and within both social and ecological systems are vital and are poorly understood. This may seem on
the surface a rather arid scientific dispute but the implications could
be profound:

> The research interest in the field of ecosystem services is rapidly
> expanding, and can contribute significantly to the sustainable
> management of natural resources. However, a narrow disciplinary

approach, or an approach which does not consider feedbacks within and between ecological and social systems, has the potential to produce dangerously misleading policy recommendations. In contrast, if we explicitly acknowledge and address uncertainties and complexities in the provision of ecosystem services, progress may appear slower but our models will be substantially more robust and informative about the effects of environmental change. (p. 1139)

It will be apparent by now that these concerns about the ecosystem approach do not amount to a unified and consistent body of argument. Some fear that the approach might lead to too much (negative) change as the forces of economics extend their tentacles ever more deeply into human and non-human spheres. Others fear that a stasis, derived from a misunderstanding of ecosystems themselves, may prevent us from developing our ability to discern and work with processes of ecological change. Some would argue that many of these criticisms are premature in that the ecosystem services approach is still in an early stage of development both scientifically and politically. Hopefully the criticisms will serve to influence positively the way in which the approach is framed and implemented in practice. It is the contention of this chapter that the ecosystem approach is here to stay, certainly in terms of its influence within policy circles, and that working within this paradigm requires a critical engagement in which other framings of the environment problem are developed simultaneously.

Land, morality, people: a return to stewardship

It is timely, therefore, to return to the land and particularly to its stewardship. The language of land management and stewardship long pre-date the development of the ecosystem services approach. As signalled in the introduction to this chapter, there is a fundamental problem at the heart of this, namely the absence of a moral or normative imperative without which radical change in human relationships or human–land relations is hard to envision. This is only partially addressed by bringing well-being into the equation, not least because the economic methods used to establish well-being are not adequate to take on board the prescriptive, some might argue utopian, notions of well-being put forward by the NEF. However, land management, as a discipline in both practice and the academy, has long concerned itself with processes *and* with ends. Often, it is true, these have been deeply conservative ends but they are not intrinsically so. The insights of land management as an approach to our relations with the environment, with creation, are simply stated:

- Most of what we value from land is a result of some form of human intervention.
- Humans intervene in processes, and while their interventions may comprise single actions they have longer-term consequences.
- Different land-management activities will have differential consequences for societies and individuals connected to that land.

In other words, land management is a human enterprise based around decisions and choices and therefore is essentially an activity that will be governed by norms of behaviour. It is an ethical undertaking and as such takes place in historical and geographical settings, in relationship and in community, which provides the 'essential context of ethics' (Carruthers, 2009, p. 312). Of course, this ethical context for our relationship with the land has been developed in biblical theology in particular by the seminal work of Walter Brueggemann (2002). His biblical reflections on the people of Israel coming into their 'promised' land have remarkable resonances for us as we grapple with our own relations with the land. He identifies land as gift, as temptation, as task, and as threat. As gift, land surely should not be seen solely in terms of its economic and servicing properties. The temptation in our time is to take land for granted, to abuse and over-use, to ignore the richness of land as community. The tasks are many: land management, land stewardship, the proper application of science, the promotion of justice. And the threat is not, as Lovelock (2009) so graphically sets out, that the land will disappear or even that ecosystems will cease to function, but that with rampant climate change and natural resource depletion they will no longer function in ways that suit human existence.

To accept gifts, to resist temptation, to engage in working relationship in land and community, and to build resilience in the face of threat are the characteristics of the 'good' life. To achieve this, intimacy or, to return to Kant, dignity is required. We need to dignify the land through intimate relationship and intimate knowing, for that is what lies at the heart of good land management and stewardship. This is an enterprise that is both scientific and theological. As Winter and Lobley (2009) have explained, land has been neglected in research and this neglect is manifest in all sorts of ways. As Nicholson *et al.* (2009) remind us, 'the dynamics of the soil microbial community still require substantial research if we are to understand and predict the processes underlying decomposition' (p. 1142; see also Brussaard *et al.*, 1997). And not only decomposition, for the behaviour of microbes is important to our understanding of movement of water across and through catchments (Kay *et al.*, 2007) and thus of environmental risks associated with water pollution (Fish *et al.*, 2009). To microbes add soil physics and chemistry, field processes, landforms, hydrology; the list could go on.

Intimate knowledge through science allows us to scope the management actions that might be taken to promote healing of the 'the land' and of our relations with it. Intimacy is equally important to the rejuvenation of the relationship between people and land through a proper understanding and, indeed, promotion of people in place; what it means to be an individual, a family, a community within a locality. So we turn to theology and sociology in the final part of this section. The theologian Mark Wynn (2009) has sought to explain how 'our encounter with particular places, each characterized by its own phenomenology and distinctive possibilities for bodily appropriation, may prove to be religiously significant' (p. 44). He outlines three ways in which this might be the case. First, particular places may come to hold a religious significance because they carry some microcosmic significance, epitomizing in some way the nature of things more generally. Second, God is taken to be presupposed in some particular material context – places or features that appear to point to God. Third, there are those places that re-present the meaning of past religious events that took place there. In all three contexts, religious experiences can have positive implications for faith, relationships and action. In the first and second of these possibilities, outdoor and open places may be more important than the traditional built or enclosed sites of religious devotion.

Empirical social scientific evidence of the extent and nature of these religious encounters are much harder to find, especially in the UK context. This paucity of quantitative or even qualitative data is, of course, rooted in the historical and contemporary sociology of religion. At the risk of gross simplification we can identify two key issues, both legacies of the reformation. The first is the uncertain status of sacred space in Protestant theology and ecclesiology, issues that have been rehearsed at great length in contemporary writings (examples include Brown, 2004; Inge, 2003; Sheehy, 2007; Wynn, 2007, 2009). The second is the rise of new forms of religiosity and religious pluralism which give more importance to land and space. This primarily concerns New Age spirituality with its particular emphasis on holism and 'connectedness' to nature (Heelas, 1996). It is not explored further in this chapter, where the focus is on Christian approaches (but see Heelas and Woodhead, 2005).

Protestant Christianity has not historically been sympathetic to a theology of sacred places as efficacious, in and of themselves, to religious well-being. Thus it stands in contrast to the importance attached to religious sites and places in pre-reformation Britain so graphically portrayed in the works of Eamon Duffy (1992). Sadly, Duffy provides little comment on the legacy of some of the sites and practices he explores. However, the twentieth century has witnessed a modest reassessment of space within mainstream protestant denominations (including the Anglican Church), and pilgrimage, retreats and ideas of sacred space have become more acceptable.

A few studies are now focusing empirically on the motivations and experiences of those for whom religious experience is linked in some way to particular places and ecosystems. Wynn (2007) talks of the 'localization of divine presence' that is implied in pilgrimage. Where research on motivation and experience has been undertaken there is a tendency to focus on the built environments that are pilgrimage destinations, such as churches and cathedrals (Winter and Gasson, 1996). However, there has been an increasing focus on the journey through nature or land rather than solely the destination (Coleman and Eade, 2004), although not yet researched in Britain. Frey (1998) has studied those walking to Santiago de Compostela and found the sacred goal to be less important to many than the journey through wild and beautiful terrain. More recently, Bremborg (2008) has looked at the experiences of pilgrims in Sweden. Pilgrimage, banned in Sweden at the Reformation, has been re-assimilated in the Lutheran church in a way that puts more emphasis on the walking than on specific pilgrim places. Participants in Bremborg's study were asked to evaluate eight pilgrimage activities. All were evaluated highly positively, but 'silent walking' was at the top of the list, ahead even of prayer and celebrations of the Eucharist. Linked to this, 'get out in nature' headed a list of twelve motivations. Ross-Bryant (2005), in a very different context, has examined the role of nature in pilgrimage in the context of US national parks. He sees nature as set apart in parks as 'the embodiment of an archetypal America, which is the ever-pristine source of the greatness of the nation and the people. As such, it serves as a sacred site and a unifying symbol in US American culture.' Similar claims for the importance of 'natures' and the countryside to national identity occur in political, social and literary writings in twentieth century Britain, some of which are explicitly linked to religious discourses. Matless (1998) shows how a number of advocates of organic farming and ruralism both drew from and further developed Christian thinking: 'the model is of a universal parochial church, attentive to often semi-pagan seasonal ritual, with place itself becoming a church to belong to and revere' (p. 128). Moore-Colyer (2001) has examined one of these thinkers, Rolf Gardiner, in more detail, and his attempts to enlist Church leaders and people in a greater understanding of the spirituality of nature and of rural living (see also Jefferies and Tyldesley, 2010).

Alongside the growth of pilgrimage as 'moving though nature', there has also been a marked growth in recent years in religious retreats to particular places in nature. There are approximately 130 places of Christian retreat in Britain listed by the Retreat Association, located in both urban and rural locations. A project by David Conradson at Southampton University is examining four retreat centres in southern England, looking at how retreat centre staff view the growing public interest in the experiential environments they make available; what guests experience when they visit retreat centres; how their visits relate to notions of making space for stillness; and the ways in which guests' experiences of visiting retreat centres endure beyond the period of visit. In one of the first chapters from this project, Conradson (2008) looked at two Benedictine places of retreat in southern England – Alton Abbey and Elmore Abbey. Conradson's work is particularly important because it is based on empirical research – participant observation and interviews with monks and guests on retreat. His work demonstrates clearly the spatiality of these religious places, not just the abbey buildings themselves but also the surrounding gardens and countryside. So for those on retreat the 'stillness' they seek may be found in both the Benedictine monastic liturgy but also in the abbey grounds and gardens. Conradson couches his research in terms of the therapeutic role of stillness and so, by implication, religious places are important to human well-being in their provision of 'therapeutic stillness'.

Conclusions

Early in my academic career, indeed at the time of the Archbishops' Commission on Rural Areas, to which I contributed research, I taught in a land management department at the Royal Agricultural College, Cirencester. I am not sure whether my erstwhile colleagues in land management would relate their practical management concerns of land surveying and management to a discussion of pilgrimage and retreat in nature, but they would readily acknowledge that this, like any other land use, requires appropriate management and is consistent with the notion of stewardship that properly lies at the heart of all land management. However, the connections are more profound than that since land management as a profession deals in both intimacy and in intricacy. The pursuit of management requires attention to detail in the sciences of valuation, property law, agronomy and forestry, applied to particular cases and places. It is also about property relations. The land management profession presupposes land occupancy based on private ownership; indeed its bedrock is the delineation and protection of property rights. To many concerned with social justice and access to land, existing private property relations and the unequal distribution of property rights will raise profound ethical and political questions at a national and global scale.

The Church is caught up in the inevitable tensions that derive from its ownership of land while exercising a prophetic ministry of social justice. Too often this debate has revolved only around justice for people in terms of land access and occupancy, but there is also a justice issue with regard to the land itself, its own integrity and inherent value. It would be foolish to maintain that land management could be neutral on such issues, but it can contribute the knowledge necessary to inform such debates. If the ecosystem services approach runs the danger of being an amoral marriage of convenience between a certain strand of economics and a certain strand of ecology, then the land management discipline has the potential to provide that added depth necessary for an ethical undertaking. Land management that makes the case for place, locality, intimacy and intricacy in our relationships with the land moves us away from narrowly utilitarian conceptions.

Thus at a time when global land grabs are in the news, when the demands on land for all sorts of purposes are so exacting and potentially conflicting, we need to take stock of how we relate to land and why; and to what end do we think about the land. By making that end human well-being, notwithstanding the wholly secular terms in which that paradigm has been developed, the contemporary proponents of ecosystem services offer at least a means for those who wish to reclaim the land as an ethical enterprise and a theological one. If this is also grounded in that older discipline of land management, we may yet resolve some of the profound political and ethical dilemmas we confront. However, this is not easy territory to navigate. As an ethical project, 'reclaiming' the land for human goodness and the glory of God may provoke powerful vested interests. Nor are the relationships we as church people need to cultivate likely to be either comfortable or always welcome. After all, natural science weaves its way through this chapter. The religious quest and the scientific quest might be comfortably aligned for many of us but not for all – but that is another chapter for another time! Meanwhile, seedtime and harvest, the land, endures, at least for now.

Acknowledgement

I am grateful to my two close colleagues in the Centre for Rural Policy Research at the University of Exeter, Matt Lobley and Rob Fish, without whose longstanding research collaboration this chapter would have been the weaker. All shortcomings are, of course, entirely my own.

References

Beddington, J., 2009, 'Food, energy, water and the climate: A perfect storm of global events?' – Keynote Speech to Sustainable Development UK 09, QEII Conference Centre, London.

Bremborg, A.D., 2008, 'Spirituality in silence and nature: Motivations, experiences and impressions among Swedish pilgrims', *Journal of Empirical Theology* 21, pp. 149–65.

Brown, D., 2004, *God and Enchantment of Place: Reclaiming Human Experience*, Oxford: Oxford University Press.

Brueggemann, W., 2002, *The Land: Place as Gift, Promise, and Challenge in Biblical Faith*, Minneapolis: Fortress Press.

Brussaard, L., Behan-Pelletier, V.M., Bignell, D.E., Brown, V.K., Didden, W.A.M., Folgarait, P.J., Fragoso, C., Freckman, D.W., Gupta, V.V.S.R. and Hattori, T., 1997, 'Biodiversity and ecosystem functioning in soil', *Ambio* 26, pp. 563–70.

Bulte, E.H., Lipper, L., Stringer, R. and Zilberman, D., 2008, 'Payments for ecosystem services and poverty reduction: Concepts, issues, and empirical perspectives', *Environment and Development Economics* 13, pp. 245–54.

Carruthers, P., 2009, 'The land debate – "doing the right thing": Ethical Approaches to land-use decision-making', in M. Winter and M. Lobley (eds), *What is Land for? The Food, Fuel and Climate Change Debate*, London: Earthscan, pp. 293–317.

Coleman, S. and Eade, J., 2004, *Reframing Pilgrimage: Cultures in Motion*, London: Routledge.

Conradson, D., 2008, 'The experiential economy of stillness: Places of retreat in contemporary Britain', in A. Williams (ed.), *Therapeutic Landscapes*, Aldershot: Ashgate.

Duffy, E., 1992, *The Stripping of the Altars: Traditional Religion in England 1400–1580*, Yale: Yale University Press.

Fish, R., Winter, M., Oliver, D.M., Chadwick, D., Selfa, T., Heathwaite, L. and Hodgson, C.J., 2009, 'Unruly pathogens: Eliciting values for environmental risk in the context of heterogeneous expert knowledge', *Environmental Science and Policy* 12, pp. 281–96.

Fonte, S.J. and Six, J., 2010, 'Earthworms and litter management contributions to ecosystem services in a tropical agroforestry system', *Ecological Applications* 20, pp. 1061–107.

Frey, N.L., 1998, *Pilgrim Stories: On and off the Road to Santiago*, Berkeley: University of California Press.

Gomez-Baggethun, E., de Groot, R., Lomas, P.L. and Montes, C., 2010, 'The history of ecosystem services in economic theory and practice: From early notions to markets and payment schemes', *Ecological Economics* 69, pp. 1209–18.

Heelas, P., 1996, *The New Age Movement*, Oxford: Blackwell.

Heelas, P. and Woodhead, L., 2005, *The Spiritual Revolution: Why Religion is Giving Way to Spirituality*, Oxford: Blackwell.

Inge, J., 2003, *A Christian Theology of Place*, Farnham: Ashgate.

Jefferies, M. and Tyldesley, M. (eds), 2010, *Rolf Gardiner: Folk, Nature and Culture in Interwar Britain*, Aldershot: Ashgate.

Kant, E., 1785, (1948 edn), *Groundwork of the Metaphysics of Morals*, London: Hutchinson.

Kay, D., Edwards, A.C., Ferrier, R.C., Francis, C., Kay, C., Rushby, L., Watkins, J., McDonald, A.T., Wyer, M., Crowther, J. and Wilkinson, J., 2007, 'Catchment microbial dynamics: The emergence of a research agenda', *Progress in Physical Geography* 31, pp. 59–76.

Kosoy, N. and Corbera, E., 2010, 'Payments for ecosystem services as commodity fetishism', *Ecological Economics* 69, pp. 1228–36.

Liu, Y.Y., Wang, W.N., Ou, C.X., Yuan, J.X., Wang, A.L., Jiang, H.S. and Sun, R.Y., 2010, 'Valuation of shrimp ecosystem services: A case study in Leizhou City, China', *International Journal of Sustainable Development and World Ecology* 17, pp. 217–24.

Lovelock, J., 2009, *The Vanishing Face of Gaia: A Final Warning*, London: Allen Lane.

Matless, D., 1998, *Landscape and Englishness*, London: Reaktion Books.

McAfee, K. and Shapiro, E.N., 2010, 'Payments for ecosystem services in Mexico: Nature, neoliberalism, social movements, and the state', *Annals of the Association of American Geographers* 100, pp. 579–99.

Millennium Assessment, 2005, *Ecosystems and Human Well-being: A Framework for Assessment*, Millennium Ecosystem Assessment.

Moore-Colyer, R., 2001, 'Rolf Gardiner, English patriot and the Council for the Church and Countryside', *Agricultural History Review* 49, pp. 187–209.

Nichols, E., Spector, S., Louzada, J., Larsen, T., Amequita, S. and Favila, M.E., 2008, 'Ecological functions and ecosystem services provided by Scarabaeinae dung beetles', *Biological Conservation* 141, pp. 1461–74.

Nicholson, E., Mace, G.M., Armsworth, P.R., Atkinson, G., Buckle, S., Clements, T., Ewers, R.M., Fa, J.E., Gardner, T.A., Gibbons, J., Grenyer, R., Metcalfe, R., Mourato, S., Muuls, M., Osborn, D., Reuman, D.C., Watson, C. and Milner-Gulland, E.J., 2009, 'Priority research areas for ecosystem services in a changing world', *Journal of Applied Ecology* 46, pp. 1139–44.

Norgaard, R.B., 2010, 'Ecosystem services: From eye-opening metaphor to complexity blinder', *Ecological Economics* 69, pp. 1219–27.

O'Neill, J., 2007, *Markets, Deliberation and Environment*, Routledge, London.

O'Neill, R.V., 2001, 'Is it time to bury the ecosystem concept?', *Ecology* 82, pp. 3275–84.

Pearce, D. (ed.), 2006, *Environmental Valuation in Developed Countries*, Cheltenham: Edward Elgar.

Posthumus, H., Rouquette, J.R., Morris, J., Cowing, D.J.G. and Hess, T.M., 2010, 'A framework for the assessment of ecosystem goods and services: A case study on lowland floodplains in England', *Ecological Economics* 69, pp. 1510–23.

Ridder, B., 2008, 'Questioning the ecosystem services argument for biodiversity conservation', *Biodiversity and Conservation* 17, pp. 781–90.

Ross-Bryant, L., 2005, 'Sacred sites: nature and nation in the US National Parks', *Religion and American Culture – a Journal of Interpretation* 15, pp. 31–62.

Sheehy, J., 2007, 'Sacred space and the incarnation', in P. North and J. North (eds), *Sacred Space: House of God, Gate of Heaven*, London: Continuum.

UK National Ecosystem Assessment, 2010, *Progress and Steps Towards Delivery*, Cambridge: UNEP-WCMC.

Winter, M. and Gasson, R., 1996, 'Pilgrimage and tourism: cathedral visiting in contemporary England', *International Journal of Heritage Studies* 2, pp. 172–82.

Winter, M. and Lobley, M., 2009, 'Conclusions: The emerging contours of the new land debate', in M. Winter and M. Lobley (eds), *What is Land for? The Food, Fuel and Climate Change Debate*, London: Earthscan, pp. 319–30.

Wynn, M., 2007, 'God, pilgrimage, and acknowledgement of place', *Religious Studies* 43, pp. 145–63.

Wynn, M., 2009, *Faith and Place: An Essay in Embodied Religious Epistemology*, Oxford: Oxford University Press.

3

How should we eat? The principles and practice of just food[1]

ELIZABETH DOWLER

'Food issues' have a wider social and political resonance these days, both in the UK and around the world: rising prices, falling yields, struggling local shops and small farmers, riots in the streets and old anxieties about feeding a growing global population. The problems pose difficult questions, which challenge complacency and certainties. Yet 'food' is such a fundamental, its relative intellectual and theological neglect is surprising. It is essential to our lives: the cement of relationships, an index of status and love and the basis of livelihoods and much trade. At individual and household/community level, food is fundamental to identity; it is taken into the self as the ultimate 'intimate commodity' (Fischler, 1988); ways of growing, processing and consuming food can contribute to group self-recognition and patterns of co-living (Pretty, 2002; Kneafsey *et al.*, 2008). As Riches (2003, p. 3) argues, 'Food is not only essential to human existence but to the quality of our lives, to cultural identity and freedom itself. To deny access to the means of life is also to deny community and democracy.' All these ideas are reflected in Max-Neef's 1992 call to recognize human requirements as being for: 'subsistence, protection, affection, understanding, participation, creation, recreation, identity and freedom'; that which we describe as basic needs (food, shelter, clothing, etc.) are only 'satisfiers' of these requirements. The ways in which they are met have to fulfil what he terms the human core needs of 'being, having, doing and interacting' (Dowler and Tansey, 2003, p. 197). Thus the biological, social, cultural and economic demands of food should be achieved using means which fulfil rather than violate these other more fundamental needs (Dowler and Tansey, 2003). Such an understanding offers a framework for re-examining Christian perspectives on and contemporary practices towards food. Not least, it challenges narrow mechanistic or utilitarian tendencies which emerge from a focus on creation as fodder to satisfy human needs, and which have been used at times to justify exploitative agricultural practices (Gorringe, 2006, pp. 91–3; Tudge, 2007). By contrast, the celebration of creation, fecundity, hospitality and God's generous love is symbolized throughout the Bible and in daily life by the growing, harvesting, rearing, trading and sharing of food. This is ultimately represented of course in the Eucharist, a shared meal in which all are invited to participate. Biblical narratives of fertile lands, running water, richness of soil, animal fertility and teeming nets may reflect the agro-pastoral and fishing subsistence and trading societies from which they emerged; but they also point to just and thriving communities, where social, economic and individual well-being are markers of grace. Barren lands or animals, dried up water sources, poor food security and unjust market trading are indicators of human failure to emulate God's creativity and the stewardship enjoined in creation. They are a powerful indictment of human failure to live and eat justly – which arguably includes those in rich countries such as the UK, who can buy and eat much of the food they want at the expense of people and environments ruined elsewhere.

Thinking and practice among faith communities is often very good on support for international aid, campaigns to 'Drop the Debt' or purchase Fairtrade commodities, but there are larger questions and challenges. Increasingly, the way contemporary societies shape, and are shaped by, the food system is under review (Tansey and Worsley, 1995; Pretty, 2002; Tudge, 2003, 2007). Arguments seem to be polarized between perspectives which endorse highly technologized and industrialized systems, based on economic efficiency, and those taking a more agro-ecological approach, based on small-scale, mixed farming and human development (see above and Lang and Heasman, 2004; Shiva, 2005). These debates have heightened as climate change, resource sustainability and population growth become more urgent. This chapter summarizes some of these polarities, and focuses on three overarching trends: increasing inequalities; turning a blind eye to the invisibilities of poor food-experience and its complexities; and 'reconnection'. These issues link UK practice with the wider, international scene, and point up, beyond individual ethical choices or group campaigns, the larger biological, social and political forces which shape the food system and the task of mitigating or changing them. It is with these challenges that we begin.

Challenges in the food system

Contemporary anxieties about food now feature regularly in the press and increasingly in academic inquiry, in ways which were less common a decade ago. This is partly because, until recently, policy makers and the public simply regarded the food system as hugely successful: more people can now choose from the greatest range of safe foodstuffs in history, and populations of previously unimaginable size are fed through the application of technology, largely in the private sector (Spielman and Pandya-Lorch, 2009; Paarlberg, 2010). That same technological innovation is already being used to reduce greenhouse gas (GHG) footprints, and industrial regulatory systems, focused on consumer interests, are efficient.[2] This view has been, and to some extent remains, the dominant position of most European, American and Australasian governments, as well as many large international and civil society organizations. Nevertheless, challenges to it have emerged from NGOs (particularly those addressing environmental issues and corporate justice), grassroots local food movements, and from individuals/academics working in food systems, environment, planning, public health and food inequalities. Broadly, the argument is that systems for producing, storing and distributing food are socially and environmentally unsustainable and deeply divisive; that fewer and fewer corporations own the means of food production for, and control the livelihoods of, large numbers of people who have no say in the process or its outcome; and that technological changes are driven by shareholder profit rather than human needs (Pretty, 2002; Shiva, 2005; Tudge, 2003, 2007; Gorringe, 2006; Patel,

2007; Roberts, 2008; Tansey, 2008; FEC, 2010). Despite national and international regulatory systems, it is argued that food contributes to both infectious and chronic diseases of various kinds, and is a critical factor in health inequalities (Lang and Heasman, 2004; Dowler *et al.*, 2007).

There is now considerable concern about the sustainability of the food system. This is usually couched in terms of the security of key inputs such as energy and water, accelerating decline in agricultural and processing skills, and the potential impact of global climate change. The latter includes threats to production, processing and transport, since the food system generates some 20%–30% of GHG, but the food system also has potential mechanisms for mitigating some effects of climate change (Garnett, 2008). Nevertheless, long-term, almost universal, state neglect of the agricultural sector has resulted in increased migration to already overcrowded urban areas, particularly in the global South, with loss of capacity on the land (skills, energy, entrepreneurship, etc.), to which sickness, especially HIV/AIDS, has added further problems. Growing public health challenges (particularly increases in Type II diabetes and obesity), which in some places co-exist with malnutrition, are also emerging, along with conflict over access to resources, especially land (Cotula *et al.*, 2009; Friends of the Earth Europe/Africa, 2010). In particular, questions are being raised over the sustainability of increased meat and dairy consumption in richer countries (USA, Canada, UK and elsewhere in Europe) and among a growing middle class in places such as India and China, since meat consumption places very large demands on grain markets, water and oil (D'Silva and Webster, 2010). In response, the food chain is implementing technical innovation, and typical advice to consumers on eating in ways which do not worsen the effects of climate change is couched as follows (this from the UK): 'if eating red meat then choose grass fed, eat more plant based foods, eat more of what you buy [that is, waste less], consider seasonality' (CFPA, 2009, p. 9). Recent responses from major philanthropic donors towards the global South are said to draw on solutions based on industrialized agriculture which have been viewed as part of the problem (Vidal, 2010[3]).

Furthermore, as is well known, in recent years world food prices have increased rapidly and differentially, in some instances by as much as 80%. Although grain prices have fallen since the 2007/08 spike, the volatility continues. These price increases have been variously attributed to rising oil prices, land and resources diverted to biofuels, grain going to animal feed (rising meat demand), and low stocks following droughts in major producing areas such as Australia (Ambler-Edwards *et al.*, 2009, among many). More recent research has pointed at futures trading and speculation as contributing to commodity price instability (Jones, 2010; de Schutter, 2010). The food price crisis has to some extent been eclipsed in the media by the international economic crisis; nevertheless, the consensus is that it is still very much with us, and that '[o]ver the next few decades the global food system will come under renewed pressure . . . Expectations of abundant and ever cheaper food could come under strain. The UK can no longer afford to take its food supply for granted' (Ambler-Edwards *et al.*, 2009, p. 5).

Thus 'food' is a powerful lens through which to view many bigger issues within society, including the social, economic and environmental sustainability of livelihoods and systems of production, trade and consumption, as well as more arcane issues such as the governance of, investment in, and practice of science and technology. Hunger and malnutrition, distorted labour markets, poor working conditions, and loss of access to resources are perhaps more familiar territory for Christians. The rest of the chapter largely concentrates on UK matters, but as shown, these are inextricably linked to wider problems in the food system and potential for change.

Food inequalities

The Hebrew prophets and Jesus had harsh words for those who ignored or short-changed the hungry and whose actions perpetuated the problems of the poor; yet food inequalities and injustice are, some argue, still at the heart of the food system. The benefits of technological change for increased productivity have not been evenly experienced, and its application has probably contributed to environmental and social problems which increasingly undermine food security for poorer people. Even before the recent commodity price rises and economic crisis, the numbers who are hungry were increasing, but the UN Food and Agriculture Organization (FAO) now estimates that over a billion poor people lack access to sufficient food (FAO, 2009). In the global South the majority are in fact likely to be involved in food production: marginalized farming families, landless workers, pastoralists, fisherfolk or forest-dwellers. In addition, as hungry urban poor experience worsening conditions from the economic crisis, they migrate back to already impoverished rural areas (FAO, 2009; EHDC, 2009). Women are particularly likely to bear the brunt, as producers, processors and providers. As is now widely acknowledged, the chances of reaching the Millennium Development Goal of halving the proportion of people who are undernourished by 2015 are very slim.

Many more live with chronic malnutrition, which stunts intellectual and physical development and makes the effects of infectious disease worse, so contributing to early death (Patel, 2007; Save the Children, 2009). This is particularly true in the global South of HIV/AIDS, where those most at risk both of infection and who are less likely to obtain appropriate testing, drugs and support are poor and female (Gillespie and Kadiyala, 2005). HIV/AIDS usually affects productive workers, draining time and energy from others who then have to do the food producing / earning work while caring for orphaned children and the sick. Thus: 'HIV/AIDS and food and nutrition insecurity are becoming increasingly entwined in a vicious cycle, with food insecurity heightening susceptibility to HIV exposure and infection, and HIV/AIDS in turn heightening vulnerability to food insecurity' (Gillespie and Kadiyala, 2005, p. 4). Good nutrition, on the other hand, enables those living with HIV to remain healthier for longer, and respond better to treatment, thus generating a 'virtuous cycle'.

In addition, food and health problems which have hitherto been equated with the richer North are also increasing rapidly in the global South: obesity, coronary heart disease, Type II diabetes and cancers (Popkin, 1998; Lang *et al.*, 2009). This can be linked to changing agricultural practice and food imports and exports (Hawkes, 2005), alongside changing cultural aspirations in response to marketing and (sometimes) urbanization (Popkin, 1998). These 'chronic diseases', markers for food environments as well as food patterns and nutrient intakes, are now among the leading causes of mortality worldwide. They are also often likely to affect lower income groups, who are also more susceptible to infectious diseases and the least likely to receive appropriate health care and treatment from national welfare systems. Thus the food system, while providing well for the richer world's populations, increasingly and systematically fails to meet the needs of the majority, and, with the drive to maintain 'cheap food' cultures following the economic crisis, seems likely to perpetuate rather than address inequalities.

It is difficult to identify straightforward personal or collective responses in the rich North to such inequalities, beyond giving to and supporting NGOs and charities, and buying fairly traded goods. Nevertheless, being better informed, joining campaigning or lobbying initiatives, both within local or professional communities and with local MPs or MEPs, to ensure national trading practices are just, and support for science and technological innovation governed by respect for the needs of small producers, especially women, are more time-consuming but essential tasks (Biggs, 2008; FEC, 2010). For church communities, a closer, more informal but ongoing engagement with a community in a country in the global South can also be a powerful means of enabling understanding of how difficult it is to sustain viable livelihoods which enable people to feed themselves with dignity and celebration, while maintaining the integrity of local physical and social environments. Such links can be enlightening and life changing, challenging what are sometimes implicit, often rather simplistic, notions of 'too many mouths to feed, with backward agricultural practices', and can also provide insights which help resist knee-jerk responses based entirely in rich country (and company) technology.

Yet food inequalities are not always far away, beyond reach: they can be found in Britain too. People here can have insufficient money for food, particularly for food that is better for health, or they may be unable to reach shops which sell a good range of healthy food;

they are unlikely to enjoy the choice of cuisines or opportunities for celebration most take for granted. Many deny such a circumstance is possible in a country with a longstanding welfare state, seeing the problem as more to do with poor budgeting, shopping or cooking skills. Nevertheless, continual academic and NGO research has shown that those living on state benefits or on the minimum wage for any length of time are unlikely to have enough money for food, however carefully they budget, particularly as food prices have risen over the past two years. Utility costs (water, gas, electricity, fuel) have risen at the same time and these increases affect food prices too. The recent update report on minimum income standards (MIS) shows that, largely because of the disproportionate effect of rising food prices, the costs of meeting a basic, consensually defined standard of living have risen much faster than official inflation over the last decade. Since the latter is the basis for updating benefits and the minimum wage, people on low incomes have increasingly found themselves unable to afford to live decently (Davis *et al.*, 2010). By April 2010, a couple with two children needed an income of £29,700 a year to afford a basic but acceptable standard of living (including childcare costs); this equates to £7.60 per hour, but the minimum wage is only £5.80 per hour, and in 2009 about 23% of full-time workers and 39% part-time workers aged 22 and above were paid less than £7 per hour. MIS uses average costs, but in fact the price of food can vary from shop to shop – the larger supermarkets, traditional markets and discounters are usually cheaper for basics (Dowler *et al.*, 2007). If those on low income cannot easily get to such stores (because of disability, or where they live), they may have to pay considerably more for the same goods in smaller local shops which lack larger retailers' economies of scale, and thus be further disadvantaged. This can be particularly true in rural or semi-urban communities, local produce markets notwithstanding.

These facts make clear the probable impact of low pay and current benefits levels on household well-being. People manage in different ways, but many forego a varied, healthy diet, relying instead on monotonous, cheap diets likely to be high in saturated fats, sugar and salt. Despite oft-stated desires to the contrary, people have to prioritize paying other bills, such as rent, fuel, debts, etc.; thus they buy familiar, low-cost food they know will be eaten (Dowler *et al.*, 2007), and cannot afford to try different foods or 'luxuries' such as five portions of fruit or vegetables a day. In a UK-wide national survey in 2005 of people living in multiple deprivation, almost a third said they didn't have enough money to buy enough varied and suitable food for an active and healthy life, and two out of five regularly worried about running out of money for food (Nelson *et al.*, 2007); and this was before the recent food price and utility increases, the economic crisis or forthcoming public sector cuts.

In 2009 over 5 million people claimed an out-of-work benefit in the UK, through being sick or disabled, unemployed or a lone parent, and more than three million claimed pensioner credit.[4] Almost 13 million people in the UK live in households whose income is less than 60% of the median after housing costs (the European definition of poverty), many of whom are benefit claimants or earning the minimum or low wages. Public attention is seldom directed to the circumstances of people having to live in these conditions, other than to lament the national welfare bill. If these issues are discussed, the response is often disbelief ('the only really poor people in Britain are rough sleepers or asylum seekers') or that the fault lies in people's own hands ('they need to learn how to cook'). It is probably the case that younger parents have grown up in a culture which does not value food skills of any kind (although many schools have recently begun to address this failure). Yet anyone who has tried to manage on benefits, a state pension or low wages for any length of time knows how difficult it is to eat properly or to feed growing children when money is scarce. Many who work in the Church, education, health or social care with hard-up households, or who run community food projects, school breakfasts, homework clubs or healthy school meals, recognize these complexities of managing on low incomes.

Turning a blind eye: invisibilities and ignorance

Here, then, is a blind eye turned: whether or not the circumstances are recognized, few in Britain protest, campaign or work to redress this food injustice. Of course, many people do help rough sleepers or asylum sleepers – rightly so – and faith groups are prominent in distributing free food parcels and hot meals to those who need them. But a substantial proportion claiming such charity are not in the distressing and difficult circumstances those categories imply; they are ordinary citizens and maybe taxpayers, but they just don't have enough money to eat properly.[5] Sometimes this is temporary, because of benefit problems or difficulties when starting a job. The Trussell Trust, for instance, a recent example of a Christian charity whose work has grown exponentially to meet needs, has campaigned about the need for food banks to feed households during benefit delay (see box below). They seem to be having some success, in that the current Government has endorsed its activities (Lewis, 2010). However, sometimes people's need for material help, including for food, is much more permanent, in that they are without sufficient money for long periods. This is often recognized by those handing out food, but seldom acknowledged by government or the general public. It is a critical challenge to ask why people should have regularly to accept charitable food – essentially others' food cast-offs – in order to survive; indeed, to question whether it is right that the Government recognize the inadequacy of the benefits system by allowing distribution of vouchers for food banks through Job Centre Plus offices (Riches, 2011). In rural areas the problem is exacerbated because these offices are not easily accessible but require either an impossible or an extremely costly journey by public transport.

The Trussell Trust: emergency food due to benefit delay

The Trussell Trust charity runs a network of community-led foodbanks across the UK which provide emergency food to people in crisis. Foodbanks work in partnership with frontline care professionals such as doctors and social workers who identify to the foodbank people who are going hungry. The care professionals issue a food voucher entitling people to a minimum of three days of emergency

---

food and signpost to other organizations who are able to resolve the underlying cause of the crisis. Clients are referred to foodbanks for a variety of reasons including redundancy, benefit delay, ill health, low income, homelessness and debt. Food is donated by schools, churches, businesses and individuals in the local area and sorted by volunteers. Each foodbank is led by a local church and encourages help to the community by the community. Currently over 100 foodbanks have been launched nationwide and this number is growing rapidly. The goal is for every town to have a foodbank (www.trusselltrust.org).

Last year 60,000 people across the UK received emergency food from Trussell Trust charity foodbanks, a 50% increase on the previous year. Over a third of people were referred due to benefit delay. As a result of pressure from the Trussell Trust, the previous Government's directive which stopped Job Centre Plus issuing food vouchers to eligible clients, has been rescinded in 2011 (www.trusselltrust.org/resources/documents/Press/PRESS-RELEASE-Jobcentre-to-give-out-food-vouchers.pdf).

Such social injustice is very hard to grasp. It is often unseen; people find it shameful to admit to not having enough to eat decently or even at all and 'food' is a private concern for many, especially poorer people. This is not to condemn giving food to those who need it: such action appeals to people's basic instincts to help those less fortunate, and clearly meets an immediate, urgent need. However, the reasons why people are in the position of requiring such help are less transparent and harder to challenge. Nevertheless, the consistent biblical message is not only to 'feed the hungry'; it is to understand and address *why* people are hungry. Even when 'rescue feeding', Jesus' actions were towards hospitality and dignity, not minimalism or shame – which is the UK state's approach on behalf of its citizens.

These complexities of contemporary British circumstances need to be better understood and acknowledged. Some of the evidence that benefits and low wages are in themselves insufficient for decent living, including having enough food, has been outlined; in addition, there can be indignities and problems from systematic delays or miscalculations in the money people receive. A quite different set of problems, often compounding low income, arises from the poor economic sustainability of food retail and other services in areas of multiple deprivation (Dowler *et al.*, 2007). This has also not been a policy priority, even to the former Labour Government with its commitment to reducing poverty and inequality. In terms of public sector food, work on improving school meals has moved in good directions, with appropriate standards for public health and local procurement, and some beginnings have been made with hospitals. However, at the time of writing much of this activity faces an uncertain future: school meal and social care standards, widening provision of free meals, sustainability (environmental and social) in public procurement, and local initiatives supported by Primary Care Trusts all face potential cuts under the impending public sector spending cuts. This is the more disappointing because the social pleasures and delight from growing and cooking, as well as eating food have also begun to emerge as important, with, for instance, healthy school growing and cooking initiatives.

The commercial food sector plays a complex role. Over recent decades it has increasingly been driven by the need to keep food 'cheap': the four major retailers (Tesco, Sainsbury's, Walmart/Asda and Morrisons) usually compete mostly on price, and this is often achieved both by squeezing suppliers (producers and processors) and by paying low wages to workers. Some argue that keeping food 'cheap' suits governments because it keeps benefits and wages down. But food has also been cheap only because we do not pay the full costs of its production, manufacture, processing, transport and retail. These and other externalities – such as the well-being of producers and transport workers overseas, animal welfare, carbon emissions, waste and congestion, as well as subsidies – are not reflected in the prices in the shops but borne by other people and the environment, elsewhere. For instance, recent work by Lawrence (2010) examines allegations of environmental damage, union-busting, chemical poisoning and poverty wages in Costa Rica as a result of a 'pineapple price war' in European supermarkets. Even

Fairtrade production does not always solve the issue: in this instance price differentials with non-Fairtrade pineapples (largely sold through two major US multinationals) are £1 or more. The major retailers insist they audit production and working conditions and investigate breaches of regulatory standards, but such detailed study of a commodity chain is difficult and expensive – as is litigation if complaints cannot be substantiated.

Some of these issues were addressed in a recent inquiry into food and fairness by the Food Ethics Council (FEC, 2010), which, to help clarify the nature of important inequalities, adopted a social justice framework in terms of 'fair shares' (equality of outcome), 'fair play' (equality of opportunity) and 'fair say' (autonomy and voice). These conditions were applied to the three key food policy strands: food security, sustainability and public health. The inquiry examined the symptoms and causes of food-related injustice, and attempted to analyse the complex relationships between unfairness, environmental degradation and ill-health. It drew on a wide range of evidence submitted in response to a public call, as well as the very different perspectives of the members of the 14-strong inquiry panel, half of whom were leading players in sectors and bodies in food and farming (the remainder were members of the FEC). The process of deliberating from very different viewpoints and having to engage with a variety of oral witnesses and written evidence was a critical feature of the inquiry's work, and enabled the challenges posed by conflicting understandings of these different interests to be made explicit and creatively addressed. The key messages from the inquiry, whose report by the FEC secretariat includes recommendations for government, businesses and civil society, are set out in the following box.

Food Justice: The Report of the Food and
Fairness Inquiry

Key messages
'The Food and Fairness Inquiry was motivated by the concern that policy debate around sustainable food and farming does not attach due weight to issues of social justice. In addition to . . .

---

the recommendations . . ., the Inquiry committee . . . formulated a series of "key messages" that encapsulate how the debate about food policy needs to change, in order to reflect the seriousness of social justice issues, and the ways in which they relate to concerns about environmental sustainability and public health.

- Food policy is central to meeting recognized ecological sustainability challenges.
- Social justice issues around food are at the heart of recognized environmental and health challenges.
- Addressing food-related social injustice mainly requires wider social and economic policy solutions.
- Social justice does not mean treating everyone the same.
- We need to find ways to engage people, and society as a whole, with food policy.
- To enable people to change their behaviour, we need to address the inequalities that underpin their behaviour.
- "Cheap food" is no longer a legitimate social policy objective.
- The market, including the financial market, has to work differently.
- There are limits to what can be achieved through market mechanisms, so we need government leadership.
- The current international trade regime presents significant obstacles to addressing social injustice in food and farming.
- All stakeholders face limits to what they can achieve themselves but, for their commitment to social justice to be credible, they must openly support whatever measures are necessary but beyond their own capacity.

The UK is an unfair society in a deeply unfair world. The Food and Fairness Inquiry has shown how all of us – in government, business, and civil society – are to some extent implicated. This means that we all have responsibilities for doing something about it. We can each do much more before we run up against the limits to our responsibilities.' (FEC, 2010, pp. 17–18)

The main summary message is a call to recognize the causes and consequences of social injustices within the food system, in the UK and elsewhere, and the imperative to do something about them, at every level. Of course, the intense pressures on all involved (consumers, producers, processors, scientists, retailers, workers) and the factors driving the system in current directions, have to be acknowledged. These trends, which are national and international, include:

- Agricultural employment (fewer farmers and landowners, more landless labourers with fewer skills, demands for high flexibility so that producers bear more and more of the risk).
- Processing and retail (high levels of regulation which militates against small businesses remaining in the system, increasing short-termism from shareholders).
- Consumerism (increasingly values-driven, but with many unable to afford to put their values into practice).

All these trends are well documented, including to an increasing extent in policy and government circles (CFPA, 2010; Scottish Government, 2009), but are much less acknowledged by the general public. Again, these complexities need to be recognized and engaged with because, in the longer term, rising oil and other input costs, water and land scarcities and the impact of climate change induced instabilities, will mean that global and national food supply are less assured, and that more imaginative, just solutions will rapidly become essential if the trend towards polarized consumption is to be halted, and growing international middle-class affluence does not increasingly deprive international poor classes of food.

Although poverty-driven food inequalities in Britain have similar causes, if not yet such desperate effects, as those in the global South, both public systems and welfare, and the public in general, have grown used to paying less for food bought for daily consumption, year on year, as the promotion and pleasures of eating out have grown alongside purchase of expensive cookery books and luxury ingredients. On average the UK spend on food is about 10% of income (though those in the lowest income groups spend 16% or more) but, as mentioned earlier, having to pay more for food over the last couple of years has had severe economic and social effects (Gentleman, 2009; IGD, 2009). In other parts of the world rising food prices have led to civil unrest which destabilize governments. The cheap food culture (in all senses) has to be challenged, but this has to be done fairly so as not to make the circumstances of the poorest even worse. Solutions have to encompass both better understanding of the forces and contradictions producing cheap food and externalized costs, and creative social justice so that the answer is not simply 'high-tech' production-led and top-down (FEC, 2008). On the contrary, the FEC and others argue that what is needed is an agro-ecological approach which moves beyond familiar calls for corporate-dominated systems of industrial agriculture locking producers and processors into vertically controlled global markets, to a more equitable system placing food for people at the centre of policy and practice (UK Food Group, 2010).

Reconnection

This, then, marks the 'reconnection' potential of new ways of 'doing food', for:

> biologically diverse 'agro-ecological' farming and grazing methods, especially those practised sustainably by small-scale food producers, particularly women, make agriculture more resilient, adaptive and capable of eliminating hunger and rural poverty . . . policy and institutional failure has limited the use of sustainable practices; it could also be argued this is the underlying reason why people are malnourished, farmers are poor and the price of food is rising. (IAASTD, 2008)

These words come from a summary of the 2008 report from the International Assessment of Agricultural Knowledge, Science and Technology for Development which was sponsored by the Food and Agriculture Organisation, Global Environment Facility, United Nations Development Programme, United Nations Environment Programme, United Nationals Educational, Scientific and Cultural Organisation, the World Bank and the

World Health Organisation. IAASTD presents radical, agro-eco-logical approaches as solutions to the current food crisis. The UK Government (previous and present) has so far shown little overt interest in implementing it (in fact the chair of the report commit-tee, Professor Robert Watson, is now Chief Scientist at Defra). But such solutions find much resonance with practices among small producers here in the UK and elsewhere, as well as, in fact, echoing biblical principles of resilience, social fairness and holistic views of creation (McIntosh, 2001; Gorringe, 2006; Clark and Morley, 2008).

Such approaches reflect the growing desire from producers and the public to 'reconnect' to each other and to their food: its sourc-ing in soil, water, the biosphere; a concern for decent ways of rearing animals and harvesting their products; a respect for 'the earth' (Kneafsey *et al.*, 2008; Dowler *et al.*, 2010). Many in Europe and North America now use farmers' markets, farm shops, box schemes, or try to grow more of their own food. In England, Big Lottery funding has enabled the Food for Life Partnership[6] and Making Local Food Work Partnership[7] to develop and build com-munity support and practice in growing, sourcing and consuming local food, and transforming food cultures. Churches have also been urging their congregations to buy from local producers so as to improve understanding and change practices over valuing food. Although 'local' food may not effect the major reduction in GHG footprints as sometimes claimed, purchasing or growing it provides an opportunity to help maintain viable livelihoods in the UK and elsewhere, and to contribute to improved well-being and justice in society (Steedman and MacMillan, 2008; Edwards-Jones, 2010). Again, as with communities in the global South, links between lo-cal producers and church groups can be revealing, supportive and life-changing. Such processes can take time and effort to effect: 're-connection' is not just about structures and distance but also in-volves feelings, perceptions and the work of building relationships which generate and maintain trust and regard. Furthermore, the time spent using local suppliers outwith the main supermarkets for collecting, cleaning and cooking food, which also builds confidence and skills, embodies a practical way to challenge the industrialized contemporary food culture and system, where economic efficiency, denying seasonality and minimal consumer effort are paramount (Kneafsey *et al.*, 2008).

Academic study of people's reasons for being involved in 're-connection' in its different forms has explored the multiplicity of drives and desires. Unsurprisingly, many talk about a desire for better health as a key motivation for engagement, but this under-standing of health is much broader than mere absence of disease or poisoning, which is how 'health' is usually seen in public policy. Rather, people talk about 'being healthy' as being part of a thriv-ing and sustainable ecosystem, where the integrity of the soil and other living creatures is respected; this is health in its most holistic sense, as true wholeness and well-being for creation and not just the individual. Second, many people who use farm shops, com-munity supported agriculture, local food hubs or co-operatives, even those living in highly urban areas, say they value produc-tion systems which are less dependent on non-renewable resources, which waste less and which promote social as well as environ-mental growth and well-being. In this they demonstrate that, even for people in a long-industrialized society, a true agro-ecological way of living can be imagined and put into practice (Kneafsey *et al.*, 2008). This is perhaps more remarkable given the increasingly industrialized nature of the food system: although it is hard to give numbers, there is clear evidence of a more grassroots, community-based desire for different ways of growing, processing, retailing and consuming food.

Furthermore, people value transparency and integrity in food systems, particularly over science and technology, and their gov-ernance (Dowler *et al.*, 2010). Thus, for instance, much of the reaction against genetically modified (GM) food is not so much 'anti-science' as showing deep concern at corporate control of the scientific and technological processes as well as the outputs – what might be rather construed as 'anti-Monsanto' (Tansey, 2008; UK Food Group, 2010).

Finally, but also crucially, food is associated with, and essential to, pleasure, both for individuals, in taking delight in growing, pre-paring or eating particular foods, and as part of hospitality – even for those who are not very wealthy – and to be denied this is to be denied humanity. Consensual budget standards include being able to invite people to celebrate birthdays or festivals, and being able to eat out occasionally. Max-Neef's (1992) fundamental needs for 'being, having, doing and interacting' echo these elements, and challenge parsimonious definitions of poverty and basic needs, as well as pointing up possibilities for change. That our relationships to food need to change is unequivocal: we need visions which respect creation and sustainable living, and ways of putting them into effect. Taking part in a community-supported agriculture scheme, joining a local bread-hub, helping children grow vegetables in a school garden and cook them for their school café are all ways to live differently where food is concerned. Even those who are very poor in Britain, who live what might seem chaotic lives, sometimes with no regular address, can be transformed by growing, cooking and sharing food, gaining skills, self-respect and pleasure. These practices contribute to building a sense of celebration in food provision and an understanding of plenty without profligacy, learning how to eat more simply and in ways which are less demanding of resources (Pretty, 2002). They support more diversified agriculture and husbandry, in the UK and elsewhere – systems which in fact have a history of re-emerging as intensification and monocultures fail (see Thirsk, 1997, for a clear account).

Conclusions

There is currently an almost apocalyptic visioning of the future for food, with profound implications for human security. Food security is seen as under threat from social instability and environmental unsustainability, conflict over access to resources of land, water and fossil fuels and the growing protest from the hungry and poor in a world technically able to feed itself. Concern over population growth contributes to building what powerful people are describing as the 'perfect storm' (Beddington, 2009). The many national and international meetings and reports point up these challenges to the global food system: a system, as Tansey (2008) points out, which has both an economic and social history as well as a future.

The latter does not have to be dictated by the former; many argue the need to order things differently. The real challenge is to know how.

This chapter has drawn attention to the need to make social justice and reconnection explicit and tangible, both in public policy and in governance of science and technology. This is hard, but the real difficulty is breaking out of notions of poverty and scarcity, recognizing them to be human constructions which maintain inequalities of resources and power. Indeed, the politics of food is precisely located here. Instead, processes which enable emotional and economic imagination to focus on abundance, rather than limitations and scarcity, are needed, so that ideas of possibility are enabled (Campbell, 2003). The participative and democratic processes which are embodied in the international Food Sovereignty movement, with all its limitations and challenges (Patel, 2009; Pimbert, 2010); which were espoused by the IAASTD report (2008); which govern operations of the UK Food Group (UK Food Group, 2010) and were used in the Food Ethics Council's inquiry (FEC, 2010), need to be replicated in policy practice within the UK and more widely. In the Bible, images of feasting, delicious food and overflowing wine signal deliverance and reconciliation, as do production, land and trade justice. We have to find ways of realizing the creative potential of 'caring' for food – not as a reductionist way of avoiding ill-health but as active contribution to well-being and delight, in a world that really can produce enough for everyone's needs.

To help achieve this, consensually defined minimum income standards (MIS) should be widely used in the UK at national and local levels, by government and other actors in public and private sectors, to ensure all households have sufficient money to live decently. MIS have been endorsed by over 70 NGOs, including trade unions and church governing bodies. They are the basis of the living wage, and have implications for the minimum wage, levels of benefit and, for instance, court practices in imposing fines on those whose incomes are low. Change can be achieved through campaigning, advocacy and example.

Churches would benefit from exploring what it could mean to a eucharistic community to build resilience in ecosystems, common knowledge and spirit, in relation to food. This notion of resilience in 'soil, soul and society' draws on Alastair McIntosh.[8] The ideas can relate to a specific locality, or to wider groupings of congregations. 'Resilience' can mean many things, but has the key notion of building and sustaining capacity to withstand shocks, changes and uncertainties. It might include increasing self-sufficiency, and taking stock of what we have and need, rather than just what we want.

References

Ambler-Edwards, S., Bailey, K., Kiff, A., Lang, T., Lee, R., Marsden, T., Simons, D. and Tibbs, H., 2009, *Food Futures: Rethinking UK Strategy*, London: Chatham House.

Beddington, J., 2009, 'Food, energy, water and the climate: A perfect storm of global events?' Speech to the Sustainable Development Conference UK 09, QEII Conference Centre, London, 19 March 2009, www.webarchive.nationalarchives.gov.uk/ and www.dius.gov.uk/news_and_speeches/speeches/john_beddington/perfect-storm

Biggs, S., 2008, 'The lost 1990s? Personal reflections on a history of participatory technology development', *Development in Practice* 18, pp. 489–505.

Campbell, C., 2003, *Stations of the Banquet: Faith Foundations for Food Justice*, Collegeville, Liturgical Press.

CFPA, 2009, *First Report from the Council of Food Policy Advisors*, London: Defra, www.archive.defra.gov.uk/foodfarm/food/policy/council/pdf/cfpa-rpt-090914.pdf

CFPA, 2010, *Food: A Recipe for a Healthy, Sustainable and Successful Future: Second Report from the Council of Food Policy Advisors*, www.archive.defra.gov.uk/foodfarm/food/policy/council/pdf/cfpa-rpt-100315.pdf

Clark, E. and Morley, L., 2008, *The Significance of Food*, briefing paper, Churches Regional Commission for Yorkshire and Humberside, www.crc-online.org.uk/downloads/Significance%20of%20Food.doc

Cotula, L., Vermeulen, S., Leonard, R. and Keeley, J., 2009, *Land Grab or Development Opportunity? Agricultural Investment and International Land Deals in Africa*, London/Rome: International Institute for Environment and Development / Food and Agriculture Organization / International Fund for Agricultural Development, www.pubs.iied.org/12561IIED.html

Davis, A., Hirsch, D. and Smith, N., 2010, *A Minimum Income Standard for the UK in 2010*, York: Joseph Rowntree Foundation, www.jrf.org.uk/sites/files/jrf/MIS-2010-report_0.pdf

de Schutter, O., 2010, *Food Commodities Speculation and Food Price Crises: Regulation to Reduce the Risks of Price Volatility*, Briefing Note 02, www.iaahp.net/uploads/media/20102309_briefing_note_02_en.pdf

Dowler, E. and Tansey, G., 2003, 'Food and poverty', in P. Mosley and E. Dowler (eds), *Poverty and Social Exclusion in North and South*, London: Routledge, pp. 189–207.

Dowler, E., Caraher, M. and Lincoln, P., 2007, 'Inequalities in food and nutrition: challenging "lifestyles"', in E. Dowler and N. Spencer (eds), *Challenging Health Inequalities: from Acheson to 'Choosing Health'*, Bristol: Policy Press, pp. 127–155.

Dowler, E., Kneafsey, M., Cox, R. and Holloway, L., 2010, '"Doing food differently": reconnecting biological and social relationships through care for food', in N. Charles and R. Carter (eds), *Nature, Society and Environmental Crisis*, Sociological Review Monograph, Chichester: Wiley-Blackwell, pp. 200–21.

D'Silva, J. and Webster, J. (eds), 2010, *The Meat Crisis: Developing More Sustainable Production and Consumption*, London: Earthscan.

Edwards-Jones, G., 2010, 'Does eating local food reduce the environmental impact of food production and enhance consumer health?', *Proceedings of the Nutrition Society*, volume 69, issue 04, pp. 582–91, Cambridge Journals Online, 10 August 2010, doi:10.1017/S0029665110002004

EHDC (Eradicate Hunger Drafting Committee), 2009, *Policies and Actions to Eradicate Hunger and Malnutrition*, working paper, www.eradicatehunger.org

Evans, A., 2008, *Rising Food Prices: Drivers and Implications for Development*, London: Chatham House.

FAO, 2009, *The State of Food Insecurity in the World 2009: Economic Crises – Impacts and Lessons Learned*, Rome: Food and Agriculture Organization, www.fao.org/publications/sofi/en/

FEC, 2008, 'The food crisis', *Food Ethics Magazine*, summer, www.foodethicscouncil.org/node/215

FEC, 2010, *Food Justice: The Report of the Food and Fairness Inquiry*, Brighton: Food Ethics Council, www.foodethicscouncil.org/node/465

Fischler, C., 1988, 'Food, self and identity', *Social Science Information* 27, pp. 275–92.

Friends of the Earth Africa, Friends of the Earth Europe, 2010, *Africa: Up for Grabs: The Scale and Impact of Land Grabbing for Agrofuels*, Brussles: Friends of the Earth Europe, www.foeeurope.org/agrofuels/FoEE_Africa_up_for_grabs_2010.pdf

Garnett, T., 2008, *Cooking up a storm: Food, Greenhouse Gas Emissions and our Changing Climate*, Food Climate Research Network, Guildford: University of Surrey, www.fcrn.org.uk/fcrn/publications/cooking-up-a-storm

Gentleman, A., 2009, 'A portrait of 21st century poverty', *The Guardian*, 18 March.

Gillespie, S. and Kadiyala, S., 2005, *HIV/AIDS and Food and Nutrition Security: From Evidence to Action*, Washington: International Food Policy Research Institute, www.ifpri.org/publication/hivaids-and-food-and-nutrition-security

Gorringe, T., 2006, *Harvest: Food, Farming and the Churches*, London: SPCK.

Hawkes, C., 2005, 'The role of foreign direct investment in the nutrition transition', *Public Health Nutrition* 8, pp. 357–65.

IAASTD, 2008, *Agriculture at a Crossroads: Global Summary for Decision Makers*, Washington: Island Press for the International Assessment of Agricultural Knowledge, Science and Technology for Development (IAASTD), www.agassessment.org/reports/IAASTD/EN/Agriculture%20at%20a%20Crossroads_Synthesis%20Report%20(English).pdf

IGD, 2009, *Shopper Trends 2009: Food Shopping in a Recession*, Watford: Institute of Grocery Distribution.

Jones, T., 2010, *The Great Hunger Lottery: How Banking Speculation Causes Food Crises*, London: World Development Movement, www.wdm.org.uk/food-speculation/great-hunger-lottery

Kneafsey, M., Venn, L., Holloway, L., Cox, R., Dowler, E. and Tuomainen, H., 2008, *Reconnecting Consumers, Producers and Food: Exploring Alternatives*, Oxford: Berg.

Lang, T., Barling, D. and Caraher, M., 2009, *Food Policy: Integrating Health, Environment and Society*, Oxford: Oxford University Press.

Lang, T. and Heasman, M., 2004, *Food Wars*, London: Earthscan.

Lawrence, F., 2010, 'Bitter fruit: The truth about supermarket pineapple', *The Guardian*, 2 October (Colour Magazine pp. 40–7), www.guardian.co.uk/business/2010/oct/02/truth-about-pineapple-production

Lewis, P., 2010, 'Ministers consider scheme to hand out food vouchers to unemployed', *The Guardian*, 2 July, www.guardian.co.uk/politics/2010/jul/02/ministers-food-vouchers-unemployed

Max-Neef, M., 1992, 'Development and human needs', in P. Ekins and M. Max-Neef (eds), *Real-Life Economics: Understanding Wealth Creation*, Routledge: London, pp. 199–200.

McIntosh, A., 2001, *Soil and Soul: People versus Corporate Power*, London: Aurum Press.

MIS current project on rural minimum income standards, www.minimumincomestandard.org/mis_rural.htm

Nelson, M. *et al.*, 2007, *Low-Income Diet and Nutrition Survey: Executive Summary*, London: The Stationery Office.

Paarlberg, R., 2010, *Food Politics: What Everyone Needs to Know*, New York: Oxford University Press.

Patel, R., 2007, *Stuffed and Starved: Markets, Power and the Hidden Battle for the World Food System*, London: Portobello Books.

Patel, R., 2009, 'What does food sovereignty look like?' *Journal of Peasant Studies* 36, 3, pp. 663–73.

Pimbert, M., 2010, *Towards Food Sovereignty: Reclaiming Autonomous Food Systems*, London: International Institute for Environment and Development.

Popkin, B.M., 1998, 'The nutrition transition and its health implications in lower income countries', *Public Health Nutrition* 1, pp. 5–21.

Pretty, J., 2002, *Agri-Culture: Reconnecting People, Land and Nature*, London: Earthscan.

Riches, G., 2003, *The Human Right to Food: Engaging the Debate about Globalization, Employment and the Quality of Life*, paper for FAO Right to Food, www.fao.org/eims/secretariat/right_to_food/eims_search/details.asp?lang=en&pub_id=213064

Riches, G., 2011, 'Thinking and acting outside the charitable food box: hunger and the right to food in rich societies', *Development in Practice* 21:4–5, pp. 768–75.

Roberts, P., 2008, *The End of Food: The Coming Crisis in the World Food Industry*, London: Bloomsbury.

Save the Children, 2009, *Hungry for Change: An Eight-step, Costed Plan of Action to Tackle Global Child Hunger*, London: Save the Children, www.savethechildren.org.uk/en/54_9544.htm

Scottish Government, 2009, *Recipe For Success: Scotland's National Food and Drink Policy*, Edinburgh: The Scottish Government.

Shiva, V., 2005, *Earth democracy: Justice, Sustainability and Peace*, London: Zed Books Ltd.

Spielman, D.J. and Pandya-Lorch, R. (eds), 2009, *Millions Fed: Proven Successes in Agricultural Development*, Washington: International Food Policy Research Institute (IFPRI), www.ifpri.org/publication/millions-fed

Steedman, P. and MacMillan, T., 2008, *Food Distribution: An Ethical Agenda*, Brighton: Food Ethics Council, www.foodethicscouncil.org/node/401

Tansey, G., 2008, 'Farming, Food and Global Rules', in G. Tansey and T. Rajotte (eds), *The Future Control of Food: A Guide to International Negotiations and Rules on Intellectual Property, Biodiversity and Food Security*, London: Earthscan, pp. 3–24.

Tansey, G. and Worsley, T., 1995, *The Food System: A Guide*, London: Earthscan.

Thirsk, J., 1997, *Alternative Agriculture: A History from the Black Death to the Present Day*, Oxford: Oxford University Press.

Trussell Trust, The, 2010, *Jobcentres to Give Charity Food Vouchers to Neediest Clients*, www.trusselltrust.org/resources/documents/Press/PRESS-RELEASE-Jobcentre-to-give-out-food-vouchers.pdf

Tudge, C., 2003, *So Shall We Reap: What's Gone Wrong with the World's Food and How to Fix it*, London: Penguin Books.

Tudge, C., 2007, *Feeding People is Easy*, Grosseto, Pari Publishing.

UK Food Group, 2010, *Securing Future Food: Towards Ecological Food Provision*, London: UK Food Group Briefing, www.ukfg.org.uk/ ecological_food_provision.php

Vidal, J., 2010, 'Why is the Gates foundation investing in GM giant Monsanto?' *The Guardian*, 29 Sept, www.guardian.co.uk/global-development/poverty-matters/2010/sep/29/gates-foundation-gm-monsanto

von Braun, J., 2008, *Food and Financial Crises: Implications for Agriculture and the Poor*, Washington: International Food Policy Research Institute.

Notes

1 The paper draws on an earlier version published in 2008 in *The Reader* (E. Dowler, 'Getting food right: social challenge in the contemporary food system', *The Reader* 105/3 (2008), pp. 18–19); and on presentations at Blackfriars, Oxford, January 2010; National Justice and Peace Network conference, Swanwick, July 2010.

2 See for example webpages of IGD, www.igd.com/; the UK Food and Drink Federation, www.fdf.org.uk/priorities_sus_comp.aspx

3 See also Community Alliance for Global Justice (CAGJ) AGRA watch. AGRA promotes food sovereignty and farmers' self-determination. CAGJ is 'an alliance of individuals and organizations working in Seattle and the region who believe the global economy should embody the core values of social justice, environmental sustainability, democracy and self-determination'. www.seattleglobaljustice.org/agra-watch/

4 These data are all taken from the UK Poverty Site funded by the Joseph Rowntree Foundation, www.poverty.org.uk/index.htm

5 See Zacchaeus 2000 work, among others, www.z2k.org/

6 'The Food for Life Partnership is a network of schools and communities across England committed to transforming food culture. Together we are revolutionising school meals, reconnecting children and young people with where their food comes from, and inspiring families to grow and cook food.' www.foodforlife.org.uk/

7 'Making Local Food Work helps people to take ownership of their food and where it comes from by providing advice and support to community food enterprises across England.' www.makinglocalfoodwork.co.uk/

8 Alastair McIntosh developed this notion of resilience in 'soil, soul and society' in a presentation at the National Justice and Peace Network Annual Conference 2010 themed 'Our Daily Bread: food security, people and planet'.

4

No one is a *sustainable* island: a theological perspective on the sustainability agenda in the rural context

DAGMAR WINTER

Sustainability and sustainable development

Rural communities are feeling the pressure. In this they do not differ from other parts of society but the mix of perceptions and expectations of a rural way of life and the intensified relationships brought about by a much lower population density all conspire to heighten the experience of threatening change.

Change inevitably brings conflict with it – conflicting visions of the future, conflicting influences and interests. The popular word which seeks to combat threat is 'sustainability'.[1] It is a word that has come down from many high-level international reports and entered common parlance and policy making. Indeed, the sustainability of rural communities was the shortest and most accurate way of describing the focus of the erstwhile Commission for Rural Communities. This is continued in the new report by the Rural Coalition: *The Rural Challenge: Achieving Sustainable Rural Communities for the 21st Century*. Are rural communities sustainable and if so, what might this mean?

Clearly, rural communities, in their particular context and with their particular issues, need to play their part in lowering their carbon footprint and gaining greater environmental sustainability, and in a difficult economic climate services will only have a future if they are economically viable. However, while these environmental and economic matters need to be implicit in any consideration of flourishing communities, this chapter addresses the question of whether there is insight to be gained by seeking a theological understanding of the sustainability of community life.

The history of the concept of sustainability

The roots which led to the creation of the word 'sustainability', linking 'sustain' and 'able', are fascinating (Simonis, 2002, p. 32). How did this semantic innovation come about? For this (see Grober 2001 and 2007), we need to go back to the seventeenth and eighteenth centuries when European forests were harvested to such a degree that their survival was in question, thus severely threatening a timber-reliant economy and society. In the middle of the seventeenth century, both the Royal Navy and the French navy generated a huge demand for timber which their respective national forests could not satisfy. In the 1660s, John Evelyn of the Royal Society was put in charge of solving the timber problem. He wrote *Sylva* (1664). In it, he lambasts destructive exploitation of woodland and states:

> men should perpetually be planting, that so posterity might have Trees fit for there [sic] service . . . which it is impossible they should have, if we thus continue to destroy our Woods, without this providential planning in their stead, and felling what we do cut down with great discretion, and regard to the future.[2]

The book was a bestseller in the seventeenth century. At the same time, Jean-Baptiste Colbert, a minister of French King Louis XIV, designed a *grande reformation des forêts*, since he feared the French might perish for lack of timber. He coined phrases like *bon ménage* and *bon usage*, with a sense of responsibility for future generations (*passer le fruit à la posterité*).

On his European travels, one Hanns Carl von Carlowitz had become acquainted with the work of both Evelyn and Colbert. As head of the mining administration in Saxony, he too saw the danger of seeking short-term profit resulting in massive deforestation. In 1713 he published *Sylvacultura oeconomica*, dedicated to 'dear posterity'. In this his life's work he pleads for timber to be treated with care (*pfleglich*), with the aim of a continuous, constant and sustained usage (*eine continuirliche beständige und nachhaltende Nutzung*).

In eighteenth-century German forestry the word *nachhaltend* changed to *nachhaltig* and became the key word for this concept of forest management.[3] As German forestry gained international reputation, the beginning of the nineteenth century saw the translation of the concept *nachhaltig* into French as *production soutenu* (Adolphe Parade), and by the mid nineteenth century into English as 'sustained yield'. Von Carlowitz is therefore seen as the originator of the term sustainability, which gradually spread into a fledgling forestry service in the United States in the early twentieth century.

Sustained yield is a stewardship concept which seeks to maintain productivity in perpetuity. By 1960, the Multiple-Use Sustained Yield Act was enacted in the United States. Based on a principle of human benefit sustainability, it identified five categories of human benefits: timber, fish and wildlife, outdoor recreation, range and fodder, and watershed protection.

So we see American forester William Duerr formulating a classic definition in 1968:

> To fulfill our obligations to our descendents and to stabilize our communities, each generation should sustain its resources at a high level and hand them along undiminished. The sustained yield of timber is an aspect of man's most fundamental need: to sustain life itself. (quoted in Simonis, 2002, p. 32)

It is important to note that von Carlowitz was motivated not only by the sheer economic necessity of preserving the forests but also by a deep reverence for nature. He rejected a view of nature as a mere supply store for resources but urged his people to work with nature in the spirit of Genesis 2.15: cultivating and preserving the earth. Von Carlowitz's approach was essentially a conservative one as he fought to avoid the destruction of the present goods and sought to extend the present into the future.

The word and concept of sustainability was first publicized in the global context by the Club of Rome and its 1972 Report *The Limits to Growth*. The Club of Rome was a group of people concerned 'about the dilemma of prevailing short-term thinking in international affairs and, in particular, the concerns regarding unlimited resource consumption in an increasingly interdependent world'.[4] The report stated: 'We are searching for a model output that represents a world system that is: 1. sustainable without sudden and uncontrollable collapse' (Meadows *et al.*, 1972, p. 158).

The report was a bestseller and a World Council of Churches (WCC) consultation in Bucharest in 1974 picked up the concern, which in turn led to agricultural scientist and ecologist Charles Bird calling for 'a just and sustainable society' at the 1975 WCC assembly in Nairobi. Bird's insistence on the word 'sustainable' guided the WCC's thinking, resulting in its work on climate change and in the adoption of a process called Justice, Peace and Integrity of Creation (JPIC) at the 1983 Vancouver assembly (see WCC, 2010).[5]

Churches had hereby made the important link between socio-economic justice and ecological sustainability. This link proved to be vital for the work and benchmark definition of the 1987 UN World Commission on Environment and Development, known as the Brundtland[6] Commission, which was particularly exercised by the global division between rich and poor. The Rio Summit in 1992 finally ensured that the term 'sustainability' became firmly embedded in common parlance, in global as well as in national and local discussions and policy making in the UK. For the declaration from the Rio Summit, human beings are at the centre of concern for sustainable development, entitled to a healthy and productive life in harmony with nature.

The widely accepted and used definition of 'sustainable development' as articulated by the Brundtland Commission is:

Sustainable development is development which meets the needs of the present without compromising the ability of future generations to meet their own needs.

It contains within it two key concepts:

- the concept of 'needs', in particular the essential needs of the world's poor, to which overriding priority should be given;

- and the idea of limitations imposed by the state of technology and social organizations on the environment's ability to meet present and future needs. (UN World Commission, 1987 p. 43)

It is difficult to argue against considering the needs of the poor to-day as well as needs of future generations – the intragenerational as well as intergenerational approach. Nevertheless, it is worth taking a closer look at the focus of this statement which has been used so widely.

It is *development* rather than yield, consumption, production[7] or indeed growth that is described here as sustainable. Thinking back, the old term 'sustainable yield' describes ultimately an economic concept whereby no more is used than can be regenerated. Thus the present or a fairly recent past situation and condition is perpetuated, an equilibrium achieved. It is, however, arguable that even von Carlowitz's 'sustainable yield' is a too simplistic concept for forestry if it focuses on timber yield alone and does not consider, for example, the function of old trees for biodiversity and health of the forest habitat, or a changing market for timber. The term development, on the other hand, implies change and possibly a goal for the future. Does 'sustainable development' suggest that there is a 'natural' state to which we should revert or can we only ever speak of a process? The Brundtland Commission speaks of development as a progressive transformation of economy and society. This tension between a basically unchanging state and a constant process is an important point to consider when we turn to the ideas of sustainable rural communities where we encounter precisely these different models: from the idea of preserving a (usually glorified) past to developing a vision for a different future.

Using *needs* as the key word begs the question how these needs are defined: are they the needs of a remote mountain tribe or of a global city? The focus in the Brundtland definition is clearly on the present generation, wherever they are. It is worth noting that the statement would read quite differently if it were reversed: 'which meets the needs of future generations without compromising the needs of the present'! This in turn leads to the question whether or how we could possibly forecast future needs. Finally, it has been stated frequently that the definition is anthropocentric. Does the environment not have an intrinsic value other than for satisfying human need?

The 2005 World Summit, following on from the Millennium Development goals, formulated the three pillars of sustainability as economic, environmental and social, three overlapping areas (Figure 4.1). This suggests that there is a balance to be sought and a formula to be found which reconciles these three areas which mutually constrain each other.

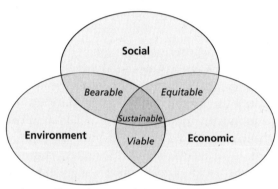

Figure 4.1: Three pillars of sustainability, Johann Dréo (2006).[8]

Environmental and social sustainability we have mentioned. Social sustainability is seen today not only as addressing poverty and inequalities in our world but also well-being and quality of life. For instance, the 2005 Sustainable Development Strategy in the UK includes the concept of well-being, with indicators as far ranging as pensioner poverty, fear of crime, cultural participation and life satisfaction.[9]

We have moved a long way in our understanding of the term 'sustainable' in the forests of Saxony or under Louis XIV. Or have we? Grober (2009) wryly observed that the concept of sustainability appears when there is a crisis, as in the Peak Timber crisis of the seventeenth century or the ecological crisis we are facing today. In our world today we have undoubtedly become increasingly aware of interrelatedness of global problems and issues.

However, 'sustainable' has become over-used and has suffered as a consequence – it can even be used to sell a product in order to communicate to the consumer that this product may be consumed without a guilty conscience. Sustainability is not a neutral word but is caught up between a marketized concept and an idealist and moral understanding: 'we invest it with meaning and value' (Bryden and Shucksmith, 2000). On the level of social systems, it is a political concept seeking to reconcile different interests; on the level of groups and individuals, it describes a choice of lifestyle with concern for the environment (Raudsepp and Heidmets, 2005).

To summarize our findings so far: a sustainable community is one that offers a positive present and future for all people. It is responsive to the needs of all and it cares for the environment (whether out of necessity or out of belief in its implicit worth).

What can 'sustainable' mean for a rural community in changing times? Can we develop any coherent vision what this might be? It is time to look for insight from the Christian tradition.

Biblical perspectives on sustainability

The scope of this chapter allows for only a selective snapshot of the understanding, values and concepts which inform the biblical texts of the Old and New Testaments. Our question is: what makes for a biblical view of a sustainable human community?

Serve and protect: interdependence and relationship

The most often quoted passage from the Old Testament about the relationship of human beings to their environment is the one from Genesis 1.28. What is translated as subduing and dominating has ever since served to accuse the Judaeo-Christian faith as having given encouragement if not actually having instigated the unsustainable exploitation of the planet. Environmentally concerned Jews and Christians have responded by interpreting the role described in Genesis 1 as one of careful stewardship and responsibility rather than cruel and selfish behaviour in a self-service store. If the *opinio communis* of Old Testament scholarship is correct, then surely the background and context to this creation narrative, exile by the waters of Babylon, is an important factor as it likens human beings to kings, thus rendering this passage not the most immediately helpful for our purposes.

We therefore turn to the creation narrative of Genesis 2, where we find a key passage for a Hebrew understanding of sustaining: 'The LORD God took the man and put him in the garden of Eden to *till* it and to *keep* it.' (Genesis 2.15, NRSV). The two words used here, *abad* and *shamar*, could also be translated as 'serve' and 'protect' respectively, or 'watch over' or 'take care of'.

Serving the land is a notable counterbalance to the monarchic account of Genesis 1. Serving indicates a relationship of dependency, so 'serving the land' places the notion of dependence in the Garden of Eden, not as a negative (postlapsarian) idea but as part of life in its best sense. The fact that *abad* is also commanded to Adam after the Fall (Genesis 3.23) is a mere continuation rather than part of the consequence of the Fall outlined in Genesis 3.17–19.

The command to *shamar* is a command that creates another close relationship with responsibilities and duties attached. It is worth noting that life before the Fall is thereby not described as an experience of splendid self-sufficiency, self-reliance and isolation but as one of interdependence and relationship, with all the duties and responsibilities pertaining to this.

This is further emphasized in the story of Cain and Abel where Cain asks 'Am I my brother's keeper?' (Genesis 4.9). The same word, *shamar* is used here as a noun, *shomer*, but this time with another person as its object: to protect, watch over and take care of.

Human well-being is thus inextricably linked to the needs and the well-being of the environment and of other people.

Two key passages from the book of Numbers and from the Psalms illustrate that *shamar* is also a divine action. The word occurs in the Aaronite blessing, Numbers 6.24, and six times in Psalm 121. God's protecting, watching over and taking care of are prized and prayed for, for the flourishing of life. This means that humans reflect and join God's doing when they *shamar* their environment and one another.

Loads and burdens: solidarity and responsibility

An example from among the earliest of New Testament writings offers pertinent advice for community living. In Galatians 6.2 and 6.5, Paul presents two seemingly contradictory verses: 'Bear one another's burdens', and 'All must carry their own loads'. At first glance this seems contradictory but it is not. Everyone, by himself or herself alone, should carry whatever load has been placed on them: the *phortion* is the daypack of a soldier, something that each can and should carry. It is what Jesus refers to as a light burden in Matthew 11:30. The burden of Galatians 6.2, however, is a *baros*, a crushing heavy burden. This is the type of burden which requires sharing. It is too much for one person to bear without the loving help of others. This is an excellent illustration for the interplay of personal responsibility and mutual solidarity which is needed for a community to thrive.

Jubilee and one body: equity and inclusion

The concept of the Jubilee is expounded in Leviticus 25. It is the name for every fiftieth year when all property sales shall be reversed, land returned to its original families, debts cancelled and servants liberated. It is quite unclear whether the rules set out in Leviticus 25 were ever realized. Nevertheless, they reflect a prophetic norm of relationships between people, land and wealth which is expressed in Isaiah 61 and picked up in Jesus' Nazareth manifesto, Luke 4.16–21.

The principle of the Jubilee imposes limits on the personal creation of material wealth in favour of realizing the memory of the equity of all before God: all were once servants brought out of the land of Egypt, and all depend on God who remains the ultimate owner (Leviticus 25.23: 'the land is mine; with me you are but aliens and tenants'). Social exclusion is thus barred by impressing on everyone every 50 years in very concrete ways that everyone is a stakeholder. In the light of this understanding of the Jubilee, a sustainable community needs to keep working on enabling all its members to participate economically and socially.

A not dissimilar message comes from Paul's admonition to the Corinthians in 1 Corinthians 12.12–30; it is the passage about *one body – many members*, and I maintain with its funny dialogues between ear, eye, hand and foot, it is humorous! (Personally, I would plead for humour to be an essential element of a sustainable community.) The image of the many different parts of the one body conveys that all need to work together for the good of the whole. Difference is appreciated and treasured rather than tolerated, since the different abilities are all required for the body to function well. In the humorous and bitter dialogue Paul creates, one member says to the other that it doesn't need the other, implying that needing another is not a good thing in the first place since it confers power on the one who is needed. The inference for the hearer is clear: the mutual need of one another is not a weakness but strengthens the whole, adding to the sustainability of the community.

The message of participation and inclusion is brought together as one of the points of Jesus' parable of the Samaritan (Luke 10.25–37). The brilliance of the parable lies in the fact that it is not a poor beaten up Samaritan, already marginalized by virtue of being a Samaritan, who is being cared for by a 'normal' person who would thus be modelling the desired behaviour as a neighbour doing good to a poor and needy Samaritan. Rather, it is a 'normal' person who is in need and who is aided in an exemplary way by the normally marginalized Samaritan. Clearly, helping others in need is an important aspect of any healthy community. But the parable of the Samaritan goes a step further with a message of humility for those who think they do not need a neighbour and a message of empowerment for those who might often only be able to see themselves at the receiving end of charity or even condescension and hostility. They also are included and they have something to offer; they have an active participating role in community life.

Servant leadership: responsive to the needs of others

Despite famous leaders featuring in the scriptures, they are invariably flawed: from Moses or David to Jesus' disciples. There is an inherent scepticism in the biblical narrative against a form of leadership that puts one above the other. The story of Abimelech in Judges 9, who sets himself up as king and has his brothers killed, leads to the parable of the Trees (Judges 9.7–15): a group of hapless trees who want to anoint a king over themselves, but end up anointing a destructive bramble rather than one of the more fruitful trees.

The classic text in the New Testament in this respect is of Jesus saying of the Gentiles that 'their great ones are tyrants over them. But it is not so among you; but whoever wishes to become great among you must be your servant' (Mark 10.42f. NRSV). The servant leadership that Jesus models is a form of leadership that seeks to build up and strengthen the community rather than make it dependent on big individuals. It is most likely shared leadership.

Service is a response to human need. It is no coincidence that the Old Testament recognizes need as a basic characteristic of the human soul and calls it *nephesh*, a dry thirsty throat.

Servant leadership obviously bears fruit so that what the individual achieves by understanding his or her leadership as service is responsive to the needs of those it relates to. But it has an impact beyond the individual by inspiring others to join in serving others. As with individuals, organizations and institutions can equally take on the mantle of such servant leadership.

Prejudice and injustice: communities in conflict

We began by describing rural communities as being in a state of change and resulting conflict because people with different backgrounds, expectations and values suddenly find themselves thrown together in a small population. With Mark 7.24–30 we are in the interesting position of having before us a text which shows us a rural community in Jesus' time at a time of change, with Jesus caught up in the issues. The passage of Jesus' encounter with the Syrophoenician woman deserves a closer look. It is found both in Mark's Gospel and in Matthew 15.21–28. Assuming, with most commentators, Markan priority, I will concentrate on Mark's passage.

The purpose of the story in its current form clearly deals with issues of Jewish superiority over the Gentile world. The inclusion of the Gentiles is here prefigured, if with some reluctance, in Jesus' exorcism, as is the conflict between Jewish and Gentile Christians. The passage is not generally a favourite since it appears to show Jesus in a rather unfortunate discriminating light, verbally abusing a desperate mother asking for her daughter's healing. The pericope also causes untold difficulties to commentators. The earliest illustration of this is in Matthew's Gospel: Matthew clearly feels compelled to soften Jesus' gruff behaviour by explaining how Jesus was really only sent to the lost sheep of the people of Israel. Some commentators claim Jesus was only joking. Of those who accept the depth of conflict expressed in the passage, some opt for a salvation history interpretation in which the woman becomes the symbol for Gentile Christians. The image is then one of the Gentile church praying for exorcism on behalf of her children, the Gentile peoples, that they may be liberated from the demon of unbelief. Other exegetes see in the Syrophoenician woman a model of faith and perseverance, succeeding in the trials of faith.[10]

However, both of these interpretations are symbolic and abstract from the social realities of the encounter.[11]

In contrast, a feminist interpretation (Tolbert, 1992, p. 269) draws attention to the gender of the Syrophoenician whose request, while in conventional posture, is unconventional and shameful: she is usurping the role of a male family member by going out to seek help. Consequently, Jesus reacts with disdain, before the woman's appropriate christological (*kyrie* Lord) and clever response brings about a change, even teaching Jesus about his own mission. However, this still does not address the incongruence of the woman's asking for her child to be restored and Jesus' responding by speaking of food being given to dogs rather than children. Not only does the image of food not fit the context of a sick daughter, Jesus' cruel dismissal of the Syrophoenician child also appears to be in blatant contradiction to his valuing of children (Mark 9.36–37; 10.13–16).

Gerd Theissen's study of the social and economic background to this passage casts an interesting light on the difficult encounter, which is located in the region of Tyre (Theissen, 1989). Tyre was a rich Gentile trading city, despised by Jewish people, along with the other Hellenistic cities, for its Gentile ways. Despite its wealth, Tyre had a problem: it had little agricultural land and was therefore dependent on imports from the rural hinterland. Much of Tyre's grain came from Jewish Galilee and whenever there were crises, Tyre was wealthy enough to flex its economic muscle and buy grain even if this left the rural Jewish population going without or led to the enslavement of parts of the Jewish population. Galilee thus shared in the fate of much of the rural hinterland of the major Hellenistic cities in that they were the losers in the battle for resources. Hence, Jesus' saying that food should not be taken from the children and thrown to the dogs really means: don't take food away from the poor rural Jewish families and give it to the rich Gentiles in the cities.

Economic dependence, attempted political expansion and cultural and religious distance were the perfect breeding ground for aggressive prejudice on the side of the Jewish population towards their urban Gentile neighbours. Likewise, the people of Tyre were full of fear and mistrust towards their rural Jewish trading partners following various incidents with Jewish freedom fighters.

Against this backdrop, the miracle performed and the demon to be overcome is clearly not only about the woman's daughter. The miracle also lies in the demon of barriers between peoples being overcome. The Syrophoenician woman manages to pick up the – literally – cynical image used by Jesus and restructure it. She behaves like a tenacious, faithful dog and claims the crumbs for her daughter, also a child. The Syrophoenician woman's need of Jesus is in contrast to the overpowering economic might of her people vis-à-vis Jesus' people. The woman no longer shares in the corporate denial of interdependence between the two sides.

Jesus' overcoming a sense of Jewish superiority and prejudice towards her and her people means overcoming his people's defensiveness and aggression. 'Jesus and the Syrophoenician woman defy first-century conventions of power and deference, suggesting potential renewal in the form of new commitments to social and economic co-operation' (Hicks, 2003, p. 83). As a result, a real relationship is born in which neither side dominates the other and a child is healed.

Mutual recognition is the only possible basis for a relationship between individuals, as between different groups and peoples. A sustainable community can only be achieved where injustice is addressed, prejudice named, defensiveness and a sense of superiority left behind – and where a sense of interdependence and mutual support flourishes. There are times when one side needs the other more than vice versa. This is the situation the Syrophoenician woman finds herself in: the Jewish Galilean rural community, suffering under her people's economic stranglehold and yet dependent on Tyre, can offer her Jesus, who has got what she absolutely needs, namely the ability to exorcize her daughter. In the end, the conflict is resolved, a relationship established and the prospect of a future opens up, symbolically very powerfully for the daughter of the Syrophoenician woman.

The passage is of particular interest because it is not difficult to find parallels in our world today, with rural communities feeling misunderstood and left behind in the allocation of resources. And within the rural communities some feel usurped by newcomers with urban and suburban values who have come in with more economic and social power, purchasing property out of reach for the next generation of the indigenous population and dominating the democratic and other representative bodies and councils.

Sustainable community life needs to overcome these issues of prejudice and injustice which militate against cohesion.

Summary of the biblical perspective

In summary, the biblical perspective has pointed us to the following aspects of sustainable community life:

- embracing local, regional and global interdependence (Genesis 2; Mark 7)
- assuming its own responsibilities while sharing the burdens of others (Galatians 6)
- including all and creating a climate in which all are empowered to participate (Leviticus 25; 1 Corinthians 12)
- serving, cherishing and blessing the world and its people (Numbers; Psalm 121; Mark 10).

A suitable image for a sustainable community, a community with a future, is thus not a strong rock or a selection of self-contained hard pebbles, but a web. The more connections there are and the stronger they are, the stronger and the more sustainable the web is. In a web, tensions are not equally balanced. The weight any fixed point has to bear may vary and other points may have to take the slack. Most importantly of all, dependency: as interdependence is a virtue rather than a vice, it goes to the very essence of its life.[12]

A theological shaping of the sustainability agenda

A church addendum?

One often hears a sentiment expressed along these lines: 'Sustainability has an economic, an ecological and a social angle – oh, and we must not forget our faith communities, also a spiritual angle.'

However, promoting the spiritual angle is not the point of this chapter. Of course, churches and other faith groups add to the social capital and vibrancy of community life. Equally, they may suffer from issues of sustainability if their numbers are dwindling, their ageing members do not find the next generation, they operate with a deficit budget or their property is crumbling. This is the typical problem of lack of resources of people, time, money, commitment and so on which makes it impossible to sustain any organization. This could be the institutional way of speaking of spiritual sustainability. A cultural way would be to speak more generally of the need for (spiritual) values to infuse a community in order to add to its sustainability.

So while it makes sense to speak of this kind of sustainability, to do so reduces the spiritual to being seen simply as a separate compartment of life, comparable or alternative to economy, environment or social aspects.

The more interesting question is whether a theological perspective can add inherently to the general understanding of sustainable communities.

Creatio originalis – continua – nova

An exploration of the rich understanding of creation offers a theological framework for the sustainability debate. Used simply and creatively, the old categories of *creatio originalis*, *continua* and *nova* can hold together meanings of sustainability which both affirm and critique the current use of the term and concept.

Creatio originalis

This aspect speaks of God as the original creator of the world. Genesis almost immediately puts the created world in a relationship with human beings who are part of this created world, and it is the human task to serve and protect the earth. The worth of the natural environment is implicit, it is good.

It is beyond the scope of this chapter to enlarge on the mediating role of Christ in creation as expressed in the New Testament (Colossians 1.15–20), suffice it to say that the implicit worth of the created world is thereby reinforced since it puts the whole of creation rather than just humanity into the frame of God's loving attention. For our understanding of sustainable development this means that there is more to say about the world than its being reduced to a resource for the fulfilment of human need. Indeed, we are only beginning to discover some of the complexity of life and our human interdependence with the rest of creation and its biodiversity. In this light, focusing sustainability purely on the immediate fulfilment of human need appears not only irreverent towards the whole of the created order but also shortsighted for the well-being of humanity. We endorse the reverence for creation expressed by von Carlowitz. A sustainable community must embrace a complex understanding of what it is that is to be sustained.

Creatio continua

Continuing creation is traditionally understood as God's ongoing conservation and preservation of the world from moment to moment. It clarifies that the Creator was not merely involved at the point of *creatio ex nihilo* (the initial act of creation out of nothing) as in Deism, but shows continued involvement in the care of the world.

There is an obvious danger in giving conservation and preservation a rather passive and backward-looking meaning, as though there were a perfect point in time in the past which ideally needed to be preserved or replicated. Instead *creatio continua* needs to include proactive and innovative behaviour. This is expressed in the words of the Brundtland Commission: 'progressive transformation of economy and society'. In the image of the web, it is an organic living being for which stagnation is death. Maintaining the present undiminished, as Duerr suggested earlier, is not enough. New connections are constantly to be made which allow the web to grow in different directions. Ridley (2010) makes just this point that the assumption of unchanged continuation is deeply flawed. Rather, we live and survive by constant adaptation and innovation which cannot be predicted. Therefore, predicting the needs of future generations, as most definitions of sustainability imply, is an impossible concept. The future brings a new dimension with it.

Sustainable development cannot be imposed but requires the participation of the whole community. The web makes this very clear. Any efforts towards sustainable development of communities must make people subjects rather than objects of such development. Everyone has something to contribute, and without appreciating, encouraging and cherishing this, the sustainability of a society is weakened. It is here that the loads and burdens of Galatians 6 converge with the best of the Big Society idea by encouraging that mix of personal responsibility and mutual solidarity. Not many years ago, the term many policy papers would have used in the place of 'sustainability' would have been 'regeneration', a word also suggesting a return to some former state of affairs. Regeneration is associated with considerable intervention and financial investment. In contrast, sustainable development is usually understood to be less costly to the public purse by encouraging the local community to take responsibility for itself – possibly therefore also the preferred option in our day, coupled with the Big Society. As a result, sustainability can run the risk of becoming too closely linked to the mythical ideal of self-reliance, with the needs of some regarded as an unwelcome constraint.

However, while there is no sustainability without people being empowered to take responsibility and carry their own load, the responsibility remains for sharing the burdens of those who have too much to carry. Interdependence should not be seen as a restraint but as a resource towards innovative progress. Dependability is a vital asset for a sustainable community, though it may be costly.

Creatio nova

One of the abiding elements of sustainability is its concern for the future, often interpreted as a continuation of the present in perpetuity. With *creatio nova* we speak of the new creation in Christ and the new heaven and the new earth. An important contribution of the theological perspective is its open-eyed acceptance of limitation and death which at the same time does not foreclose the future. Jesus could be said to have lived a sustainable life: it led him to death but it also opened up a new future. The servant leadership model consciously puts the needs of others before the needs of self and accepts that sacrifice will be involved. The model of the web illustrates that the good of one is closely interwoven with the good of the other.

So this eschatological viewpoint is, invariably, an entry point for ethics, asking us what our vision for the future and of the greater good might be. It is this greater good and the knowledge that the fulfilment of human need is not the final word which offer a liberating framework: there are limits to our lives and to human need; they are not absolute. There will be a day when the human soul characterized as *nephesh*, a needy dry throat, will no longer thirst.

The eucharistic community: symbol of a sustainable community

The eucharistic community can be seen as a symbol of a sustainable community: the values of the new world are mediated in the Eucharist. The characteristics of the eucharistic community can be described as follows.

- *Thankful and appreciative for gifts of earth and love*: the acknowledgement of gifts unearned and unachieved and valuing, that is blessing them, are an essential starting point for any community.

- *Remembering*: in its remembering the Eucharist brings together past, present and future, the focus on the now nevertheless brings in those before and those after us. The memory of history and culture gives people roots, meaning and identity and the intergenerational links strengthen the bonds of the web. It is a re-membering, making members again.

- *The Peace*: the eucharistic community does not deny tensions and conflict arising out of differences of its members but is there to model proactive peacemaking with and alongside conflicting arguments. A sustainable community is not one that pretends to be homogenous but one which embraces diversity and in conflict does not fail to recognize the essentially human, the child of God, in the other.

- *A place for everyone at the heavenly banquet*: the eucharistic community prefigures the heavenly banquet where there is a place for everyone, where everyone participates and where human need is answered by gratuitous grace. This is the vision and the mission to inspire life in and work for a sustainable community today.

- *Serving*: there is no human community without need and no human community can flourish without service. In the Eucharist, Christ serves his friends and sends them out to follow his example. It has long been shown that church members are essential in rural communities for strengthening the bonds of community by responding to human need.

- *Death and resurrection*: death is acknowledged rather than denied while celebrating new life out of defeat. A sustainable community cannot live without hope and vision.

Practical outlook and conclusion

Rural churches at their best are personally known and corporately embedded in their local communities. They share in the experience of similar issues: economic viability, reduction of services, especially of paid staff, encounter of urban and suburban culture and expectations. The rural church has to make a decision on how to deal with this: look back and retell the Golden Age story, act dependently and whinge? Settle for 'hospice care' or look to its resources and its partners locally, regionally, nationally and globally and build on these gifts?

It is the role of the church to model a sustainable community and to nurture individuals and a people who will contribute to a strengthening of bonds within and between communities.

There are excellent examples[13] of churches offering their premises for a community hub: from a farmers' market to a Post Office, from a community library to an advice centre. There are churches supporting the local development trust, working in partnership with local small businesses, offering a film club together with the village hall, or using glebe land for affordable housing and being a broker for the plans in the community. There is the eco-congregation initiative and churchyards managed for wildlife. All these add to the economic, environmental and social sustainability of village communities.

Many rural churches are vestiges of community history, identity and meaning. The focus offered to the whole of the community at important times in people's lives, communal occasions and occasional offices is an invaluable specific contribution to sustainable rural life. In many rural communities, the integration of the incoming residents with urban and suburban visions on one side and of the indigenous residents with a traditional rural mindset on the other is a key task. People begin appreciating one another best when 'doing things together', and if the church can offer such opportunities, even such mundane but necessary activities as tidying up the churchyard, this will strengthen the bonds and provide a basis for tackling more difficult and serious issues in the community. A divided community where each fights their own corner is not sustainable.

The acknowledgement of being part of an interdependent web is a particularly important issue for rural communities who, like any human community, can easily be inward-looking when feeling threatened. The value of partner churches overseas in especially poor parts of the world is well documented. Additionally, there is significant value in rural parishes linking with urban ones, to visit one another, to learn from one another's life and to appreciate each other's and their own gifts.

Understanding the issues around the sustainability of rural communities is an important project which is significantly enriched by a theological perspective. At its best, the rural church embodies trust, dependability and hope. The very being of the church can contribute to the sustainability – economic, environmental and social – of rural community life. At its best, the rural church stands for trust, dependability and hope. Perhaps the church's most important contribution to a sustainable community is its open acknowledgment of needs and limitations and a wholehearted embrace of interdependence rather than individualism and the pretence of self-reliance. Such interdependence needs to be modelled by the church itself by daring to ask for help from others beyond the Sunday congregation. Few things are more powerful than to be told: 'We need you!' No one is a sustainable island.

References

Barton, J. and Muddiman, J., 2001, *The Oxford Bible Commentary*, London: Oxford University Press.

Bosselmann, K., 2008, *The Principle of Sustainability: Transforming Law and Governance*, London: Ashgate.

Bryden, J. and Shucksmith, M., 2000, 'The concept of sustainability in relation to agriculture and rural development in the European Union', in M. Forbord and T. Stavrum (eds), *Rural and Regional Development in Northern Periphery*, Report 4/00/ Centre for Rural Research, Norwegian University of Science and Technology, Trondheim, Norway.

Club of Rome, 1972, *The Limits to Growth*, www.clubofrome.at/about/limitstogrowth.html

Club of Rome, 2009, *The Story of the Club of Rome*, www.clubofrome.org/eng/about/4/

Davoudi, S., 2001, 'Planning and the twin discourses of sustainability', in A. Layard, S. Davoudi, S. Batty (eds), *Planning for a Sustainable Future*, London: Spon Press, pp. 81–93.

Department of Environment, Food and Rural Affairs (2008), *Sustainable Development Indicators in your Pocket. An Update of the UK Government Strategy Indicators*, London: Department of Environment, Food and Rural Affairs.

Dréo, J., 2006, *Sustainable Development* graphic, www.en.wikipedia.org/wiki/File:Sustainable_development.svg

Evelyn, John, 1664, *Sylva or a Discourse of Forest-Trees and the Propagation of Timber in His Majesties Dominions*, ed. A. Ward, edition 1786, p. 205; quoted in Bosselman (2008), p. 17.

Gnilka, J., 1978, *Das Evangelium nach Markus*, EKK II/1, Köln, Benziger.

Grober, U., 2001, Die Idee der Nachhaltigkeit als zivilisatorischer Entwurf, *Aus Politik und Zeitgeschiche* B24/2001, pp. 3–5.

Grober, U., 2007, 'Hanns Carl von Carlowitz – ein Blatt, ein Bild, ein Wort', in U. Simonis (ed.), *Ein Blatt, ein Bild, ein Wort. Vor-Denker der Ökologiebewegung*, Wissenschaftszentrum Berlin für Sozialforschung, Juli 2007, www.bibliothek.wzb.eu/pdf/2007/p07-005.pdf

Grober, U., 2009, 'Der Erfinder der Nachhaltigkeit', *Die Zeit*, 9.11.2009, www.zeit.de/1999/48/Der_Erfinder_der_Nachhaltigkeit

Hicks, J.E., 2003, *Moral Agency at the Borders: Rereading the Story of the Syrophoenician Woman*, Word & World, Vol. 23/1, pp. 76–84.

International Union for Conservation of Nature and Natural Resources, 1980, *World Conservation Strategy: Living Resource Conservation for Sustainable Development*, http://data.iucn.org/dbtw-wpd/edocs/WCS-004.pdf

Meadows, D.H., Meadows, D.L., Randers, J. and Behrens, W.W. III, 1972, *The Limits to Growth*, New York: Potomac Associates.

Nussbaum, M. and Sen, A. (eds), 1993, *The Quality of Life*, Clarendon Press: Oxford.

Nussbaum, M., 2000, *Women and Human Development: The Capabilities Approach (The Seeley Lectures)*, Cambridge, Cambridge University Press.

Raudsepp, M. and Heidmets, M., 2005, 'Sustainability as a regulative idea and norm of behaviour: social and psychological aspects', in W.L. Filho (ed.), *Handbook of Sustainability Research*, Frankfurt: Peter Lang, pp. 205–34.

Ridley, M., 2010, *The Rational Optimist: How Prosperity Evolves*, London: Fourth Estate.

Shorten, J., 2006, 'It's not just about transport, is it?', in *What are Sustainable Rural Communities? How can we Achieve Them?*, Cheltenham: Commission for Rural Communities.

Sen, A., 2009, *The Idea of Justice*, Allen Lane: Penguin.

Simonis, U.E., 2002, 'Festvortrag: Nachhaltigkeit in internationaler Sicht', in: *Schriftenreihe des Deutschen Rates für Landespflege*, Heft 24, pp. 32–6.

Theissen, G., 1989, *Lokalkolorit und Zeitgeschichte in den Evangelien: Ein Beitrag zur Geschichte der synoptischen Tradition*, Fribourg, NTOA 8.

The Rural Coalition, 2010, *The Rural Challenge: Achieving Sustainable Rural Communities for the 21st Century*, London: Town and Country Planning Association, www.lga.gov.uk/lga/aio/13131403

The UN World Commission on Environment and Development, 1987, *Our Common Future*, The United Nations, www.un-documents.net/wced-ocf.htm

Tolbert, M.A., 1992, 'Mark', in C. A. Newsom and S.H. Ringe (eds), *The Women's Bible Commentary*, London: SPCK, pp. 263–74.

Wilkinson, R. and Pickett K., 2009, *The Spirit Level: Why More Equal Societies Almost Always Do Better*, London: Allen Lane.

Wiersum, K.F., 1995, *200 Years of Sustainability in Forestry: Lessons from History*, http://hydrology.lsu.edu/courses/rnr7071/Papers/WiersumKF_EnvironManage1995.pdf

Working Group on Economic Environmental and Social Issues of the European Ecumenical Commission for Church and Society (EECCS), 2000, *Sustainable Development and the Market Economy: Integrating Environment in EU Economic and Employment Policies*, Brussels, www.pcsc.ceceurope.org/fileadmin/filer/csc/Globalisation/Sustainable1-3.pdf

World Council of Churches, 2010, *Climate Change and the World Council of Churches: Background Information and Recent Statements*, March 2010, www.oikoumene.org/fileadmin/images/wcc-main/programmes/P4/climate/1003%20-%20Cl%20chg%20booklet%20-%20all%20-%20final.pdf

Notes

1   It would warrant another essay to reflect on the way 'sustainability' has replaced 'regeneration' as the current buzzword, with 'regeneration' also having a notable theological background.

2   Evelyn, John: *Sylva or a Discourse of Forest–Trees and the Propagation of Timber in His Majesties Dominions*, ed. A. Ward, edition 1786, p. 205; quoted in Bosselman (2008), p. 17.

3   In fact *nachhaltig* was applied to the economy by another forester, Wilhelm Gottfried Moser, who spoke of a 'nachhaltige Wirtschaft', a sustainable economy.

4   As stated on the History page of the Club of Rome's website, www.clubofrome.org/eng/about/4/

5   In 1980 the UN published a World Conservation Strategy subtitled 'Living Resource Conservation for Sustainable Development', and in this document it speaks of sustainable utilization of species and ecosystems.

6   Named after the Commission Chair, Gro Brundtland, the then Norwegian Prime Minister.

7   It is interesting to note that UK government sustainable development indicators 2005 include indicators for sustainable consumption and production, seemingly asking the question: how much can we get away with.

8 Other models show the environmental circle constraining the other two.

9 Compare the work of Nussbaum and Sen (1993) and Sen (2009). Nussbaum's and Sen's earlier work had a big influence on the development which followed the Brundtland Commission's report.

10 For an overview, see Gnilka (1978), p. 294; also Theissen (1989), pp. 64–8, and Barton and Muddiman (2001), ad loc.

11 For a full discussion, see Gnilka, and also Theissen, pp. 63–8.

12 This defies the western 'illusion of self-sufficiency' (Alastair MacIntyre) and lies at the heart of the capabilities approach of Martha Nussbaum.

13 See the magazine *Country Way* with many examples in every issue.

5

Planning and housing: power and values in rural communities

MARK SHUCKSMITH

The supply of affordable rural housing has long been identified as essential to the vitality and sustainability of rural communities. It is also crucial to the life-chances of many of the less prosperous members of rural societies and to the socially inclusive character of the British countryside (Newby, 1985; Shucksmith, 1981, 1990a). Unfortunately, affordable housing is sadly lacking in many rural areas. Despite efforts over more than 25 years, the situation continues to deteriorate. These issues have been highlighted in several recent reports, including those commissioned by the government from the Affordable Rural Housing Commission (2006) and Matthew Taylor MP (2008), as well as by the Rural Coalition (2010). This chapter explores why this remains such an intractable issue in terms of who gains and who loses from the perpetuation of these problems; how power is exercised and in whose interests; and how this relates to fundamental values of social justice, stewardship and sustainability which are widely believed to characterize rural communities.

Unaffordable rural housing and its consequences

'Only 22 of the 52 characters in *The Archers* can now afford to live in Ambridge.'

House completions have fallen under successive governments since the 1960s and now stand at a historic low, while the need for houses increases (due to our ageing population, increased longevity, inward migration and smaller households). Recent research by Oxford Economics (2010) for the National Housing Federation suggests that current 21-year-olds will have to wait until their 40s or 50s before they can qualify for a mortgage, unless their parents can provide the deposit. The coalition government cut the affordable housing budget by 50% in the Comprehensive Spending Review of 2010, but has stated its aim is 'to increase the number of houses available to buy and to rent, including affordable housing' by encouraging 'more individuals to take responsibility for meeting their own and their families' housing needs' (CLG, 2011).

This challenge is most severe in areas of high demand, whether urban or rural, and where supply is constrained. Because of the value placed on a rural lifestyle, most rural areas experience high demand. A rural location is consistently found to be the residential preference of the majority of English people: 89% of people living in the countryside would prefer to continue to live there, while only 21% of city dwellers wish to stay in cities, with 51% aspiring to live in the countryside (Best and Shucksmith, 2006, p. 4). For 50 years there has accordingly been outward movement from our urban areas to the suburbs and to rural areas (Bate, Best and Holmans, 2002). The professional and managerial classes – whether in retirement or commuting to towns nearby – can outbid those earning a living in the countryside and are thus displacing the rural working classes.

The gap between supply and demand is therefore often at its greatest in rural areas, resulting in a well-established affordability gap in such areas. The Affordable Rural Housing Commission (ARHC) and the Commission for Rural Communities (CRC) have identified significantly higher affordability ratios (the ratio of house prices to incomes) in rural areas than in urban areas (ARHC, 2006; CRC, 2007, 2010; but note that Bramley and Watkins, 2009, disagree). Generally most researchers acknowledge the unaffordability of housing as an issue in rural England (Satsangi *et al.*, 2010). The most recent CRC (2010) analysis of government statistics on average house prices and affordability is shown in Figures 5.1 and 5.2 respectively.

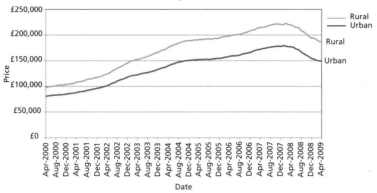

Figure 5.1: Average house prices for rural and urban England, 2000–09 (CRC, 2010).

Figure 5.1 shows that, uniquely among OECD countries, average house prices in rural areas have exceeded those in urban areas of England by around 25% every year since reliable figures first became available in 2000. Indeed, the smaller the settlement size, the higher the price (CRC, 2010).

Figure 5.2 presents a measure of housing affordability for lower income households, which is the ratio of house price to income for a household in the lower quartile of income, buying a house in the lower quartile of house prices. So, for example, the price of a (lower quartile) house in the smallest settlements in sparsely populated areas in 2008 was 10.7 times (lower quartile) household income on average. Since 2007 affordability has improved (i.e. the ratio has fallen) but remains worse in rural areas than urban, systematically worse still in smaller settlements and sparser areas, and well beyond lower income groups' ability to pay.

Across all rural England only 55% of newly forming households are able to afford a house in their own ward (Roger, Tym and Partners, 2006), leaving an affordable housing need of 22,800 homes per annum, on top of a backlog of a further 40,000 houses then required to meet existing needs. In the south-east, south-west and east regions the proportion unable to afford to buy local

93

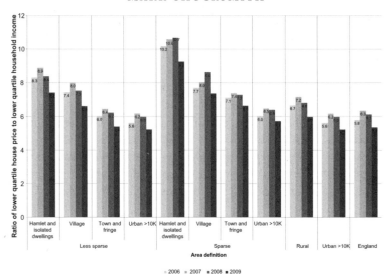

Figure 5.2: Lower quartile housing affordability, 2006–09 (CRC, 2010).

housing in rural areas was estimated to be nearer 70%. Research for Defra in 2006 (ARHC, 2006) showed that average rural earnings of £17,400 would only have allowed the purchase of a home in 28% of rural wards in England. More recent estimates from CRC (2010a) indicate that between 2006 and 2031 demand for new housing as a result of projected household change will grow more in rural than urban districts, with 356,000 new households emerging every five years in predominantly rural districts.

So the majority of these new rural households will be unable to afford to buy in the open market, and for them the alternatives are to rent or to leave. Few rent from private landlords in the UK for a variety of reasons, and the provision of social housing has historically been far lower in rural areas, both by councils and by registered social landlords (RSLs) who are now the main providers. Meanwhile the small stock of social housing has been further depleted, as four rural homes have been sold under the right to buy (RTB) for every three built by RSLs (ARHC, 2006), and in some areas the stock of affordable housing has almost disappeared. The provision of affordable housing in rural districts did increase from

2004/5 to 2008/9, but this was focused on the larger settlements (CRC, 2010a), through requiring developers of market housing to include a quota of affordable housing in their schemes.

The most recent figures for housing tenure disaggregated by rurality (i.e. settlement size and population sparsity (ONS, 2004)) derive from the 2001 Census (CRC, 2005), as shown in Table 5.1.

The most striking feature is how little social rented housing is available in smaller settlements, which are becoming increasingly socially exclusive. A small town's social rented housing thus has crucial importance in meeting not only the housing needs of its own new households but also of those priced out of the villages and surrounding countryside. Only by seeking social housing in the nearest town is it possible for many newly forming households to find housing relatively near to their place of work and to family and friends. Even this may lead to reverse commuting and a fracturing of social support networks. Such small towns may now be the only places in large parts of rural England where mixed-income communities remain a possibility, with most villages and smaller settlements becoming exclusive enclaves divorced from wider society. This raises questions for churches and their members, and for government, about where best to meet housing needs and about how desirable it is for settlements to become so socially polarized in what Professor Sir Peter Hall warned in 1973 would become 'this very civilized British version of apartheid' (Hall *et al.*, 1973, p. 409).

Table 5.1: Housing tenure by rurality.

Sparsity	Settlement type	Owned %	Social rented %	Private rented %
Less sparse	Urban settlements of >10k	67	21	10
	Town and fringe	77	15	7
	Village	78	10	9
	Hamlet and isolated dwelling	78	5	13
Sparse	Urban settlements of >10k	70	16	12
	Town and fringe	68	18	12
	Village	73	11	13
	Hamlet and isolated dwelling	71	5	19

Of course, these tendencies are not uniform in all parts of rural England. Demand is greatest in the more accessible rural areas and in the more scenic of the remoter areas, while supply is most constrained by planning in areas designated as green belt, national parks, Areas of Outstanding Natural Beauty (AONBs) and such-like (amounting together to about 40% of England and Wales). In the 1990s, to capture this diversity, the then Department of the Environment commissioned the derivation of a ward-level typology of rural housing markets in England (Shucksmith *et al.*, 1995), and associated housing market case studies (DTZ Pieda, 1998). This was updated by Bevan *et al.* (2001) as part of the Joseph Rowntree Foundation's (JRF) Action in Rural Areas programme.

In summary, six classes of rural housing markets were identified on the basis of the degree of supply-side constraints, the sources of housing demand, and the change in the stock of social housing between 1981–91 (Bevan *et al.*, 2001). Case studies validated this analysis and elaborated the issues. The six types may be summarized as in Table 5.2.

A new Defra-funded study (Buchanan, 2010) has largely confirmed this pattern, finding in all its case studies that housing is not affordable by local people on local wages, especially in villages and where there is commuter pressure. However, people were reluctant to concede that an affordability problem exists since this would risk inviting new development, preferring instead to talk about the needs of known, named individuals.

The strong messages emerging from these studies are: (1) the overwhelming importance of planning constraints to affordability in most of rural England; (2) marked north–south differences, modified by national park designation; (3) the effect of accessibility to urban labour markets in north and south; and (4) socio-spatial sorting within rural districts as smaller settlements become increasingly unaffordable to all but the most wealthy.

Figure 5.3 and Table 5.3 each present some evidence of this socio-spatial sorting by settlement size in rural England. Figure 5.3 takes Census super output areas (SOAs – the smallest scale available for analysis) and for each size of settlement shows the proportion of SOAs in each income quintile: for example, among villages,

Table 5.2: Typology of rural housing markets.

Type	Characteristics of wards	Location
1	Lower demand. Sustained high proportion of social housing. Most residents live in larger settlements.	Former coalfields in NE, Y & H; northern Fenland; military bases.
2	High but declining proportion of social housing, with vigorous right to buy sales.	Mainly in southern England.
3	Strong demand from commuters and severe housing supply constraints. Little social housing. Prosperous.	Home counties, commuting villages around London and Bristol.
4	Strong demand from commuters but milder supply-side constraints. Little social housing. Prosperous.	Northern commuting villages, around cities north of London.
5	Strong demand from retirement or holiday buyers and severe housing supply constraints.	Mainly in south but includes northern national parks.
6	Strong demand from retirement or holiday buyers but lower supply-side constraints.	Mainly residual areas of north, remote from major cities.

hamlets and isolated dwellings, 35% are among the richest fifth of SOAs, and 39% are among the next richest fifth of SOAs. It can be seen that among these smallest rural settlements, 74% are among the richest 40% of SOAs while only 4% are among the poorest 40% of SOAs – that is their residents are disproportionately well paid. This demonstrates clearly the degree to which smaller rural settlements are becoming the preserve of richer residents, even though we know that scattered and hidden poverty remains even here.

While Figure 5.3 showed the proportion of areas (SOAs) in each income band, Table 5.3 presents information for individual households. It shows the mean weekly household income in 2009/10 by Defra's rural definition (CRC 2010). It can be seen that household incomes are systematically higher the smaller the settlement, whether in sparse or less sparse areas, and that household incomes

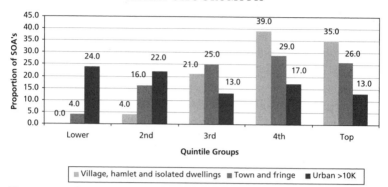

Figure 5.3: Census super output areas by settlement size and income quintile (CRC, 2005).

are lower in more sparse areas. The table also shows weekly wages, both for those who work in the area and for those resident in the area. Wages paid for work in rural areas are lower than wages earned by rural residents who commute to work elsewhere, with the exception of villages in sparse areas.

Table 5.3: Mean household income and mean wage by settlement size and sparsity, 2009/10.

Sparsity	Settlement type	Household income £/week	Work-based wage £/week	Resident-based wage £/week
Less sparse	Urban settlements of >10k	666.54	496.90	483.80
	Town and fringe	686.26	422.80	483.30
	Village	755.23	458.00	556.10
	Hamlet and isolated dwelling	801.01	470.30	580.90
Sparse	Urban settlements of >10k	540.28	350.50	334.40
	Town and fringe	547.12	316.20	356.60
	Village	610.83	438.80	397.80
	Hamlet and isolated dwelling	634.01	350.60	436.10

Taken together, the evidence in this section establishes that housing is least affordable and social (affordable) housing least available in smaller rural settlements, and accordingly the people who can afford to live in these smaller settlements tend to have higher incomes. So richer people are moving into and poorer people are moving out of rural England, in an ongoing gentrification which is particularly marked in its villages and hamlets. The housing market is the principal engine of this social change in rural England (Shucksmith, 1990a).

Perpetuating an intractable problem: the exercise of power

A recent book entitled *The Rural Housing Question* (Satsangi, Gallent and Bevan, 2010) observes that these social consequences for rural areas were foreseen and have been well documented for 30, 40 or even 50 years. This leads the authors to ask why the rural housing question has persisted and proved so intractable. Twenty years ago, for example, another book, *Housebuilding in Britain's Countryside* (Shucksmith, 1990a), offered a range of alternative policies to address these issues. But the book concluded, pessimistically, by anticipating a need for further research which would 'explain why such alternative policies will not be implemented and so to understand why rural housing disadvantage will persist' (p. 207). So why has this problem proved so intractable? Why has it persisted?

This question can be pursued both on a technical level and at a political level. Many writers have looked for, and identified, technical fixes which could help to ameliorate the problems evidenced above; but despite such innovations (exception sites, quotas of affordable housing in private developments) the problem has worsened. Rural housing has become ever less affordable and the chances of finding affordable housing have diminished, such that there are fewer and fewer opportunities for low- and middle-income households to find homes in rural England. This suggests that the rural housing question is not essentially a technical question but rather a political question, concerning the exercise of power. Sociologists tend to approach such questions by asking who gains and who loses from perpetuating the situation, and through what mechanisms do the gainers exercise power to ensure their favourable position is maintained. Why might society at large, including those whose interests are harmed, acquiesce in such a process?

Sturzaker and Shucksmith (2011) suggest some answers by drawing on the theories of Steven Lukes and Pierre Bourdieu. In his book, *Power: A Radical View*, Lukes (2005) showed that dominant groups exercise power both through prevailing in decisions and by excluding other groups from decision making in many cases; but beyond these there is a 'third dimension of power' which is 'the most effective and insidious use of power' (p. 27) because it is largely invisible. This works discursively through powerful groups shaping the way that other groups think, forestalling potential dissent 'by shaping their perceptions, cognitions and preferences in such a way that they accept their role in the existing order of things' (p. 28), seeing it as natural or inevitable. In other words, people subscribe to the values which oppress them.

Bourdieu's concept of 'symbolic violence' is closely related to Lukes' third face of power, defined as 'the violence which is exercised upon a social agent with his or her complicity' (Bourdieu, 1992, p. 167). This does not refer to physical violence, but to domination of more subtle forms. Thus, people

> are subjected to forms of violence (treated as inferior, denied resources, limited in their social mobility and aspirations), but they do not perceive it that way; rather their situation seems to them to be 'the natural order of things'. (Webb *et al.*, 2002, p. 25)

For example, in gender domination, 'women misrecognized the symbolic violence to which they were subjected as something that was natural, simply "the way of the world". Consequently they were complicit in the production of those things [gender roles or dress, for example] which worked to reinscribe their domination' (Webb *et al.*, 2002, p. 25). It is important to note that the dominant class may be equally unaware of the symbolic violence exercised, also seeing gender roles (in this example) as natural and taken-for-granted.

Bourdieu (1977, 1992) argues, and illustrates in his work, how the power of the dominant class succeeds in defining, through symbolic violence, what counts as legitimate knowledge, what social relations are valuable, and what symbols confer prestige and social honour. These symbols are socially constructed to suit the interests of the dominant class. Another example he offers is in education, where the power of the dominant class defines the curriculum and what constitutes success, and those who acquire through socialization within families a cultural capital which conforms with this will appear more gifted, while others will not (Lee, 1989). Moreover they will appear to be 'naturally' gifted and deserving of success, so concealing the power relations underlying the outcome (Bourdieu, 1977). Their progress to better qualifications and better jobs is widely seen as only fair. 'Misrecognition', as Bourdieu puts it, is thus at the heart of the exercise of the third face of power. Not only does this further the interests of a dominant class, but this is achieved in a way which masks the power relations involved and so appears legitimate. Could the perpetuation of rural housing disadvantage similarly be a result of symbolic violence and misrecognition?

One thing we all take for granted is the need to protect the countryside from development. Ever since the 1940s, planning for rural England has given the greatest priority to urban containment. In the immediate post-war period the justification for this was the protection of farmland to ensure food supplies and the prevention of urban sprawl. When in the 1980s the Government determined that too much land was being farmed, the justification changed first to protection of the countryside for its own sake, and then to sustainable communities and an urban renaissance. It is important to note whose interests are served by such policies.

In their seminal study in 1973, Hall and his colleagues saw urban containment deriving from an 'unholy alliance' of urban councils seeking to divert resources to the cities together with the rural middle classes seeking to preserve an exclusive countryside and to enhance their own property values. The major gainers were identified as wealthy, middle-class, ex-urbanite country dwellers and the owners of land designated for development. The principal losers his team identified were non-home-owners in rural England (including future generations) and people forced to live in dense urban areas despite the widespread aspiration to rural, or at least suburban, living. Summarizing, they concluded that the effects had been regressive in that 'it is the most fortunate who have gained the benefits from the operation of the system, while the less fortunate have gained very little' (Hall *et al.*, 1973, p. 409). Newby (1985, p. 239) similarly observed that 'the rural poor had little to gain from the preservation of their poverty but were without a voice on the crucial committees which evolved the planning system from the late 1930s onwards.' These analyses reveal the first and second faces of power, in Lukes' terms, whereby powerful groups prevail in planning decisions and less powerful groups are generally excluded. But there is also evidence of the exercise of the third face of power – symbolic violence.

In the 1940s the overall stance of urban containment and prevention of rural development was informed by 'a hopelessly sentimental view of rural life among nature-loving ramblers and Hampstead-dwelling Fabians' (Newby, 1985, p. 225). This dominant discourse has recently been strengthened through becoming deliberately linked to new agendas of environmental sustainability. Of particular interest is the role played by the Campaign for the Protection of Rural England (CPRE) in the initiation, development and implementation of these policies. The CPRE, as its *raison d'être*, has always sought to prevent house building in rural areas, deploying a range of symbolic concepts to pursue this objective, including 'urban sprawl', 'concreting over the countryside' and 'light pollution' among others. Through analysis of documentary evidence and interviews with former and current CPRE staff, Murdoch and Lowe (2003) revealed the various ways in which CPRE has managed to set the agenda for rural planning since the 1940s, when it promoted the idea of a rural/urban divide and the desirability of separation of nature and society, as exemplified in green belts and urban containment policies. During the 1980s it altered it's tactics away from a preservationist argument to take advantage of the growing environmental awareness. Thus it sought to 'ecologize' its arguments by arguing an environmental case for containment, essentially through the exercise of discursive power over the concepts of sustainability and sustainable communities.

The concept of sustainability had gained currency in the work of the Brundtland Commission, which proposed a notion of sustainable development with social justice at its core, comprising three elements: (1) intergenerational equity; (2) intragenerational equity; and (3) avoiding uncompensated transnational spillovers. In practice, however, sustainability has become understood overwhelmingly in narrower environmental terms, with little attention given to the social justice values at its heart, reflecting the capture of this concept by powerful environmental and other interests. In line with their 'ecologizing' tactical shift, CPRE staff explained to Murdoch and Lowe (2003) how they had deployed the argument that building in rural areas was incompatible with sustainable development, since inadequate public transport in rural areas would require residents to use cars, with environmentally damaging CO_2 emissions. Key arenas in which they were able to promote this discourse included the Urban Task Force under Lord Rogers (a senior officer of CPRE was Deputy Chair), the Urban White Paper, the Sustainable Communities White Paper, the drafting of Planning Policy Guidance Note 3 (PPG3) on planning for housing, Regional Spatial Strategies (RSSs) and Local Development Frameworks (LDFs). One CPRE staff member told Murdoch and Lowe that the Urban White Paper was the key arena for ensuring anti-development policies were implemented in rural areas (Murdoch and Lowe, 2003), and indeed this did recommend higher urban densities and stronger protection of greenfield sites. CPRE was highly effective in framing debates in this way, and in influencing government policy at all levels. Thus Murdoch and Lowe heard how CPRE had lobbied to ensure that 'most new housing should be concentrated in existing conurbations ... One CPRE policy officer claimed: "We invented all the key planks in PPG3. PPG3 is basically CPRE policy"'. (Murdoch and Lowe, 2003, p. 327).

In this way the overall stance of urban containment and prevention of rural development has been strengthened through becoming linked to new agendas of environmental sustainability. In this approach, found by the ARHC (2006) to be widespread throughout rural England, local authorities have been categorizing rural settlements into those which they regard as 'sustainable' (and therefore suitable for new housing and investment) or 'unsustainable' (effectively red-lined), on the basis of crude checklists of service availability. This was widely believed to be required by Office of the Deputy Prime Minister (ODPM) guidance on sustainable communities, defining these principally in terms of presence of services and access to public transport, so discouraging new investment in rural settlements, but the Department for Communities and Local Government (CLG), the successor to ODPM, maintained that this was not intended. Indeed, CLG had softened its stance somewhat in Planning Policy Statement 3 (PPS3) and in its response to the first Barker Report, following representations by the ARHC and others. Despite this, CLG's website on 'sustainable communities' until recently listed the essential characteristics of a sustainable community as follows:

> A sustainable community is a place where people want to live and work now and in the future . . . For communities to be sustainable, they must offer: decent homes at prices people can afford; good public transport; schools; hospitals; shops; a clean, safe environment. (CLG, 2008)

Few rural communities have all of these, and yet they are overwhelmingly where people want to live.

Critics have viewed this dualistic construction of sustainable communities as an acceptance in planning policy and practice of a discourse of sustainability which privileges the environmental over the social, and of exclusivity over inclusion (Best and Shucksmith, 2006; Satsangi and Dunmore, 2003; Owen, 1996).[1] A letter to *The Economist* in 2007 took this to the extreme, asserting that 'villages and rural communities are inherently inefficient . . . It is therefore clear that we should abolish villages and make everyone live in towns of at least 25,000 people' (*The Economist*, 31 May 2007). The distinguished academic and columnist Germaine Greer similarly argued in 2009 that for sustainability reasons, people in future should live in high-rise blocks in 'groovy places downtown for preference, so you can walk to work and the shops and don't need a car' (Greer, 2009).

Worryingly, the ARHC, JRF, CRC and Matthew Taylor's review all found that Regional Spatial Strategies were reducing the land allocations for houses in rural areas still further in the interests of promoting urban regeneration, without regard to the impact on affordability of rural housing. In turn, local planners are applying sustainability checklists as described above with the effect of preventing any new housing outside the towns, and these are being approved by the Planning Inspectorate as government policy. Both JRF and the ARHC warned that there was a real danger that the powerful role given to regional bodies by Labour (and now the ascendancy of the 'city-region' agenda) facilitates urban interests' collusion with rural elites to limit the supply of housing in rural areas, so assisting the 'unholy alliance' of urban districts and rural elites, to the detriment of affordability and the life-chances of poorer and middle-income groups (Hall *et al.*, 1973; Newby, 1985).

The capture of the concept of 'sustainable communities' by urban districts and rural elites, for example CPRE, can be conceptualized as Bourdieu's misrecognition and symbolic violence and as Lukes' third dimension of power – shaping the way people think, such that they acquiesce and do not recognize the power relations involved. Moreover, the planning system is the crucial arena for the exercise of this form of power. Constructing the meaning of sustainable communities as self-evidently those which have a broad range of services and frequent public transport masks the way in which the real objective is to prevent development in rural areas, and that those who benefit most from this are those who already have privilege and wealth. Bourdieu's analysis of symbolic violence thus offers an explanation of how the deployment in planning arenas of a partial concept of sustainable communities may be a means of not only furthering the interests of a dominant class (and so exacerbating inequalities and exclusion), but also of masking the power relations implicit in this process and making it appear legitimate to those who 'misrecognize' it.

Of course, it is easy to point the finger at an organization like CPRE to illustrate the way in which power is exercised invisibly, subtly and discursively. But there are challenges here for us all.

This analysis of power relations can be applied just as readily at the community and individual levels. When Tynedale Council announced its list of sustainable villages, residents of some villages were quoted in the press celebrating the designation of their settlements as 'unsustainable' because this meant there would be no housing built there. The ARHC encountered residents in many villages around the country unwilling to accept affordable housing in their villages for fear of 'unsuitable people' or 'asylum seekers'. The widespread fierce local opposition to new housing in the countryside is renowned.

And there is a widespread belief that the countryside is already 'concreted over', against the evidence. A survey found that 54% of people think that more than half the English countryside is already built-up, and only 13% thought that less than a quarter is built-up: in fact the proportion of developed land is 9.8%, and half of that is gardens (Foresight, 2010).

The economist Kate Barker was asked by the then Prime Minister in 2004 to review issues underlying the lack of supply and responsiveness of housing in the UK. Apart from private housebuilders' failure to respond to market signals, the Barker Report found that: 'the relationship between supply and affordability is not always recognised in debate: the lack of market affordable housing is bemoaned, while, at the same time, new housing developments are fiercely opposed'. Nowhere is this truer than in rural England. Barker notes that this has the characteristics of 'an insider-outsider problem, where those inside the housing market have more power over any decisions than those outside and their decisions naturally reflect their own interests rather than those of the wider community', let alone generations to come. 'Wider affordability', she concludes, 'can only be sustainable over the longer term by increasing the supply of housing' (Barker, 2006, p. 5). Moreover, 'the benefits of a less constrained supply are not just cold efficiency arguments. Access to decent housing, in a location that sustains social networks, adds to individual welfare. Improving stability in the market would bring important economic benefits to all' (Barker, 2006, p. 6). This challenge is explored in the final section of this chapter.

What values define an ever more exclusive countryside?

Love thy neighbour?

This chapter has argued so far that power is exercised on various levels to exclude middle- and lower-income groups from rural areas, and so to diminish their life-chances. The planning system provides an arena for overt struggle, and opposition to new housing is often effectively mobilized during development plan and development control processes. But power is also exercised in more covert and insidious ways in the form of discursive power which shapes people's perceptions and understandings of the world. For example, it is taken as axiomatic in Britain that rural communities are 'unsustainable' if they lack public transport and services, and generate car journeys. Yet on closer inspection, the deployment in planning arenas of such a partial concept of sustainable communities may be seen to further the interests of a dominant class (exacerbating inequalities and exclusion), while also masking the power relations implicit in this process and making it appear legitimate to those adversely affected. The final part of this chapter contrasts these ways in which power is exercised with the values popularly ascribed to rural communities, notably that of neighbourliness. What values define an ever more exclusive countryside?

Ever since people first gathered to live in urban settlements, contrasts have been suggested between urban and rural life, and between urban and rural values. At different stages in our history rural life has been disparaged as primitive and rude, or praised as idyllic and virtuous. Today the predominant view of rural life is highly romanticized. As one writer has suggested:

> to delight in a rural heritage, albeit without giving too much thought to the people who live and work in the countryside, may be a necessary antidote to the urban environment which is home to the majority of the nation's population. The rural myth has been fondly nurtured for many decades, supported by many social and commercial devices, even to the picturesque village churches, thatched cottages and rose garden portrayed on innumerable calendars and chocolate boxes. (Jones, 1973)

Since the poets and artists of the Romantic Movement, a dichotomy has often been proposed between rural and urban life, by social scientists as much as in popular discourse. The best-known of these is the contrast proposed by Ferdinand Tönnies in 1887 between *Gemeinschaft* and *Gesellschaft*. The urban category, *Gesellschaft*, is seen as characterized by each person being an isolated individual, in a condition of tension against all others, interacting primarily through exchange, rational calculation and formal function, with status deriving from personal achievement. In contrast, the rural category, *Gemeinschaft*, is typified by a sharing of responsibilities and a furtherance of the common good through consensus and understanding, with an emphasis on kinship, locality and neighbourliness.

Researchers soon found that this dichotomy was over-simplistic, finding 'urban' aspects in rural communities (such as Surrey and Hertfordshire) and 'rural' aspects in urban communities (the East End of London). The rural–urban continuum and the notion that the values and sociological characteristics of a place could be 'read off' from its relative location along this continuum was demolished by the weight of contradictory evidence (Pahl, 1968; Newby, 1985; Halfacree, 1993). Moreover, Hoggart (1990) has argued that the social and economic processes underlying change cut across urban–rural boundaries. Most rural clergy will be well aware of the mythical status of the rural idyll (Archbishops' Council, 2005; Gaze, 2006).

And yet people living in rural communities continue to proclaim supposed rural values. Respondents in a study of rural Scotland (Shucksmith *et al.*, 1994, 1996), for example, were anxious to emphasize the existence of rural values which they saw as being quite different from the values held by urban residents. Indeed, their representation of rural life and values (as opposed to urban) followed closely the dichotomy of *Gemeinschaft* and *Gesellschaft* as summarized above. Rural people, it was stated, were less materialistic than urbanites, placing greater importance on family and community than on material possessions and wealth. There was a strong sense of family and community support, and connected to this was a strong sense of self-sufficiency: in times of need the family and then the community were seen as the sources of support and help. Thus people who had faced homelessness had sometimes found solutions to their housing difficulties through family and community networks, and this was seen as preferable to approaching official agencies for help. As well as rural communities being perceived to be more caring, respondents felt that life went at a slower pace and that people had more time for others, and consequently had a greater personal knowledge of neighbours and friends. Rural life was seen as being safer than urban life, and more relaxed. These, together with peace and quiet, pleasant surroundings, a sense of space and absence of crime, were felt to contribute to a higher quality of life than would be possible in an urban area, despite poorer housing and employment opportunities and an absence of transport. Such views are repeated in many other studies across Europe, and underpin many people's desire to move to rural areas.

So on the one hand sociologists observing rural and urban communities find there are no inherent differences between rural and urban life and rural and urban values; while at the same time people believe strongly that such differences do exist, and that they echo Tönnies' ideal types of *Gemeinschaft* and *Gesellschaft*. Pahl (1968) sought to explain this paradox in terms of people's 'village in the mind', constructed in the imagination as much as in day-to-day experience. Similarly, Halfacree (1993, p. 30) explains that our view of what is rural derives from 'a disembodied, but none the less real, social representation of the rural', which however distorted and idealized both guides and constrains our actions. It is for this reason that conflicting interests put forward competing representations of rurality (a part of our heritage to be preserved, or a resource for commodification, for example). Most people perceive rural life and rural values to be under threat. In studies in Scotland, many feared the social changes in rural areas as the number of commuters increased, as it was felt that commuters had 'urban values' and these would ultimately subvert indigenous values. Another fear was that each successive generation's values would become more 'urban' as television influences young people and presents a different, more materialistic world. Furthermore, it was widely suggested that as more women went out to work, either because of choice or economic necessity, support networks would become weakened, as 'voluntary' work was mainly undertaken by women. People commented on the pace of these changes, as the rural way of life 'slipped through their fingers' (Shucksmith *et al.*, 1996, p. 508).

The social construction of the countryside, in accordance with dominant rural ideologies, is clearly a pervasive influence on perceptions of rural life. The majority of respondents to surveys and studies present rural communities as inherently 'good', 'caring', 'safe' and advantaged, while presenting urban communities as inherently degenerate, dangerous and disadvantaged. The potential influx of people from elsewhere is therefore something to be feared,[2] as a threat to 'good communities'.

But there is a paradox in relation to values. Rural values are proclaimed as inclusive and neighbourly, and yet these can only be protected from corrosive urban values through being exclusive and drawing tight bounds around community and neighbourliness. For rural communities to retain their caring and neighbourly character, only immediate neighbours may be included while more distant or different neighbours must be kept out lest their alien values and ways of life disturb the local community's caring values. So who counts as a neighbour? Who is cared for in a caring community? Who is inside and who outside? What are the bounds of social solidarity?

Beyond the question of who is acceptable to join a rural community, there are issues of fairness and social justice. In the previous sections of this chapter we have seen how people's housing opportunities are crushed and their life-chances diminished by the failure to build sufficient houses in rural Britain. At the same time, many people gain substantially. The owners of houses in rural communities enjoy enhanced property values because of this planned scarcity of housing, our villages become more socially exclusive, our schools become more successful, our shops become organic, our pubs become 'gastropubs', and our distance from poverty, from crime, from hunger, from squalor becomes ever greater. Thus we become not only separated from disadvantage: in this process, we become a *cause* of disadvantage as we protect our own advantage and exclusivity. Again, this is a question of values. Our exercise of power, conscious or unconscious, has consequences which intensify disadvantage and social injustice. Once we cease to 'misrecognize' these power relations and become aware of their consequences, what should we do?

Conclusion

Under the Labour Government, Gordon Brown asked Matthew Taylor, the Liberal Democrat MP for Truro, to prepare a report on how to address these issues. His 2008 report, *Living, Working Countryside*, commands widespread support and should form the basis of the Coalition Government's response. Rather than the 60% cut in the social housing budget announced in the Comprehensive Spending Review of 2010, greater investment is needed in affordable rural housing, and this would help contribute to continuing economic growth. Reforms to planning guidance and planning practice are fundamental. But most important will be a recognition by those who live in rural communities of the part they can play in supporting rural housing provision, and of the values which are revealed in their (our) actions.

This is where churches can lead the way. In Tolpuddle in 2010, Stuart Burgess (as Chair of the Commission for Rural Communities) challenged churches to champion the cause of disadvantaged people in the countryside. He argued that it is important for churches to rediscover their role in the community, as a force of 'organized compassion' and social justice. He emphasized that affordable housing is vital 'if these bastions of the rural idyll are not to become ghettoes of the elderly and rich', pointing out that churches 'can have a role in this, persuading the NIMBYs that maybe social housing should have a place in their village – and not just in the next village where there is that nice little corner for it'. (as reported in *Methodist Recorder*, 5 Aug. 2010). My view too is that churches can and should play a vital role, challenging people in rural communities to act in accordance with their values, showing leadership, and preaching neighbourliness in action, through social justice and compassion. Churches may also have land and buildings with which to make a practical contribution, along with the time and commitment of their members. The *Faith in Affordable Housing* initiative is already showing what can be done. As Stuart Burgess told the congregation in Tolpuddle, 'every Circuit could start a Community Land Trust to seek to provide affordable housing' – perhaps they might also argue for more enlightened planning policies and show leadership in neighbourliness.

Acknowledgements

The author is particularly grateful to Nicola Thompson and to Jill Hopkinson for helpful comments and suggestions on earlier drafts of this chapter.

References

Affordable Rural Housing Commission, 2006, *Final Report*. London: Affordable Rural Housing Commission.

Archbishops' Commission on Rural Areas, 1990, *Faith in the Countryside*, Worthing: Churchman Publishing.

Archbishops' Council, 2005, *Seeds in Holy Ground: A Workbook for Rural Churches*, Stoneleigh Park: ACORA Publishing.

Barker, K., 2006, *Barker Review of Land Use Planning: Final Report – Recommendations*, London: The Stationery Office.

Bate, R., Best, R. and Holmans, A., 2002, *On the Move: The Housing Consequences of Migration*, York: York Publishing Services.

Best, R. and Shucksmith, M., 2006, *Homes for Rural Communities: Report of the Joseph Rowntree Foundation Rural Housing Policy Forum*, York: Joseph Rowntree Foundation.

Bevan, M., Cameron, S., Coombes, M., Merridew, T. and Raybould, S., 2001, *Social Housing in Rural Areas*, Chartered Institute of Housing / Joseph Rowntree Foundation.

Bourdieu P., 1977, *Outline of a Theory of Practice*, Cambridge: Cambridge University Press.

Bourdieu, P., 1992, 'Thinking about limits', *Theory, Culture and Society*, 9 (1), pp. 37–49.

Bramley, G. and Watkins D., 2009, 'Affordability and supply: The rural dimension', *Planning Practice and Research*, 24, 4, pp. 185–210.

Brundtland Commission (World Commission on Environment and Development), 1987, *Our Common Future*, Oxford: Oxford University Press.

Buchanan Consultants, 2010, *Research into Rural Housing Affordability, Final Report to DEFRA* (Nick Gallent, Steve Robinson *et al.*), London: University College London, www.colinbuchanan.com/rural-housing-affordability

Commission for Rural Communities, 2005, *State of the Countryside 2005*, Cheltenham: Commission for Rural Communities.

Commission for Rural Communities, 2007, *State of the Countryside 2007*, Cheltenham: Commission for Rural Communities.

Commission for Rural Communities, 2010a, *State of the Countryside Update: Housing*, Cheltenham: Commission for Rural Communities.

Commission for Rural Communities, 2010b, *State of the Countryside 2010*, Cheltenham: Commission for Rural Communities.

Department for Communities and Local Government, 2006, *Planning for Policy Statement 3: Housing*, London: The Stationery Office.

Department for Communities and Local Government, 2008, *What is a Sustainable Community?* London: Department for Communities and Local Government.

Department for Communities and Local Government, 2011, *Housing*, www.communities.gov.uk/housing/about/

DTZ Pieda, 1998, *The Nature of Demand for Housing in Rural Areas*, London: Department for the Environment, Transport and the Regions.

Faith in Affordable Housing: Using Church Land and Property for Affordable Housing, 2010, London: Housing Justice, www.fiah.org.uk

Foresight Land Use Futures Project, 2010, *Final Report*, London: Government Office for Science.

Gaze, S., 2006, *Mission-shaped and Rural: Growing Churches in the Countryside*, London: Church House Publishing.

Greer, G., 2009, 'The future of Scottish housing is high-rise', *Herald Scotland*, www.heraldscotland.com/comment/guest-commen tary/the-future-of-scottish-housing-is-high-rise-argues-germaine-greer-1.823162.

Halfacree, K., 1993, 'Locality and social representation: Space, discourse and alternative definitions of the rural', *Journal of Rural Studies* 9, 1, pp. 23–37.

Hall, P., Gracey, H., Drewitt, R. and Thomas, R., 1973, *The Containment of Urban England*, London: Allen & Unwin.

Hoggart, K., 1990, 'Let's do away with the rural', *Journal of Rural Studies*, 6, pp. 245–57.

Jenkins, S., 2007, 'Once they called it Rachmanism. Now it's being done with Taxpayers Money', *The Guardian*, Friday 16 March.

Jones, G., 1973, *Rural Life*, London: Longman.

Lee, J., 1989, 'Social class and schooling', in M. Cole (ed.), *The Social Contexts of Schooling*, Lewes: Falmer Press.

Lukes, S., 2005, *Power: A Radical View*, 2nd edition, Palgrave Macmillan.

Murdoch, J. and Lowe P., 2003, 'The preservationist paradox: Modernism, environmentalism and the politics of spatial division', *Transactions of the Institute Of British Geographers* 28, (3), pp. 318–32.

Newby, H., 1985, *Green and Pleasant Land? Social Change in Rural England*, Harmondsworth: Penguin.

Office for National Statistics, 2004, *Rural and Urban Definition*, London: Office for National Statistics.

Oxford Economics, 2010, Report for National Housing Federation: *High Rural House Prices*, Oxford: Oxford Economics.

Owen, S., 1996, 'Sustainability and rural settlement planning', *Planning, Practice and Research* 11 (1), pp. 37–47.

Pahl, R.E., 1968, 'The rural-urban continuum', in R.E. Pahl, (ed.), *Readings in Urban Sociology*, Oxford: Pergamon Press.

Rural Coalition, 2010, *The Rural Challenge*, London: The Town and Country Planning Association.

Satsangi, M. and Dunmore, K., 2003, 'The planning system and the provision of affordable housing in rural Britain: A comparison of the Scottish and English experience', *Housing Studies* 18 (2), pp. 201–17.

Satsangi, M., Gallent, N. and Bevan, M., 2010, *The Rural Housing Question*, Bristol: Policy Press.

Shucksmith, M., 1981, *No Homes For Locals?* Farnborough: Gower.

Shucksmith, M., 1990a, *Housebuilding in Britain's Countryside*, London: Routledge.

Shucksmith, M., 1990b, 'A theoretical perspective on rural housing: Housing classes in rural Britain', *Sociologia Ruralis* 30, 2, pp. 210–29.

Shucksmith, M., Henderson, M. and Watkins, L., 1993, 'Attitudes and policies towards residential development in the Scottish countryside', *Journal of Rural Studies* 9, 3, pp. 243–55.

Shucksmith, M., Chapman, P. and Clark, G., 1994, *Disadvantage in Rural Scotland*, Perth: Rural Forum (Scotland).

Shucksmith, M., Henderson, M., Coombes, M., Raybould, S. and Wong, C., 1995, *A Classification of Rural Housing Markets in England*, London: The Stationery Office.

Shucksmith, M., Chapman, P. and Clark, G., 1996, *Rural Scotland Today: The Best of Both Worlds?* Aldershot: Avebury.

Shucksmith, M., 2009, *Sustainable Rural Communities: Constructing Sustainable Places Beyond Cities*, plenary paper to European Society of Rural Sociology XXIII Congress, Vaasa, Finland.

Sturzaker, J., 2010, 'The exercise of power to limit the development of new housing in the English countryside', *Environment and Planning A* 42, 4, pp. 1001–16.

Sturzaker, J. and Shucksmith, M., 2011, 'Planning for housing in rural England: Discursive power and spatial exclusion', *Town Planning Review*, forthcoming.

Taylor, M., 2008, *Living Working Countryside: The Taylor Review of Rural Economy and Affordable Housing*, London: Department for Communities and Local Government.

The Economist, 31 May 2007, Letters page, www.economist.com/opinion/displaystory.cfm?story_id=9253741

Tönnies, F., 1887, *Gemeinschaft und Gesellschaft*, Fues Verlag, Leipzig (translated as [1988] *Community and Society*, Washington, DC: Library of Congress Publications).

Roger Tym and Partners, 2006, *Calculating Housing Needs in Rural England*, Cheltenham: Commission for Rural Communities.

Webb, J., Schirato, T. and Danaher, G., 2002, *Understanding Bourdieu*, London: Sage.

Woods, M., 2005, *Contesting Rurality: Politics in the British Countryside*, Aldershot: Ashgate.

Notes

1   Woods (2005) noted that a pro-development discourse in the countryside by 2005 was only promoted by industry groups like the Home Builders Federation, of whom the public are naturally sceptical. Since 2005 the CRC has attempted to promote homes and services in rural areas – for their efforts, they have been dubbed in *The Guardian* newspaper 'pro-sprawl' because of their counter position to the CPRE (Jenkins, 2007). Interestingly the dominant discourse is now being challenged, at least in part, by a Rural Coalition (2010) under the chairmanship of Matthew Taylor, animated by CRC and including CPRE and other groups.

2   To complicate things further, it must be borne in mind that most urban incomers to rural areas move there precisely because of the perceived value system, rather than through any desire to destroy indigenous values. Conflicts of interest arise through competing representations of 'rural life' and 'rural communities', with local residents trying to hold on to communal values and incomers trying to 'create community' through more associational means (Newby, 1985). In consequence, incomers are accused of destroying the very values which have attracted them to rural communities in the first place, but may simultaneously recreate these values in different ways, forming new associations and new traditions.

6

Climate, Jesus, and a rural prophetic alternative

EDWARD P. ECHLIN

Rural Christians are Jesus as community wherever the rural church reaches. What makes their time distinctive and unprecedented is that humans, in biblical terms God's responsible image, now have the numbers and technological powers literally to destroy the biosphere, the frail, living surface of our planet with its precious biodiverse soil communities. It is perhaps arrogant to say we literally can destroy earth; for Gaia, the frail adaptable crust of our planet, could re-stabilize climate and over millennia heal and re-evolve. But humans can literally decapitate mountains and rip and burn fossil fuels from the earth – as people now are doing – and destroy the earth community, including our own fragile, if arrogant, species.

Our contemporary context

To be Jesus Christ today, and to serve the earth community, we must understand our today. As Dermot Lane writes, 'It is important, therefore, to have some sense of the socio-cultural context in which the message of Christianity is to be taught. Faith exists only as inculturated in particular historical, social and cultural forms' (Lane, 2009, p. 11). There are no innocent traditions. Many of our contemporaries, not least environmentalists and earth-literate NGOs, criticize us trenchantly, explicitly our dilatory response to the onslaught on the earth. We who are committed to Jesus Christ may also criticize ourselves from within. In endeavouring to persuade Christians that we should be in the vanguard with the best

NGOs and caring persons in earth concern, one is painfully aware that our hands are not wholly clean!

When we regard our context, different aspects strike different people, depending on their special circumstances, interests and insights within the wider context. Here are a few salient points which impress me, as an eco-theologian and organic gardener and member of a Catholic community in the south-east. A remarkable ingredient of contemporary culture is the sudden interest in food and food security – and insecurity – especially local food production and consumption. Everywhere, not least in cities, people are interested in local food production, ranging from window ledge and roof plants to back gardens and allotments, the countryside and traditional farming regions. Yet in the UK young country people are being forced to leave the countryside.

At the recent G20 conference, Chinese country people were urged to leave the countryside and live in cities. Similarly a recent UK Prime Minister said Britain could abandon farming completely and import our food. Hopefully this will change. In a 2010 lecture at Milan, Ethiopian Environment Minister Tewolde Eqziabher said helpfully:

A new form of sustainable agricultural intensification is already taking place in Africa. This started in the badly degraded northeastern highlands of Ethiopia . . . They built terraces and bunds to prevent soil erosion; they restricted their animals to specific areas and fed them crop residues so as to allow grass, shrubs and trees to maximize growth in the rainy season, and vegetation cover improved dramatically in just one rainy season. They could then harvest the grass and add hay to the crop residues to feed their animals sufficiently.

The increased availability of animal dung and biomass made it possible for them to make and apply compost on their respective fields. Soil fertility improved and so did crop harvests. Rainwater percolated through the improved soil structure and began recharging the water table more fully. Springs and streams began to flow again and strengthen, allowing irrigation in the dry season, which increased food production further. Trees that had disappeared owing to land degradation began returning in subsequent rainy seasons. Farmers enriched the resurgent tree cover with the species of their choice, usually fruit and leguminous trees for both fodder and soil enrichment.

Here in the UK there is significant interest in explaining food production to children from towns and cities. A rural Sussex councillor, concerned with the alienation of children from soil, said that many village children, especially from what we may call exurbia, know not where chips originate, and have never seen a potato. Penelope Blossom agrees: 'The whole cycle, how we plant, nurture, harvest and consume should be able to be demonstrated to the next generation, who without this opportunity will always consider their meals to come directly from a supermarket shelf' (Blossom, 2008, p. 7).

The UN estimates that one billion people are undernourished and hungry. Environmental refugees have already begun, including from delta areas in flood-threatened Bangladesh and from island states. East Anglian agricultural land is under threat. The UK countryside is ill-equipped to accommodate migrants. One way to secure agro-ecological agriculture everywhere is to follow the proximity principle in necessary migrations, with migrants moving as close to their home country as possible, causing less disturbance of soil in distant countries and enabling a return to one's home territory when conditions permit. Estimates vary as to how many days the UK could feed its 60 million people, many of them in cities, in an emergency. Carolyn Steel observes:

> Contrary to appearances, we live as much on a knife-edge now as did the inhabitants of ancient Rome or *Ancien Regime* Paris. Cities in the past did their best to keep stocks of grain in reserve in case of sudden attack; yet the efficiencies of modern food distribution mean that we keep very little in reserve. Much of the food you and I will be eating next week hasn't even arrived in the country yet. Our food is delivered 'just in time' from all over the world: hardly the sort of system designed to withstand a sudden crisis. (Steel, 2009, p. 100)

Much of our best soil is within and 'under' population centres. Defra and the Royal Horticultural Society estimate that about 4% of soil in England and Wales is in urban gardens. Settlement gardens, parks and open spaces are a precious, potentially life-enabling resource. Yet on the Sussex coast, for example, developers, planners, and road builders are able to compulsorily purchase fertile fields some of which have been farmed since Neolithic times. 'Release', 'development' and 'regeneration' concern everyone and cry out for a prophetic alternative response to the mantra of 'economic growth'. Closely linked to soil destruction, and food insecurity, is water shortage. Dr Nicholas Grey of Wells for India observes:

> It is becoming increasingly clear that small-scale water-harvesting will be a key tool to help the rural poor adjust to climate changes not only in India but also across other parts of Asia, across Africa and South America (Grey, 2009, p. 6).

This may increasingly be the case in the UK too.

Climate change

Harmonious climate, including its harsh vagaries, is within God's creation and is celebrated in God's word in scripture, as in the Psalms:

> Who covers the heavens with clouds,
>   who provides rain for the earth,
>   who makes grass to grow on the mountains.
> He gives to the beast its food,
>   and to the young ravens which cry. . . .
> He sends forth his command to the earth;
>   his word runs very swiftly.
> He gives snow like wool;
>   he scatters the frost like ashes.
> He casts forth his ice like fragments;
>   who can stand before his cold?

He sends forth his word and melts them;
  he causes the wind to blow and the waters to flow.
(Psalm 147.8–9, 15–18, NAS)

In the opening words of the Bible we learn, through a prose poem, that within this biodiverse seed-bearing earth, women and men are enjoined to relate to one another, to become permanently *juntos* with 'the one other', and to increase human numbers until we can effectively be God's image, responsible, like ancient priestly shepherd kings, for his earth community. We are a democratized client kingship, like shepherds prepared to die for our flock, which is the whole earth or soil community. To be God's royal shepherds means that we are *within*, not technocratically above, the rest of the soil community; we are fellow creatures. 'One from among your brothers you shall set as king over you. You may not put a foreigner over you, who is not your brother' (Deuteronomy 17.15 ESV). Nor are we encouraged to over-populate.

The second, older creation story portrays our place within creation in agrarian terms. We are soil creatures, *adam*, from *adamah*. Moreover, in the Bible's birthplace, we are *adom*, of reddish tan colour like topsoil. We are soil creatures, here to work, serve, cherish, and observe garden earth. The currently popular 'guard and keep' summarizes our presence and ministry well (Davis, 2009, pp. 21–30). The garden is productive when women and men co-operate and care for the garden sustainably. When they serve other 'gods', whether their own arrogant pursuit of 'progress', 'regeneration', 'economic growth' and 'development', listening to the snake, and serving idols, the garden ceases reliable production, climate changes, animals thirst, thorns and thistles proliferate. The Bible repeatedly teaches – as does our contemporary experience – that when humans live sustainably under God, climate is stable; when humans become arrogant, their hubris brings the nemesis of climate change (Deuteronomy 11.13f.; Jeremiah 14.1–7; Echlin, 2010, pp. 82–3).

The technical term for human-induced climate damage is anthropogenic. It means human-generated. We now realize – despite those who try to deny it – that our current climate disruption is caused by anthropogenic emissions, especially from cars, lorries, planes, ships, chimneys, deforestation, overdevelopment, militarism and intensive chemo-agriculture. Less well known are the dynamics of climate change. While earth heating is induced largely by fossil-fuel emissions, methane and nitrous oxide, and other greenhouse gases, there are also mutually reinforcing feedbacks resultant from temperature rise which further exacerbate climate damage. These are called positive feedbacks. So climate change is not linear, easy to restabilize once we 'cut the carbon'. The radiation earth receives and what it returns to the atmosphere should be in balance, but since the industrial revolution and relentless human population growth they are not. We retain a surplus of radiation while constantly receiving more. That imbalance is called radiative forcing. Positive feedbacks are not directly and immediately anthropogenic and they can race beyond our control. We can cut our emissions, but feedbacks are less easy to influence. If we don't counter them immediately, they can damage and destroy whole ecosystems and one feedback can trigger another. That scary 'tipping point' is a real danger. We have at most a few years to reduce our own emissions, and equally important, to counter positive feedback by facilitating, generating and *being* negative (damping, diminishing) feedbacks.

The Arctic and Antarctic are good barometers, or white canaries. Journalist Mark Lynas puts it this way:

> Alaska is baking. Temperatures in the state – as in much of the Arctic – are rising ten times faster than in the rest of the world. And the effects are so dramatic that entire ecosystems are beginning to unravel, as are the lifestyles of the people – many of them Native Americans – who depend on them. In many ways Alaska is the canary in the coal mine, showing the rest of the world what lies ahead as global warming accelerates. (Lynas, 2005, p. 39)

In addition to reliable reports from the Intergovernmental Panel on Climate Change (IPCC) and other eminent scientists, we may also observe changes in our own climate. Sir Ghillean Prance, former

Director of Kew Gardens, said that everywhere he went people commented on strange weather. Here in England's south-east corner, experienced gardeners and allotment holders report not only the perennial afflictions of wood pigeons, jays, slugs, rodents and vandals, but also that climate change is making gardening difficult. My own garden, about the size of three allotments, is a wise teacher and an eco-theologian's workplace (Echlin, 2010, p. 97). In the 40 years I have gardened in the UK, I have noticed numerous climate-related changes, not all of them perverse, at least in the short term. In 2007, 2008, 2009 and 2010, for example, peppers and tomatoes were harvested into November, almost until American Thanksgiving. Fruit used to be planted in early November. Then as the dormant season began later, some nurserymen lifted plants later and now plant in January. Potatoes are planted and harvested several weeks earlier than before.

Among other disturbing symptoms have been excessively dry springs in the south, while rain poured in the north-west, particularly in 2008, 2009 and 2010. The crops never recovered, despite diligent hand watering. In 2008 we had traditional April weather – with a vengeance – in July. In 2009 and 2010 we suffered drought in both spring and summer, which impacted both fruit and vegetable harvests.

The IPCC notes that thermal changes in the Gulf Stream could affect Britain, perhaps temporarily deflecting some of the worst effects of earth heating. Already here on 'La Manche', sea species, themselves climate refugees, including red mullet, cuttlefish, squid, and sea bass, are colonizing. Peter Wadhams observes:

> The thing of which we are certain is that the sea surface temperature is rising globally, and this is decreasing the density of sea water and causing the ocean to stand higher. One example of ocean warming has been locally here in the North Sea. The North Sea winter temperatures have gone up by more than a degree in the last few decades and this is one of the reasons why the cod is disappearing from the North Sea because it is becoming too warm for cod to spawn. (Wadhams, 2007, p. 88)

Soil and climate change

Earth warming is especially poignant in rural areas, and for that matter in gardens, allotments and community-supported agro-ecological agriculture. Yet here in Britain we have destroyed some of our soil, especially by roads, exurban 'development' and 'regeneration', including malls, runways and asphalt carpets of car parks. Even now we 'forward stampede' with road widening, airport expansion, bypasses and link roads, and green- and brown-field construction. Graham Harvey describes the precious soil of which we are custodians:

> Fertile soils produce healthy growth. And soils don't become fertile just because they contain high levels of organic matter and available minerals. To promote healthy growth they also need large populations of microbes and other soil organisms – an underground army, which is constantly breaking down and rebuilding nutrients from plant and animal wastes; and in the process making minerals available to plants. About 5 per cent of soil is composed of organic matter – the wastes and decomposed residues of plants and animals, together with the billions of organisms that live in the air spaces between mineral particles.
>
> It is the actions of this living community that enable plants to grow. They supply plants with the nutrients they need, provide them with water and protect them against toxins and disease. Without the activity of soil organisms – from microscopic bacteria to earthworms – life on the planet would quickly grind to a halt. (Harvey, 2006, p. 106)

The precious fragility of soil, including urban soil, is a sobering challenge. Especially since the war we have become almost a nation of soil exploiters, what Edward Hyams early last century called 'disease organisms of the soil' and John Seymour later called 'soil plunderers'. Now we are responsible for what soil remains, in both urban and rural areas. We can make a healthy contribution to biodiversity by nurturing woodlands and copses, orchards and vineyards (which are themselves symbiotic habitats), ponds, hedgerows, meadows, field edges and wildlife sanctuaries (as in churchyards set aside for wildlife), and by protecting rivers and sea life.

At the end of his life renowned biblical scholar C.F.D. Moule, who had known the birds of Cambridge fens and Pevensey levels, still enjoyed a window ledge feeder in his Sherbourne care home and watched the birds in trees outside his window. Recently a dalesman from Upper Nidderdale pointed to a wooded fell on his farm: 'It used to be all like that,' he commented, 'before deforestation and intensive grazing.' In his hand was a traditional straight saw, and in his memory gems of history and wisdom through centuries on a family farm.

We can become soil and biodiversity restorers by enabling fells and meadows, grasslands, peat and heath – never forgetting kitchen gardens and local fruit varieties, such as the Sussex Forge apple. Sandra Nichols of the NFU estimates that over half of UK farmers report that changing climate – and not just weather – already impacts their fields, as growing season lengthens. The Food and Agriculture Organization echoes the NFU on the global scenario, croplands, pastures and forests are progressively exposed to threats from increased climatic variability. The IPCC predicts ominously that yields could diminish by 50% by 2020, and agriculture contributes 14% of greenhouse gases, exceeding other sources save the power industry.

In the USA, fossil-fuel interests have spent millions hindering President Obama's efforts at slight emission cuts (McCarthy, 2009, pp. 47–50).

Some crops – like some animals – adapt better to the droughts and wetness of early climate change than others. Saving seeds through seed banks preserves hereditary genetic diversity. In the EU French grower Jean de Berthelot started 'growing out' 17 cultivated wheat varieties. After searching the world's seed banks he now grows and saves seeds from 200 varieties. Some are drought tolerant, some provide ground cover or mulch as well as grain. De

Berthelot's seeds are now stored in the remarkable – and cool and protected – seed bank at Spitzbergen, Norway. Sir Julian Rose, who farms in Berkshire and heads the International Commission to Protect the Polish Countryside, comments – and this can motivate all of us: 'peasant farmers are the last line of resistance to the global corporate takeover of the food chain. The red blood that runs through their veins is the most valuable asset mankind possesses – it is quite literally, the key to our survival as sentient, loving, human beings' (Rose, 2008, pp. 7–8).

Rural dwellers, entrusted with that little land, their special fields in our Creator's garden earth (Genesis 2.15), are in many ways uniquely placed to assist our community to adapt to and mitigate climate change. We can assist our island's biosphere, and thereby the whole planet, by restoring and preserving soil. We too are soil entities, within a soil community; we are, as John Seymour used to say, soil organisms, frail members of a frail, finite community. Ours is the responsibility to lead our communities to 're-member' in the sense of re-entering creation, to 'serve' and 'observe' the soil (Genesis 2.15), and where it is crushed and 'sealed', as in disused car parks and in slabbed front gardens, to 'recover' it, by removing the covering and letting life live again. If melting glaciers and warming oceans continue to swell the waters, we may lose yet more prime agricultural land. Despite the aspirations of governments, planners and house builders, we cannot indefinitely construct dwellings on finite, shrinking land. Road and runway building, as the Green Party and better NGOs insist, should cease. Caring for God's earth, as his client priestly, royal, shepherd image, is consistent with and supportive of some of the more radical movements within society. Recent reports of the International Assessment of Agricultural Knowledge, Science and Technology for Development (IAASTD), for example, prove that small farms and holdings are at least as productive as intensive agribusiness.

The paramount contribution of the churches, which are the Jesus movement, is to be Christ as community today. Jesus showed a reverence for the countryside, its plants, animals and people, and applied the soil's wisdom in illustrating his teaching. We protect the countryside and its biodiversity in imitation of him. By helping our countryside to revive and flourish we and the whole soil community become negative feedback, mitigating climate change through our hearts, heads and hands, and in community with fellow creatures. The French Jesuit Victor Poucel said that Francis Assisi's recovery of fellow creatures *as creatures* was as important as his recovery of poverty (Poucel, 1937, pp. 19, 250–1).

The importance of the local: support local food – and other produce from as near your home as possible. Never underestimate our potential for partial self-sufficiency and encourage others here and abroad to follow the proximity principle too, instead of exporting their soil fertility and virtual water, through air and ship miles. An example is wine. In 2009, the UK won 24 medals for wines: Camel Valley Wines, Bodmin, won the first UK gold medal at the International Wine Challenge Award. We should buy and encourage local wines, including bioregional wines from the EU, never importing from beyond Europe. Jesus, in his admittedly very different culture and context, lived sustainably, supporting local food and wines.

Jesus and the earth

The whole evolutionary earth history is within Jesus' humanity, as it is in ours. 'As enfleshed, embedded in the soil like us, Jesus contains within his humanity the whole evolving earth story' (Echlin, 1999, p. 70). As a practical example of our connectedness, when we remove a piece of concrete or asphalt or slab covering soil entrusted to us, it is beneficial to the soil ecosystem and to water permeation. The early Fathers recognized the effect of Jesus' baptism on all the waters of the world, 'the cosmic Jordan'. Beginning with Ignatius of Antioch (d. AD 107) the early Fathers proclaimed that because Jesus was immersed and baptized in the river, all the waters of the earth are affected. We now know that through evaporation and precipitation all waters *are* related. There is therefore profound theological and ecological wisdom in churches calling their baptismal fonts 'the Jordan' (McDonnell, 1996, pp. 54–5). Tertullian wrote eloquently, 'It makes no difference whether a person be baptized in a sea or pool, a stream or a font, a lake or a trough; nor is there any distinction between those who John baptized in the Jordan, and those Peter baptized in the Tiber' (Roberts, 1993 pp. 670–1).

The Bible, especially the Old Testament, is water and earth inclusive. God disclosed himself in the earth and in Jewish history as concerned with human food production and self-sufficiency. God's self-bestowal comes to us in an earth-inclusive, agrarian way. An agrarian reception of revelation is the most resonant way to respond to God's word. Ellen Davis writes,

> Agrarianism is the mind-set native to many if not most biblical writers themselves. At the same time, if we who read the bible, each in our own place, stretch our minds to recognize the land as a home to be cherished, that effort will make us better readers of scripture (Davis, 2009, p. 27)

Food production and consumption, whether in carbon-sequestering grass pasture, mixed farming, smallholdings or urban gardens, gives people an affinity with the biblical writers and their message. It is especially timely to grow fruit and vegetables in our front gardens. Growing food in that precious soil contributes to food security and provides a good example.

In the primordial flood story, God enters 'an everlasting covenant' with all people, with other sensate creatures as our covenant partners. Never again will God destroy the earth with a flood (Genesis 8.21–22). Nowhere in the Bible, however, does God promise to prevent humanity from destroying the biosphere. Indeed, the scriptures repeatedly warn that human arrogance brings the nemesis of unsuitable weather or climate change (Leviticus 26.19–20; Deuteronomy 11.13–17). In brief, the dominant culture into which Jesus was born and nourished was, unlike our own, earth-inclusive, earth-dependent, and earth-respecting. In the popular wisdom of that culture, people learned from the animals, from the soil, and from wise farmers, as we learn from farmers today. An experienced grower, cultivating family fields, adapts to the wisdom of the soil (Isaiah 28.24–26), and transmits that wisdom to future generations.

As the Jewish tribes coalesced into a people, the 'good land' then available largely consisted of the 'valleys and hills' of southern Galilee, where Jesus spent most of his life, and of north Galilee, where he ministered and preached the kingdom. Galilee scholar Sean Freyne notes, 'Galilee would forever be a part of the Christian proclamation of the Good News by and about Jesus Christ . . . As a Galilean Jewish figure, he must have participated in and been affected by the everyday experiences of life as lived in that region' (Freyne, 2009, pp. 284–5).

Jesus at Nazareth

Matthew's and Luke's canonical Gospels begin with infancy narratives composed in the light of the cross and resurrection (Brown, 1993, pp. 25–32). Both infancy stories relate Jesus to creation, to the soil, fields and food production of the promised land. Matthew's brief narrative associates the holy family with Bethlehem, the 'house of bread', where cereals grew on terraced hillsides, David's city with its connotations of sacral kingship. As we noted, good kingship included good climate with concomitant soil fertility in valleys and hills (Psalm 72.3, 6, 16). Matthew's star recalls Balaam and expectations of Davidic kingship (Numbers 24.17; Matthew 2.2). The flight recalls the Joseph story with its connotations of seeds, which later feature in Jesus' parables (Matthew 13.3–9; Mark 4.2–9). When the family settles in Nazareth there is a further reference to holistic kingship in Matthew's pun on nazir, or shoot from David (Matthew 2.23; Isaiah 11.1–9). Luke's longer narrative also includes kingship; indeed Joseph's Davidic descent was the reason for the journey to Bethlehem where Jesus was born. There is also the inclusion of shepherds who connote ancient kingship, which was compared to good shepherding (Isaiah 40.11–12; Luke 2.8–20). To Luke we also owe the manger (*phatne*), which includes, as does subsequent Christian iconography, an ox and an ass (Isaiah 1.3; Luke 2.7). The visit to the temple connotes relationship to fields, for the presence of the temple on Mount Sion made fields and soils sacred. Jesus was the new temple, surpassing the old as God's incarnate presence within the soil itself, sanctifying the whole soil community.

Jesus, Luke says, was 'subject' to his parents at Nazareth. There he learned from his father and elders of his extended family about the hill country and its biodiversity and climate, especially their own share in their family fields. As the Monaghan farmer poet Patrick Kavanagh noted, there is an undying difference in the corner of a field. A rural grower literally learns God's ways from the soil itself and from the practice of wise, experienced growers. Isaiah writes:

> Does he who ploughs for sowing plough continually?
> does he continually open and harrow his ground?
> When he has levelled its surface, does he not scatter dill, sow cummin,
> and put in wheat in rows and barley in its proper place,
> and spelt as the border?
> For he is instructed aright; his God teaches him.
>
> (Isaiah 28.24–26, RSV)

Hereditary fields were shared among families. If a man sold a field to meet a debt, the field reverted to the family in Jubilee, or a relative repurchased the field (Leviticus 25.3–28). Fields, with their fertility and biodiversity, were part of the extended family. Seeds were harvested, saved and shared. The most fertile soils in southern Galilee were the valleys running east to west. These were appropriated by Romans and Herodians, hence the reference in Christ's parables to tenants and day labourers. The Jewish settlers lived and farmed on the ridges. Of the four ridges in lower Galilee, the southernmost, with Nazareth, was the most fertile. The northern ridges were alkaline. Nazareth was semi-permeable chalk and marl, with a spring and wadi. Iron Age crops were mainly cereals, olives, figs, vines, pomegranates, vegetables and perhaps a few apples, for Nazareth was near the spice route that passed through apple country, and Josephus, a first-century governor of Galilee, says Herod loved apples. I noticed a few dwarf apples in an Israeli Arab garden at Nazareth. Elder trees which still grow on the ridge would have been useful for processing of different kinds. Notable for our own time of mass urbanization, ancient Jewish culture regarded settlement living as symbiotic. Food growing, with stock, was part of the culture in larger settlements, as well as in more rural areas. And, also worthy of our consideration, the idealized new Jerusalem was a fertile city.

Jesus' prophetic alternative ministry

As a young man at Nazareth, and after leaving home, Jesus realized that he had an important role in God's forthcoming kingdom. Mark says that in the wilderness, Jesus was 'with the wild animals', another reference to the Isaian peaceable kingdom (Mark 1.13; Isaiah 11.6–9). In his ministry, Jesus' alternative lifestyle was an integral part of his teaching. He lived within the Sabbath and Jubilee tradition, sharing and trusting God, people and all creation. His lifestyle was itinerant, in the inclusive Abrahamic tradition welcoming people 'from east and west', 'sunrise and sunset'. In his inclusive ministry Jesus preached – in words and example – that all people are invited to participate in God's kingdom. We note the inclusive banquet in Isaiah's description of the kingdom (Isaiah 65.21–22). Jesus' inclusive meals, therefore, were an important part of his teaching. We note how Jesus prayed to God as Abba, 'Father', in patriarchal societies the provider of food and life's other necessities. The trusting lifestyle and shared meals continued to the very end of Jesus' ministry and life. Even as he made the last journey to Jerusalem, which he knew would probably be his last days on earth, Jesus shared a final meal with disciples in Bethany, and a final one in Jerusalem itself. This 'last supper' is what we memorialize, make present again, in our own inclusive Eucharists, in 'bread which earth has given' and 'wine fruit of the vine and work of human hands'. Significantly, Jesus ended his active life in an olive garden called Gethsemane, which he had visited often when in Jerusalem (John 18.1). The beloved disciple, probably an eyewitness of much of Jesus' ministry, who was present at Golgotha, writes that 'in the place where he was crucified there was a garden' (John 19.41). In that garden, the new Adam's side is opened, blood and water flow onto the earth, and the 'woman' and her 'son', the beloved disciple, are present, symbolizing new Eden, new creation. Jesus' resurrection inaugurates the new heaven and new earth. Henceforth, 'all flesh', including people of all faiths, and other sensate creatures, reconciled, will worship their Creator and Redeemer (Isaiah 66.23; Revelation 22.2–4).

Conclusion

To conclude, two prophetic principles are relevant, grounded in Jesus' own prophetic alternative ministry and service, one for local and national governments and their citizens, and one for the Church, all the baptized who are Jesus as community today. Governments, including local authorities, should adhere to the proximity principle. By this is meant a radical – which is what 'prophetic alternative' means – new direction from the way globalized economies have been living, which has brought the soil community literally to extinction's door. This means living and trading locally with preference for what is proximate.

Political leaders should lead in implementing – and living – the proximity principle, instead of insisting there can be indefinite economic growth on a frail, finite planet. The proximity principle is easy to disparage, but not always convenient to implement. Yet whether in north-west Europe, south-east Asia, North America or deep Africa, living and sharing in proximity is literally vital if people are to re-enter the earth community sustainably. Recall the example of wine. Think of the French (and British) vintners we can support, the ship and lorry miles eliminated by enjoying local and bioregional wine. The proximity principle also includes local, seasonal food. Here too we assist local producers and eliminate food miles and emissions. It should be noted, however that technically 'local' produce when produced out of season under glass can be climate damaging. We need both proximate and seasonal food.

To follow the proximity principle, in our age of shallow mass media, will invariably raise eyebrows and resistance. Brueggemann's dictum, prophecy challenges dominant cultures, is relevant here. As Sally McFague observes, 'Scientific predictions of matters as complex as weather can never be absolute, the "precautionary principle" advises us, as it did with the ozone issue, to act now. Climate change challenges the fossil fuel industry, as well as America's love affair with the car. Hence, denial and resistance are high' (McFague, 2000, p. 41).

Where appropriate, we must de-globalize, and certainly re-localize, practical action. Rather than promoting overseas 'development', our aid agencies should promote sufficiency for all, perhaps even changing their names to reflect this. For example: the World Development Movement would become the 'World Sufficiency Movement'. To adapt their names would itself send a prophetic alternative message. For some affluent people the most challenging part of the proximity principle is the subsidiary 'in depth principle' which means that instead of climate-damaging holidaying air or ship miles, we should enjoy and learn the historic, cultural and biodiverse treasures of one's own bioregion *in depth*.

A word about the Church itself. Christ existing as community today. We who are the Church are, or should be, a prophetic alternative to dominant unsustainable cultures. This chapter has emphasized discipleship of Jesus, for it is to him that Christians are committed. We can easily become so absorbed with the structures of discipleship that the Church virtually obscures Jesus. When the media, including some of our more reputable papers, rediscover the Church, they overlook us as his contemporary presence. It was said of the first disciples: 'See how they love one another'; and that love should include the earth. The Church can be a prophetic alternative to unsustainable consumerism — a sustainable agrarian witness. Southern African Christians have tree-planting Eucharists, where a tree is planted by a deacon or lay minister, *before* the Eucharist, remembered in the Eucharist, and most importantly, cared for thereafter (Echlin, 2000, p. 43).

The African Christians say a beautiful prayer after they plant their tree:

> You, tree, my brother . . . my sister
> today I plant you in this soil
> I shall give water for your growth
> Have good roots
> to keep the soil from eroding
> Have many branches and leaves
> so that we can:
> – breathe fresh air
> – sit in your shade
> – and find firewood.

Tree-planting Eucharists, and the admirable Living Churchyard movement, challenge us to set aside part of our chapel or church land, even if just a small corner, for a wildlife sanctuary. For some this will be a 'living churchyard', for others a bird house or feeder, perhaps an insect feeding plant – each of you knows what is especially suited to your place of worship. We can be a blessing to every community in which we live and serve, if we install solar panels on our south-facing roofs, and become a microgenerator, an energy provider in every community we serve. Plant fruit and nut trees on church land, and harvest rain from downpipes. Baptismal, and all service waters, can be returned, by children and sacristans, to a baptismal, or commemorative tree. We can baptize in harvested rainwater. And we can use harvested water for flowers, plants and cleaning. In conclusion, may the rural church, Jesus Christ as community today, be a local witness of sustainability, sharing the earth, its biodiversity, water and climate, with the earth community we serve as, in his life on earth, Jesus did.

References

Blossom, P., 2008, 'Investing in the future', *Country Way, Life and Faith in Rural Britain*, 48, p. 7.

Brown, R.E., 1993, *The Birth of the Messiah: A Commentary on the Infancy Narratives in the Gospels of Matthew and Luke*, London: Geoffrey Chapman, pp. 25–32.

Davis, E., 2009, *Scripture, Culture and Agriculture: An Agrarian Reading of the Bible*, Cambridge: Cambridge University Press, pp. 21–30.

Echlin, E.P., 1999, *Earth Spirituality: Jesus at the Centre*, New Alresford: Arthur James, p. 70.

Echlin, E.P., 2010, *Climate and Christ: A Prophetic Alternative*, Dublin: Columba Press, pp. 97, 82–3.

Echlin, E.P., 2000, 'An African church sets the example', *The Ecologist*, 30, 1, p. 43.

Eqziabher, T., 2010, *Resurgence*, no. 254 May/June 2009. Based on a speech given at the opening ceremony of Terra Madre, Turin, Italy, October 2008.

Freyne, S., 2009, 'Galilean Jesus and a contemporary Christology', *Theological Studies*, 70, 2, pp. 284–285.

Grey, N., 2009, 'Climate change in India', *Wells for India Newsletter*, 46, p. 6.

Harvey, G., 2006, *We Want Real Food: Why our Food is Deficient in Minerals and Nutrients and What we can do About it*, London: Constable, p. 106.

Lane, D., 2009, *Challenges Facing Religious Education in Contemporary Ireland*, Dublin: Veritas, p. 11.

Lynas, M., 2005, *High Tide: How Climate Crisis is Engulfing Our Planet*, London: Harper Perennial, p. 39.

McCarthy, J.J., 2009, 'Climate science and its distortion and denial by the misinformation industry', in R. White (ed.), *Creation in Crisis: Christian Perspectives on Sustainability*, London: SPCK, pp. 34–52.

McDonnell, K., 1996, *The Baptism of Jesus in the Jordan, The Trinitarian and Cosmic Order of Salvation*, Collegeville: The Liturgical Press, pp. 54–5.

McFague, S., 2000, 'An ecological Christology: does christianity have it?', in D.T. Hessel and R.R. Ruether (eds), *Christianity and Ecology, Seeking the Well-Being of Earth and Human*, Cambridge: Harvard University Press, p. 41.

Poucel, V., 1937, *Mystique de la terre, Vol. 2, La Parabole du monde*, Paris: Pion, pp. 19, 250–1.

Roberts, A. (ed.), 1993, 'Tertullian, "On Baptism"', *The Ante-Nicene Fathers*, Vol. 3, Edinburgh: T. & T. Clark, pp. 670–1.

Rose, J., 2008, 'GM crops and eugenics', *Fourth World Review*, October, pp. 7–8.

Steel, C., 2009, *Hungry City: How Food Shapes our Lives*, London: Vintage Books, p. 100.

Wadhams, P., 2007, 'Feedbacks in ice and ocean dynamics', in P. Cox, D. Rughani, P. Wadhams and D. Wasdell, *Planet Earth: We Have a Problem*, Leeds: Angus Print, pp. 71–101.

7

Older people in the country: burden or blessing?

ALBERT JEWELL

The proportion of older people in the population is rising, especially in rural areas and in churches. This chapter discusses the spiritual needs, difficulties and contributions of older people and how these issues relate to the Christian faith. It is shown how the gospel offers particular opportunities for ministry to older people, and a plea is made for a holistic approach to care.

The demographics

The title of this chapter is derived from the contribution of the former Bishop of Durham, David Jenkins, at the Second International Conference on Ageing, Spirituality and Well-Being held in Durham in July 2002. Invited to act as rapporteur for the various keynote addresses, he entitled his summary report, 'Geriatric burden or elderly blessing?' (Jenkins, 2004).

Jenkins' title is of course double-edged. On the one hand it refers to the individual whose life expectancy in the UK at age 65 has now increased to 85.2 for females and 82.6 for males (Office for National Statistics, 2010). However, whether increased quantity of days is matched by quality of life depends upon many variable factors. The title also has reference to society at large. The ratio of the number of retired people to those of working age is inexorably increasing. However, this supposed 'burden' needs to be counterbalanced by the undoubted contribution of many older people to the common good, not least in rural communities. Not everything should be measured in purely numerical and financial terms.

The report of the Oxford Consultants for Social Inclusion (2009) reveals that rural populations are older than urban populations, arising both from additional people retiring to the countryside expecting a better quality of life and the net outflow of younger people. Currently, two-fifths of the rural population is over 50, a quarter over 60, and one in twelve 85 and over. It is projected that the population of those over 65 will rise by 62% by 2029 in rural areas compared with 46% in urban areas, while the very old (those over 85, who are the most vulnerable) will increase by 114% compared with 86% in urban areas. This could be welcomed as a good advert for the quality of life in the countryside or perceived as a threat, marking an unsustainable future burden upon rural communities.

It is important to recognize that the congregations of most mainstream Christian denominations in England are ageing at a much faster rate than the population at large. In the wider community some 16% are aged 65 or over whereas among churchgoers for the Church of England, Methodist and United Reformed Church the figure is more than twice that figure (Brierley, 2000). In many individual congregations, especially in rural areas, it can be very much higher.

Spiritual needs

Over the last 30 years I have become increasingly fascinated by older church members' life journeys, which helped to explain their evident resilience. Work with Methodist Homes (MHA) brought me into contact with many remarkable individuals who might have appeared very 'ordinary' on the surface. Their life stories, usually very diffidently shared, are to be interpreted in terms of valuable resource rather than self-indulgent reminiscence.

Out of this sharing experience emerged a 'spirituality model' which was incorporated into a staff training video (Jewell, 1999; MHA Care Group, 2002) which takes as axiomatic that all human beings are spiritual beings, even if not accepting that they are 'religious' in the sense of adhering to credal statements or belonging to religious communities. 'Spirituality' is taken to include those intangibles that give meaning, purpose and direction to a person's life, including (among others) relationships, values, principles, the aesthetic, a sense of wonder and mystery, and (for many) God. Humans are of course also physical, mental, emotional, sexual and social beings. Truly holistic care, which seeks to promote the well-being of older people, will recognize that these various aspects overlap and are inter-penetrative one of another.

There is a real danger that older people can be regarded almost as a separate species. Indeed, the ageism that is rife in our society tends to do just that, denigrating or simply dismissing the aged in the community. However, the basic spiritual needs are the same in human beings whatever age they may be and whether they live in urban or rural communities, though older age does tend to give a particular focus to those needs (Jewell, 1999; Jewell, 2004; Hawley and Jewell, 2009). There is a further danger in that the very word 'needs' seems to betoken weakness and dependency rather than the positive harvest that older age can bring.

Love

Our paramount and enduring human need or instinct is for love. Without love the infant can all but shrivel up and become stunted physically, mentally, emotionally and spiritually. In old age the need is no less, though perhaps not so recognized. Many an older person will say that they have seen nobody for a week and cannot remember the last time they felt the touch of another's hand. Of course, we need to give as well as to receive love; as the first Epistle of John maintains: 'We love because we have first been loved' (1 John 4.19). That seems to be the basic principle embedded in human life by the Creator, and at a human level it appears no less significant for those who don't believe in a God.

Faith/trust

Second, there also seems built in to human beings the need to believe in or commit to something or someone. For many this will of course be God, the one to whom none is greater, but it does not need to be God. People can believe in their loved ones, democracy, a particular political creed, homeopathic medicine and 101 other things.

Hope

Third, as well as someone or something to believe in, there is the need for hope: something to look forward to. This is what kept Viktor Frankl (1964) and others in the wartime concentration camps resilient and gave them a chance of survival. Hope enables us to look forward and believe that things can change, that progress will come about, and for Christians that ultimately God's kingdom will come: hope in this life and indeed beyond. But it can come under real threat in older age.

Peace

Peace means here much more than freedom from war. All human beings seek release from over-anxiety and a tolerable degree of serenity and security: peace of mind and heart. As far as possible they want to live in and at peace. I am reminded of George Herbert's poem 'The Pulley' that pictures the strange alchemy of human life in which God has mixed all sorts of ingredients but not what the poet calls 'rest' (peace), in order that we all will spend our lives seeking it. This is also reflected in the prayer attributed to St Augustine: 'Lord, you have made us for yourself and our hearts are restless till they rest in you.' This is need which cries out for fulfilment, if not in this life then in eternity.

Worship

There does seem to be within human beings the need to recognize and bow down to that which is greater than ourselves. This means to acknowledge the mystery of life and the world; to wonder, adore and give thanks. C.S. Lewis illustrates this human instinct to worship God with the instinct in dogs to adore their master (Lewis, 1974). The ability to sense awe and reverence is not confined to those with religious convictions. Even atheistic scientists, who say that they have no belief in any God, can be moved by the sense of the numinous at the sight of a rainbow, or the intricate and beautiful patterns uncovered through minute investigation of the natural world, or exploration of space. In a newspaper interview the renowned atheist Richard Dawkins is credited with these words: 'Most scientists use the term God in the way that Einstein did, as an expression of reverence for the deep mysteries of the universe, a sentiment I share' (Crace, 2006).

Creativity

Likewise, creativity is an essential element to being human. The deep desire to make things, to be creative with materials and words, not only meets our utilitarian needs. Human creativity aspires to lift the human soul in art and music and in many other aesthetic ways. For the Judaeo-Christian tradition this is the activity of those made in the image of the Creator God.

An old-age focus

Granted that all the above contribute to giving human beings of all ages a sense of purpose in life, thus sustaining their spiritual well-being, how are these spiritual needs specifically focused in older age, and in particular for those living in a rural environment? I have suggested six ways (Jewell, 2004; Hawley and Jewell, 2009): the first three are largely determined by the circumstances in which many older people may find themselves, which can threaten their well-being. The last three are 'existential' in nature, brought into focus by death, an inescapable fact for any older person which serves to put life into perspective. In each case, the Christian gospel and the Church's pastoral care can support an older person in their particular need.

Isolation

Nothing diminishes the sense of being loved and human happiness more than social isolation, leading to loneliness and depression. This can be the situation of so-called 'third-agers' who may lose many of their social contacts when they retire, especially if they pull up their roots and move far away into a desirable rural or seaside environment. It is much more of a challenge for 'fourth-agers' as and when they can no longer get out and about independently, and as they face other isolating losses such as the deaths of contemporaries and loved ones or their mental faculties through dementia. Older people can so easily become marginalized – even, and perhaps especially in care homes, where there can be 'company' but little real companionship.

The Oxford Consultants for Social Inclusion (2009) reported that 20% of those aged over 65 have no car in rural areas compared with only 5% of those who are younger. Furthermore, 45% of those without cars are aged over 70, many being older women living on their own. It is therefore not surprising that 27% believe that the Government should prioritize public transport in rural areas and that 18% wish for improvement in shopping and other facilities in light of the closure of many village shops. The Commission for Rural Communities (2009) has found that those currently without access to the internet tend to be older people, creating a significant 'digital gap' and thereby increasing their social exclusion – though this is less likely to be true of future more 'computer literate' generations of older people. On the other hand, the Oxford Consultants (2009) pay tribute to the high level of social support older people receive from partners, families and friends in rural communities. How long this will be sustainable in view of the increasing overall age of such communities remains to be seen.

The gospel imperative concerning those who are marginalized and isolated is clearly modelled in the life of Jesus, who reached out to the marginalized of his day. The implications for the Church and its pastoral care and fellowship are evident. The Church rises to the challenge when it includes people of all ages, giving each a sense of belonging and significance. In some village communities the local church community is the only one where such intergenerational inclusivity is lived.

Affirmation

It is not always appreciated that older people are as much in need of being affirmed as children and young people. The word affirmation means saying 'yes' in regard to the person concerned: paying tribute to what they have done and are still doing and to their unique personhood. This is in stark contrast to ageist attitudes which denigrate or patronize older people and so reduce their self-esteem. Rural communities have more than enough reason to celebrate the contributions older people make. Indeed, many of our churches would be closed were it not for the faithful input of its retired members – continuing to do, give and pray.

The same is true in the case of the great majority of voluntary and charitable organizations. Research has found that older people are significant participants in many rural social enterprises, 'putting to good effect the skills and experiences they have gained during their lifetimes in the interests of their communities' (Plunkett Foundation *et al.*, 2004, p. 2).

Likewise, older people contribute to the life of their churches. They excel in friendship evangelism, getting alongside other people (whether old or young) at their point of need to offer support and hospitality, and gradually sharing with them the source of their own strength. This is surely a main reason why the organization Christian Research has found that the only age group to show real growth in the mainstream Protestant denominations in England in recent years is the over 60s (Brierley, 2000). Even well into their fourth age older people can still make hugely valuable contributions. In some churches an elderly and housebound person organizes the local church's prayer chain by means of her phone. In others older people who still write letters (a dying art) are the source of great encouragement to the recipients. These are matters for affirmation indeed.

However, alongside the sense of affirmation drawn from older people's contributions, the message of the Christian gospel is one of salvation by the grace of God who takes us, loves us and affirms us just as we are – not for what we can do or achieve. It is this kind of unconditional affirmation which older people need to be given.

Celebration

Celebration may be seen as one step further than affirmation. There is indeed so much more to celebrate in the case of older people:

retirement (*jubilacíon* in Spanish!), milestone birthdays and significant anniversaries, all that individuals have done in life, church and community, and their continued creativity. Hopefully congregations do take every opportunity to celebrate such things in their church family life rather than waiting for the funeral tribute. Churches in rural areas where everyone is 'known' can be better at this than those in more 'anonymous' urban areas.

Confirmation

The first of the existential needs of older people does not here refer to the confirmation that follows baptism but rather to the strengthening of faith. It is all too easy to believe (and perpetuate the notion) that old age for Christians is, or should be, a time of serene and confident faith. While this may be so for some fortunate individuals, the losses of the fourth age coupled with despair at the state of the world (or indeed the Church) lead many older people into times of great uncertainty and ultimate doubts: can there be a God of love in light of so much suffering; has all the work in the church been pointless; and can there really be anything beyond this life? The problem is exacerbated by the tendency of older people not to share such doubts, be it for fear of 'rocking the boat', disturbing the faith of others or shocking the vicar! Additionally, those who are housebound are unable to access church groups where their concerns might be discussed, doubts shared and faith built up. The mandate to listen and respond to older people's deepest concerns in the areas of faith and hope needs to be taken very seriously indeed (Hawley and Jewell, 2009).

Reconciliation

This relates to the peace of mind and heart that all people seek, specifically in terms of relationships. And it becomes the more urgent as we age because we are aware that time is indeed limited. Many older persons express the desire to die at peace, but this is much easier said than done. We all recognize that, as we go through life, we accumulate various hurts inflicted and received, broken or damaged relationships, as well as unfinished spiritual business. It is unhelpful to say to the old person troubled about such matters, 'Don't worry, it's best to forget about it, it doesn't really matter' – because to them it does, supremely. They desperately want to die at peace with others, with God and with themselves.

At the heart of Christian worship and truly to be celebrated is the assurance of forgiveness by God. It is something everyone needs to hear and accept repeatedly. But perhaps it is especially in the pastoral work and ministry of the Church that the need for inter-personal forgiveness and reconciliation needs to be recognized and addressed. Occasionally it may be possible to reunite estranged in-dividuals for this to be effected. Often, when the other people have died long ago, it may be a case of the healing of memories, and this can be a most powerful thing if done with true sensitivity and the assurance of confidentiality. Few spiritual needs are greater than this one for older people.

Integration

This final need relates to making sense of the whole of life and assembling it all. The developmental psychologist Erik Erikson (1982) saw what he called 'integrity' as the eighth and final life-stage, through which despair can be banished. This may be of spe-cial significance in rural areas where suicide rates in the UK have tended to be high.

When we are younger we are fully taken up with the business of that stage of our life: young people becoming educated and quali-fied, in many cases getting married or partnered, having a family and developing a career; then middle age with its multiple respon-sibilities both at work and for the older and the younger genera-tions in the family. It is probably only after retirement that we have time and space to reflect on life as a whole. And people do this in different ways: some may begin to review their life and write their autobiography – not for publication but in order to make some sense of their life journey and perhaps to share it with children and grandchildren. Others may decide on a radical change in lifestyle and establish new priorities, in the manner of Abraham who upped and departed at God's behest when he was fully 75 to start an entirely different pattern of life (Genesis 12). It can indeed be that people are more open to God in their latter years than at any time since adolescence.

Churches need to ask themselves whether this significant stage on every person's spiritual journey – probably the most significant of all – is recognized as such and whether appropriate support is given. This requires time during pastoral visiting in order to listen to the fascinating life stories told. It is in the telling of these stories that the older person can begin to make sense of life under God and ultimately offer their richly varied life back to God with a sense of integrity, feeling that they can leave the world just a little better for having lived in it.

Summary

The Christian gospel surely addresses all the circumstantial and existential needs of older people, and it is for churches to minister that gospel. In brief, the gospel incorporates: being in fellowship with God and others (countering isolation); knowing that we are of supreme value in the eyes of God (affirmation); rejoicing in the joyful news as we have experienced it (celebration); an ever deepening and progressing faith which always has mystery still attached (confirmation); finding and being at peace with God and with others (reconciliation); and ultimate wholeness (integration).

Recent research findings

The sustaining of purpose in life, continued spiritual growth, and coping in older age are concerns which can impact especially upon ageing rural communities. Research findings related to these concerns are presented here.

Purpose in life

Human beings need to find meaning in life and a sense of purpose for the future. My research among 31 individuals aged 60–94 showed a mixture of resilience and acceptance. Most continued to be very active, despite physical diminishment in many cases. Consuming interests and activities included craft work, gardening, the theatre, reading, significant church roles, the Duke of Edinburgh's discovery award and the University of the Third Age. However, they were realistic in recognizing that such activities would probably need to be curtailed or changed in future depending upon health and circumstances. Many found their fulfilment in their relationships with family and friends, though one was forthright in commenting: 'My family are still there but they are not my purpose. My purpose is to continue unfolding the gifts I have been given – and that will continue as long as I live.' One retired civil servant in his 80s declared that every day renewed his sense of purpose: 'Living in the countryside, it's alive, although to many people it may seem to be dead. Only the other day we saw a fox run across the field. I've just seen a hawk fly across. There's always life around. And I'm very fond of gardening – I love digging' (Jewell, 2010).

Rural churches can offer continuing purpose in life to their older members. They can also establish a corporate sense of purpose. One church in rural Kent, keen to 'do something' for the benefit of their community, set up a regular lunch club after consultation. Another rural church made their premises available for a daily play group, many of them helping as volunteers, and were amazed to find their congregation growing as a consequence. A further group let it be known that they would be praying at 9.15 each morning and found that prayer requests came in from near and far.

Continuing growth

Older people are easily perceived as being largely 'static' and essentially conservative in terms of their religious faith, but this is often very far from the truth. They can be among the most questioning and radical in their faith communities. Leslie Francis' useful New Indices of Religious Orientation (2007) proposes three basic orientations to aid our analysis of the approach to faith by older people:

- Extrinsic, using religion for other ends such as social status or accessing social support.

- Intrinsic, where religion governs the totality of life and is God-centred.
- Quest, which reflects a questioning approach, the acceptance of doubt and an openness to growth and change.

Interestingly, while most respondents in my research were 'intrinsic', an average of 42% of my sample responded positively to items reflecting the quest orientation, and in the case of openness to growth and change it was almost 60% (Jewell, 2010).

In the interviews conducted in connection with his investigation of the faith journeys of older church members, Hawley (2004) found that four out of his six subjects valued 'honesty, questioning and openness' in their ongoing pilgrimage. These findings give a strong indication that there should be space for older Christians to be listened to in churches, with suggestions as to how this may be facilitated through workshops and groups (Hawley and Jewell, 2009). In rural areas there should be scope for parishes and groups of churches to co-operate in such provision.

Coping with old age

People employ many different coping strategies. Folkman and Lazarus (1988) have named eight coping strategies: planful problem-solving, distancing, self-controlling, confrontive, positive reappraisal, accepting responsibility, seeking social support, and escape-avoidance. These were used in the recent Christian Council on Ageing (CCOA) study (Lowis et al., in press) involving 100 independent-living individuals aged 61–98 across England, including 19 in rural areas of the south-west. Most of the subjects belonged to churches of various denominations.

Participants were invited to rank coping strategies in relation to their own coping, and this revealed that planful problem-solving was the most favoured and escape-avoidance the least favoured mechanism. Most respondents were evidently very willing to face life's challenges. Seeking social support was the next lowest, demonstrating perhaps the independent mindedness of many older people. Three additional items were included, all of which were rated among the top five: recognizing how much worse off others are, using my sense of humour, and helping others, which also helps me. The responses to two of these items reflect a real degree of altruism on the part of the participants.

In an attempt to identify the perceptible differences between the high and low total scorers, telephone interviews were carried out with ten of the sample aged 60–84. Predictably there was a considerable difference between the two groups in regard to their present satisfaction with life and the degree to which they found life getting them down. However, the country-dwelling individual with the lowest score of all (yet grading her life satisfaction high) had learned to adapt and compensate for losses and diminishments, finding much fulfilment in musical activities. The high scorers valued the support of family and friends rather more highly but such help may have been less accessible in the case of the five low scorers. Losses of various kinds were reported across both groups but were multiple and more traumatic for the low scorers. Both groups mentioned similar helpful activities, including hobbies of various kinds, such as music and gardening, exercise to keep fit and the U3A (University of the Third Age).

Surprisingly, for a Christian-initiated study, few mentioned their religious faith or seemed specifically to value church attendance, one choosing to spend private time in the local cathedral and another finding spiritual sustenance through her personal Franciscan-based spirituality. However, when asked for her recipe for getting through in life the highest individual scorer replied, 'Without doubt, faith in God.'

The challenge of dementia

The biggest threat to well-being, as perceived by many older people, is that of Alzheimer's disease and similar old-age dementias, which the Department of Health currently estimates to affect 700,000 people in England (National Dementia Strategy, 2008).

Coping with such illnesses is partly a matter of the individual's application and resilience and partly a matter of social support

(Harris, 2008). Many manage to continue living relatively independently, especially if they remain in their own home or at least in their home area. That way their life's routine and the connections that are important to them can continue to sustain them. Andrea Gillies' recent Wellcome Prize-winning book, *Keeper* (2009), demonstrates the potentially disastrous effects of moving a relative with dementia to a remote and unfamiliar location. Diana Friel McGowin (1994) recorded how, following her mother's death, she discovered numerous notes in her house which reminded her mother how to carry out her daily tasks and how to travel to where she needed to go. It was then that she realized that her mother had been suffering from severe memory loss for some time but was determined to cope. McGowin herself then began to suffer similar symptoms and found that her computer's memory was a significant help in continuing her writing career.

As already argued, human beings are social beings who derive much of their purpose in life from 'significant others'. Indeed, all the contributors to *Spirituality and Personhood in Dementia* (Jewell, 2011) argue that personhood itself does not exist in a vacuum – it is derived in large measure, if not entirely, from relationships. If relationships diminish then so does our personhood, our unique identity. Conversely, if relationships with people with dementia are sustained then their personhood can, to a real degree, be preserved.

Nonetheless, this is far from easy and will test the empathy and commitment of families, churches and local communities (Gillies, 2009; Talbot, 2011). Short-term memory loss leads many people with dementia to ask the same question over and over again. This demonstrates an admirable desire on their part to communicate but can be very trying for those on the receiving end. There is often disorientation of time and place, so that a person may get up in the night and want to go to bed in the day. Dementia may cause them to wander and get lost continually, thus causing great anxiety to family and neighbours, and of course terror for themselves. In dementia something can seem to get in the way between thinking the thought and communicating it in words or putting it into appropriate action. People with advanced dementia may even 'forget' how to carry out simple tasks such as eating with a knife and fork or washing themselves. It is not uncommon (and a cause of great hurt) for them to fail to recognize a spouse of 60 years or a much-loved daughter, while at the same time striking up close friendships with fellow residents or staff members in their care home.

So what hope is there for families, church visitors and the persons with dementia in such a seemingly bleak landscape?

Person-centred care

Some 15 years ago, the late Professor Tom Kitwood of Bradford University pioneered a radical new approach to the care of people with dementia (1997). In place of what he regarded as a 'malignant' medical model which sought to treat patients with drugs, thereby tending to reduce them to a zombie-like state, he proposed 'person-centred care'. Staff should learn to concentrate on the person rather than the problem. Truly holistic care should be given to patients and residents in care homes. A developed system of 'dementia care mapping' based upon careful observation would help to address individual needs and lead to appropriate participation in activities. He believed that it was even possible for those with dementia to learn new skills and so go on growing as persons. Such care is not only 'person centred', it is also very much 'relationship centred'.

Kitwood's approach now holds sway in many care homes in the UK, at least in theory. However, it is costly in terms of staff training and time, expensive for local authorities and self-funders, and often it seems to be lip service rather than delivery of true person-centred care that is offered. For those living in remote rural areas, finding a suitable home may involve considerable travel.

Communication

Verbal communication can be difficult with persons with dementia, as already indicated. However, granted time and patience it is still possible until quite late on in the progress of the disease. When people with dementia find that the right words simply won't come, they can and do still communicate through body language, and can express their feelings quite forcibly when, as sometimes happens, inhibitions are removed.

Malcolm Goldsmith (1996) gives valuable guidance to those who visit persons with dementia, such as making eye contact on the same level, speaking in simple sentences, giving time for the person visited to respond or make a choice. Similar advice is to be found in a free pamphlet produced by MHA and CCOA jointly (2008).

John Killick, who worked for some years as poet in residence with Westminster Care, spent many hours sitting alongside and listening to care-home residents with dementia. He was convinced that when they could not recall the word they wanted they would often choose a connected word or metaphor to express themselves. This, he believes, is a kind of poetry, and indeed he turned many of his conversations into powerful and insightful poems (Killick, 2004).

Humour

Humour can be a great means of bonding between people. It is also in itself a coping mechanism which ranked third among 19 questionnaire items used in the CCOA study of 100 older independent living subjects (Lowis *et al.*, in press). To be able to laugh at life's misfortunes and the challenges of old age (which are great levellers) can prove both refreshing and empowering.

It is realized less that humour can play an important part in coping with dementia and in caring for people with the condition. Humour is of course best shared rather than kept to oneself, and such sharing can sweeten relationships. In *Telling Tales About Dementia* (Whitman, 2010), some 30 carers write of their experiences of caring and a number of them are very humorous and enjoyed by all parties. The 'instruction manual for keeping your mind' compiled by Gail Chester (Whitman, 2010) is frankly hilarious. Marianne Talbot in her *Saga Magazine* online blog, 'Keeping Mum', mixes grim reality and humour in equal measure. It is surely significant that Christine Bryden (2005) titles her book about her personal experience, *Dancing with Dementia*.

Worship

It has already been argued that the expression of worship, whether formal or informal, is a basic human need, and this is no less so for those with dementia. It has been my experience in conducting services in care homes to find that some of those present appeared to have no involvement at all in the worship, only to discover at the end how wrong my judgement was. However, there are obvious difficulties if, for example, the hymns are not well known, the prayers and address too lengthy, or the theology presented insensitive. Again, MHA and CCOA have produced another helpful free pamphlet on the subject (2006).

Robert Davis, an American Presbyterian minister, was the earliest writer to describe his journey into dementia (1989), which he found to resemble facing a frightening abyss which threatened his very faith in God. It may well be that many others feel the same. I have found it both moving and humbling when at the end of a service in a care home or administering communion in a small group there, everyone has joined hands as a sign of fellowship and spiritual support.

Shafts of light

One of the strange things about dementia is that, even at an advanced stage, as John Killick puts it in regard to his seeming unresponsive residents: '"the clouds part" and I have been vouchsafed words that interpret the muteness, and do so with incredible insight' (1997, p. 15). Eileen Shamy (2003, p. 20) describes how she visited her mother three days before she died in the final stage of Alzheimer's disease. She fixed Eileen with a clear eye and said: 'God never forgets us. Remember that, dear!' Significantly, her chapter's heading is 'Through a Door of Hope'.

The Notre Dame Sisters

Scientist David Snowden (2001) investigated 678 Notre Dame Sisters in the USA, the autopsies showing that some of their brains exhibited features of advanced dementia, whereas those same Sisters had shown little or no sign of it in their lives in community. Genetic, dietary and other factors were considered in an attempt to account for their sustained normality, without success. In the end he concluded that the explanation could lie only in intangible factors, including their strong fellowship and the regular liturgical pattern of their life in community.

While it cannot be maintained that the corporate life of Christian churches is anywhere near so intensive, there is surely a positive message here for the contribution that congregations, small fellowship groups and organizations like the Mothers' Union have to make in the support of those with dementia.

Dementia throws needs of older people into a particularly sharp focus. Mercifully, here as in general, the response of the gospel through the ministry of the Christian community can be seen to be at the heart of holistic appreciation of and care for older people. Churches should take steps to create 'safe places' in which older people can be honest about the opportunities and fears that face them in the latter part of their faith journeys. It is for churches to rise to the challenge and play their part by both actively caring for them and demanding a high quality of care throughout the country.

References

Brierley, P., 2000, *The Tide Is Running Out*, London: Christian Research.

Bryden, C., 2005, *Dancing with Dementia*, London: Jessica Kingsley Publishers.

Chester, G., 2010, 'An instruction manual for keeping your mind', in L. Whitman (ed.), *Telling Tales About Dementia*, London: Jessica Kingsley Publishers, pp. 183–6.

Commission for Rural Communities, 2009, *Mind the Gap: Digital England – A Rural Perspective*, Cheltenham: Commission for Rural Communities.

Crace, J., 2006, 'Beyond belief: interview with Richard Dawkins', *Education Guardian*, 10 January 2006, London: Guardian Newspapers.

Davis, R., 1989, *My Journey into Alzheimer's Disease*, London: Tyndale.

Erikson, E.H., 1982, *The Life Cycle Completed*, New York: W.W. Norton.

Folkman, S. and Lazarus, R.S., 1988, *Ways of Coping Test Booklet*, Redwood City, California: Consulting Psychologists Press Inc.

Francis, L.J., 2007, 'Introducing the new indices of religious orientation (NIRO): conceptualization and measurement', *Mental Health, Religion and Culture* (10), pp. 585– 602.

Frankl, V.E., 1964, *Man's Search for Meaning*, London: Hodder & Stoughton.

Gillies, A., 2009, *Keeper*, London: Short Books.

Goldsmith, M., 1996, *Hearing the Voices of People with Dementia*, London: Jessica Kingsley Publishers.

Harris, P.B., 2008, 'Another wrinkle in the debate about successful aging: The undervalued concept of resilience and the lived experience of dementia', *International Journal of Aging and Human Development* 67(1), pp. 43–61.

Hawley, G., 2004, 'The faith journeys of older people and their consequences for the church today', unpublished MA dissertation, University of Manchester.

Hawley, G. and Jewell, A., 2009, *Crying in the Wilderness: Giving Voice to Older People in the Church*, Derby: MHA Care Group.

Jenkins, D., 2004, 'Geriatric burden or elderly blessing', in A. Jewell (ed.), *Ageing, Spirituality and Well-being*, London: Jessica Kingsley Publishers, pp. 197–202.

Jewell, A., 1999, 'Introduction', in A Jewell (ed.), *Spirituality and Ageing*, London: Jessica Kingsley Publishers, pp. 9–13.

Jewell, A., 2004, 'Nourishing the Inner Being', in A. Jewell (ed.) *Ageing, Spirituality and Well-being*, London: Jessica Kingsley Publishers, pp. 11–26.

Jewell, A., 2010, 'The importance of purpose in life in an older British Methodist sample: Pastoral implications', *Journal of Religion, Spirituality and Aging* 22(3), pp. 138–62.

Jewell, A. (ed.), 2011, *Spirituality and Personhood in Dementia*, London: Jessica Kingsley Publishers.

Killick, J., 1997, 'Communication: A matter of the life and death of the mind', *Journal of Dementia Care* 5(5), p. 15.

Killick, J., 2004, *Dementia Poems*, London: Hawker Publications.

Kitwood, T., 1997, *Dementia Reconsidered: The Person Comes First*, Buckingham: The Open University Press.

Lewis, C.S., 1974, *Weight of Glory*, London: HarperCollins.

Lowis, M.J., Edwards, A.C., Roe, C.A., Jewell, A.J., Jackson, M.I. and Tidmarsh, W. M., 2005, 'The role of religion in mediating the transition to residential care', *Journal of Aging Studies* 19(3), pp. 349–62.

Lowis, M.J., Jewell, A., Jackson, M.I. and Merchant, R. (in press), 'Religious and secular coping methods used by older adults: An empirical investigation' (accepted by *Journal of Religion, Spirituality and Aging*).

McGowin, D.F., 1994, *Living in the Labyrinth*, Cambridge: Queen's College, Cambridge.

MHA Care Group, 2002, *Nourishing the Inner Being* (videotape), Derby: MHA.

MHA Care Group and Christian Council on Ageing, 2006, *Worship with People with Dementia*, Derby: MHA/CCOA.

MHA Care Group and Christian Council on Ageing, 2008, *Visiting People with Dementia*, Derby: MHA/CCOA.

Department of Health, 2009, *National Dementia Strategy*, London: Department of Health.

Office for National Statistics, 2010, Population and demographic data, www.statistics.gov.uk

Oxford Consultants for Social Inclusion, 2009, *Mapping the Level of Need: Assessing the Social Exclusion of Older People in Rural Areas*, Report for Cabinet Office, Social Exclusion Task Force, London.

Plunkett Foundation, Prime, Countryside Agency, Age Concern, 2004, *Rural Lifelines: Older People and Rural Social Enterprises. Their role as providers and beneficiaries of service provision in rural England*, Woodstock: Plunkett Foundation.

Shamy, E., 2003, *A Guide to the Spiritual Dimension of Care for People with Alzheimer's Disease and Related Dementia*, London: Jessica Kingsley Publishers.

Snowden, D., 2001, *Ageing with Grace*, New York: Bantam Books.

Talbot, M., 2011, *Keeping Mum: Caring for Someone with Dementia*, London: Hay House.

Whitman, L., 2010, *Telling Tales About Dementia*, London: Jessica Kingsley Publishers.

8

Rural mental health and well-being: the role of the rural church

LORNA MURRAY

The purpose of this chapter is to highlight ways in which the presence of the rural church can benefit rural mental health and well-being. The chapter considers this from the perspective of pastoral care, using the following definition:

> Pastoral care is that aspect of the ministry of the Church which is concerned with the well-being of individuals and of communities. (Campbell, 1987, p. 188)

Studies show that some aspects of life in rural areas of Scotland can have a negative impact on people's mental health (Philo, Parr and Burns, 2004; Mowat, Stark, Swinton and Mowat, 2006, pp. 19–21; Choose Life, 2007, p. 2). The high rate of suicide in these areas (Levin and Leyland, 2005; Stark, Hopkins, Gibbs, Rapson, Belbin and Hay, 2004) indicates that working to improve well-being in rural communities must be seen as an urgent priority. Improving mental health has an important part to play in reducing deaths by suicide (Scottish Executive, 2002, p. 13). Taking care of our mental health, and finding ways of removing or overcoming factors that put our mental health at risk can benefit not only individuals but also life in the community as a whole.

Where the Church works together with other agencies and organizations, its pastoral care can play a significant part in developing the mental health of individuals and the well-being of rural communities.

'Being there'

We begin by thinking about the *presence* of the Church within rural areas, emphasizing the need for such presence to be *committed*. The need for *faithful* presence is then stressed, along with the importance of reflection on the relationship between our faith and our action. In the third part of this section, we highlight the need for *shared* presence; for working together with other organizations and agencies to share insights and ideas and to learn from each other.

Committed presence

Our willingness to be *with* others, especially when they are experiencing problems or difficulties in their lives, can bring encouragement and enable people to accept themselves as valued and valuable. Our *being there* – our willingness to listen and to share their pain – can transform lives and create, or renew, a sense of hope.

The title of a book on health-care chaplaincy, *Being There*, by Peter Speck (Speck, 1988), emphasizes the importance of 'being there' relationships, as does John Swinton's focus on friendship as fundamental to caring for people with mental health problems (Swinton, 2000). A workbook about the rural church, produced by the Methodist Church, reminds us that 'Presence . . . affirms that being is as important as doing' (Methodist Church, 2004).

See Me, Scotland's campaign to 'stop the stigma of mental ill health' (www.seemescotland.org.uk), in its television promotion during Scottish Mental Health Week in October 2008, emphasized the significance of friends standing by us in times of stress or distress. In one, a young woman told viewers that 'fashions change . . . friends don't', and in the other, a male golfer is encouraged by his friend who 'kept going round' . . . 'aye, like a stuck record'. The 'being there' of friends is vital to a sense of self-worth and well-being.

'Being there', or presence, however, if it is to enable and encourage the creation of communities of mental health and well-being, cannot be passive. 'Loitering with intent', an expression sometimes used to describe the role of health-care chaplains (Pattison, 1997, p. 180), makes it clear that, for presence to be beneficial, it must be *intentional*: our 'being there' requires a clear focus and purpose. The presence of a church building that is closed, or into which people are not invited and made welcome, suggests that it is irrelevant to the local community. The presence of a congregation whose being there does not offer prayerful support, practical care and concern for others and acceptance of all, suggests to the people around them that the church – and by implication, therefore, God – has no interest in their well-being, and has no desire to help them.

As people who believe that Christian teaching about life has important and valuable insights to offer, we should have the confidence to speak out, where appropriate, about the relevance of our faith. The insights of faith can offer helpful perspectives to those struggling in difficult circumstances: they also can add an important dimension to local and national plans to improve well-being.

Presence that seeks to enable the creation of communities of well-being, demands of rural congregations a commitment to:

- prayer
- reflection on how faith directs our everyday life, as individuals and as a congregation
- theological reflection, especially on justice and love, and on Biblical accounts of healing and their relevance to our understanding of well-being
- accepting and welcoming each and every individual or group coming into our community and into our church
- caring *about* – and, where necessary, caring *for* – *everyone* who lives in, works in or visits our local area
- acknowledging our own vulnerability and our own need for care and support
- recognizing our interdependence one with another, and valuing the contribution of each individual to the life of the community as a whole
- recognizing our interdependence with the land around us and the potential benefits of closer links with our natural environment
- working with other organizations and agencies present in our community: sharing resources – buildings, commitment and

the understandings and insights of our faith – and being ready to learn from their training, skills and experience.

Faithful presence

Our biblical tradition offers a theology of caring that is both pro-active and reactive. Proactive pastoral care requires the Church to be involved in seeking the socio-political justice that God demands of us and the peaceful co-existence of all living beings as promised in Isaiah. Reactive pastoral care focuses on meeting the needs of those who are suffering and in pain, as in the parable of the Good Samaritan (Luke 10.25–37).

Pastoral care of the community as a whole, that benefits all individuals living within it, is found as an ideal in the understanding of *shalom* within the Hebrew Bible and of the *Kingdom of God* in our New Testament scriptures. God's love and justice must be shared among *all* people before loving, peaceful co-existence can be experienced to the full. Recognition of our dependence on the God who created us, and awareness of our interdependence – our human need for each another – are prerequisites for pastoral care that is given and received as we 'do what is just [and] show constant love' (Micah 6.8).

Jesus' teaching about the Kingdom makes this clear. The Kingdom of God is compared to a banquet, or feast, to which all are invited, and at which all are accepted and made welcome (Luke 14.15–24), and to a tree in whose branches all birds can live together in safety (Mark 4.30–32). The creation of this 'Kingdom community' requires that each of us love our neighbour as ourselves and that we 'do for others what you want them to do for you' (Matthew 7.12).

Love and justice go together: both are aspects of pastoral care. The proactive care of seeking justice – creating places where people can live in safety and finding ways of preventing difficulties arising or crises occurring – is as much the responsibility of the Church as is the reactive care of supporting people in distress, visiting those who are ill and listening to the worries of those who are anxious.

In relation to mental health and well-being, however, the Church in the western world has tended, in its more recent history, to focus on caring for individuals who are unwell or in distress. It has accepted and adhered to the model of western medicine, with its emphasis on care of the sick and the removal of symptoms of illness or disease, and has been influenced – sometimes over-influenced – by the disciplines of counselling and psychology. The Church has done little to challenge the individualistic, rights-based culture that is currently prevalent.

Our theology of health has been based primarily on biblical accounts of healings by Jesus: this often leading to the common assumption that a necessary indicator of health and well-being is the non-existence of symptoms of illness. While eradication of disease and removal of painful symptoms are important aims for any society, human wholeness or well-being requires far more. When Jesus healed the man suffering from leprosy he was given much more than a clear skin: he was restored to life as a member of his community. The parable of the Good Samaritan teaches us that love of neighbour goes beyond caring for our friends and extends to caring for the stranger and even for the enemy. What is also required, however, is the proactive care of the search for justice: justice aiming to ensure that in future people will not be robbed and injured on the road from Jerusalem to Jericho. If robbers attack because they are desperate to feed their starving children, ways must be found of sharing food more fairly, so that everyone has enough. If street lights or police patrols are only provided on the urban highways, but not on the rural byways, then government priorities may have to be reassessed.

To create communities of mental health and well-being, the faithful presence of the rural church, therefore, must be *informed*. Christians involved in pastoral care need to be informed by the teachings of the Bible, and informed by day-to-day circumstances and experience of life; reflection on both is essential if the message of the Bible is to be Good News in our communities today. Messages contained within scripture were intended for the cultures and contexts in which they were written. This must be remembered as we hear them today, and reflect on their meaning for our own contexts and cultures. If *that* was helpful in those circumstances then, what is most beneficial in identifying how we respond to this situation or need *today*? This is a question that must be asked, discussed and prayed about, as part of any planning or action.

Faithful presence requires that we do not act unreflectively. Busyness may make us feel good ourselves while offering little to those in need in the community around us.

Faith should be the motivator of all that we do; of how we live our lives as Christians day by day. Our faith provides the answer to the question 'Why care?' It also, as we study the Bible, pray and discuss our beliefs with other Christians, helps us to discover answers to the question of *how* to care. Discovering *how* to care, however, also requires our committed presence: our being there within our local community and our participation in all aspects of community life.

Insights from our faith and the understandings we have through our *being there* in our local community are useful guides. Vital, too, to any discussion and planning are the thoughts, feelings and experiences of those we would wish to help. It is also important to recognize that the resources and skills of organizations involved in community development and which offer care and support to people in a whole variety of ways are as necessary to the creation of communities of well-being as are the resources of the Church.

Shared presence

Creating communities of well-being means caring *about* each and every individual as well as caring *for* people during times of illness or uncertainty, need or crisis. It also requires that we challenge any prejudice or injustice that is contributing to difficulties experienced and do all we can to prevent pain and distress.

Most twentieth-century western Christians have tended to see health care as the preserve of doctors and other medical professionals, and have restricted the role of the Church to one of visiting the sick and of praying for their release from pain or disease. Some, instead, have promoted an exclusive concept of faith healing, thereby denying the presence of God in the gifts of medical care. Some Christians still hold the belief that mental illness is a sign of disobedience to God, or a punishment for wrongdoing that only faith and prayer can heal.

These attitudes – that health care is the responsibility of our National Health Service alone, or that only by faith can anyone be healed – each serve to separate the dimension of faith from the role of medicine. Such compartmentalization inhibits the holistic care that is essential to well-being. It contributes nothing to our understanding of the relationship between health and environment, health and community living, or health and the struggle for justice. Rediscovery of biblical teaching on the interrelationship between justice and love – what was referred to above as 'proactive and re-active pastoral care' – is an essential contribution of the Church to the creation of community well-being.

Separation of faith and medical care has also served to inhibit potentially helpful relationships between health-care staff and con-gregations. A psychiatrist may hesitate to allow a patient permis-sion to leave the hospital to attend Sunday worship, fearful that her Christian friends may persuade her to throw away her medication. A man, who talks to his minister about God speaking to him may be denied the help he most needs if, failing to hear also the distress this is causing, the minister interprets his experience as evidence of deep faith and not of the psychosis that may be troubling him.

Good communication is necessary, as well as the development of positive relationships between those who share a common concern for our mental health and well-being. Historic grievances need to be laid aside and attitudes of suspicion that have become accepted must be challenged.

Health care cannot be the preserve of medicine alone. The public-health work carried out in nineteenth-century Britain makes this clear: the development of indoor sanitation; the discovery of the link between dirt, germs and disease; the growing understanding of how early life experiences influence and affect our ability to cope in adult life. So, too, does health care in the two-thirds world: health care in many countries has long taken place in conjunction with social justice. However good the hospital facilities, they cannot save the lives of families starving to death because the rains have not come and there is no food to eat.

Mental health care in Scotland is moving away from what is of-ten considered to be the traditional model of medical care; it is focusing less on the management and control of symptoms and more on enabling those living with a diagnosis of mental illness to live well. Mental health improvement is a priority: the benefits to our mental health and well-being of activities such as outdoor exercise, and the finding of enjoyment and pleasure through learning about our natural environment and wildlife, are being made more widely available through the support of agencies such as the Forestry Commission (Forestry Commission Scotland, 2009).

Recent training material produced by the Scottish Recovery Network contains a list of desirable qualities for mental health workers (Scottish Recovery Network, 2008, p. 43); these echo the priorities of training in pastoral care. The concept of recovery has many similarities with holistic care – as understood from the theological perspective – with its recognition of the importance of the influence of our environment and our social and economic circumstances on our well-being. Lists of factors that have a positive impact on mental health and well-being (Scottish Recovery Network, 2008, p. 14; Scottish Executive, 2003, p. 5) are priorities that any church efforts to love one's neighbours would endorse.

The Church has much to learn from these understandings and developments in mental health care, and also from the upsurge of interest in the connection between our well-being as human individuals and the well-being of society as a whole. National and international concern about how human life is affecting our environment, and about how our environment affects us, is offering new insights that remind us of the relevance of the biblical understanding of our world as created and of ourselves as created beings.

The Church may have lots to learn, but it also has much to offer. Being there – when such presence is committed and faithful – can contribute greatly to the mental health and well-being of any community. In partnership with others, listening to stories of struggle and of celebration, of despair and of how hope was renewed, we can plan together how best to do what is just and show constant love. In collaborative relationships with other agencies working in our communities, we can share together to ensure that individual lives are enriched and our communities transformed into places of well-being.

Rural mental health and well-being

In this section, we begin by defining the terms mental health and well-being and then move on to look at aspects of rural life that may make such well-being hard to maintain.

Mental health and well-being

Freedom from mental illness is not a definition of mental *health*, although the symptoms of mental illness can, of course, have a negative impact.

Mental health can be portrayed as a continuum along which we all move: it connects with, but is not the same as, the spectrum between maximal and minimal mental illness. Our position along the mental health continuum fluctuates according to the quality of our relationships, of the support and care we receive, of our surroundings and our circumstances, and how we feel about ourselves. When our mental health is good, we can experience a sense of well-being, even within the experience of illness.

Resilience (Platt, 2008) – the ability to cope with difficult experiences and the painful emotions associated with them – is significant for our mental health. Resilience develops primarily through relationship: good inner relationship (sense of self-worth and self-acceptance) and good outer relationships (ability to care and be cared for) can sustain our mental health even in times of illness and suffering or when circumstances are difficult. Such positive relationships connect us in a beneficial way and enable us to discover a sense of purpose and of worth. Antonovsky (1987) and Frankl (1964) each stress the importance to our well-being of seeing life as having meaning and purpose.

The aim of *mental health improvement* work is to reduce factors that might put our mental health at risk and to encourage factors that benefit our mental health, thus helping us to experience well-being. Such factors impact both on individual and on community well-being, with many requiring changes at structural level in order to deal with such issues as poverty or discrimination (Scottish Government, 2007, p. 18).

What matters is whether we are living the life we want to be living. Are we achieving our personal goals? Do we have friends? Do we have connections with the community? Are we contributing or giving back in some way? (NHS Education for Scotland, 2008, p. 28).

It can be seen that mental health improvement has similar aims to those of pastoral care: both seek to create communities of well-being. Well-being and the fullness of life promised to us by Jesus are closely related.

Rural mental health and well-being

Many of the factors recognized as beneficial to our mental health and well-being – such as fresh air and exercise, green space, the natural environment – are found in rural areas. People living in more urban parts of the country are being encouraged to visit rural areas to enjoy these features.

For those living in rural areas, however, such benefits can be out-weighed by risk factors such as poverty, lack of employment opportunities, and uncertainty about the future prospects of farming or fishing. Isolation may restrict opportunities to develop positive relationships and can bring loneliness. Living a long distance from where services are provided can make accessing any necessary help or support difficult. Our current social and economic climate means that many feel no sense of control over their own lives; policies and regulations made at national and international level affect the day-to-day lifestyle of those involved in agriculture, fishing and other rural occupations.

Small communities, in which everyone knows everyone else, can be very supportive. This environment, however, may make it very difficult for people – especially those raised in a culture that perceives telling others about our problems as a sign of weakness or teaches us that real men don't cry – to ask for help or to admit they are struggling to cope.

Breathing Space (www.breathingspacescotland.co.uk), an organization offering support by telephone, aims its provision mainly at men who live and work in rural areas. The home page of the Breathing Space website, portraying a view of remote countryside and a young man gazing across the valley to wild mountains beyond, highlights some of the risks to our well-being inherent in rural life. The young man is alone: alone in an open space which many find awe-inspiring and wonderful, but which may also feel threatening or overpowering.

People who choose to come into a rural area for recreation, leisure or retirement can contribute to its well-being by bringing with them the potential for additional sources of income through tourism, or by demanding services and provision that will also benefit the resident community. They can also bring risk factors: anxiety, for example, about the security of valuable stock through their lack of concern for closing gates or the leaving of litter. Their purchase of crofts and other properties as holiday homes can drive local people away, as housing becomes less available and prices soar. As a result, family life risks breakdown: elderly members who remain become even more isolated when younger members are forced to move away to find accommodation elsewhere.

Rural life for many is not choice: it is *home*, whatever the potential benefits or risks. The rural church, present within this home area, can contribute significantly to the well-being of those whose lives are rooted there, those who settle there and those who visit to find refreshment or renewal. Commitment to the proactive pastoral care that seeks justice encourages working relationships with others involved in mental health improvement. Reactive pastoral care, offered in collaboration with other caring agencies, helps alleviate suffering and can bring comfort and hope in times of distress or despair.

Rural life and clergy stress

Such commitment to caring for others, in situations where clergy may be feeling isolated or without adequate support, can be damaging to mental health and well-being. Especially where a priest or minister has responsibility across several churches, an increasingly heavy workload can add to the problems – as outlined in the section above – associated with living and working in a rural area. It is important, therefore, that church leaders recognize that carers, too, are vulnerable, and in need of encouragement and support.

Acknowledging, and caring for, the mental health needs of clergy, however, has significant potential benefit both for the church and for the community.

Where clergy needs are recognized and appropriate support is given, their ability to meet and be sensitive to the needs of their congregation and of the wider community increases. Clergy are more likely to feel open to working in partnership when not feeling vulnerable and alone. Local ecumenical arrangements, rather than being viewed as necessary for survival, can become exciting opportunities for mission and pastoral care.

Acknowledging that *everyone* needs care and support is part of the journey towards well-being for the community as a whole. Being there – living *with* the problems and *together* seeking ways of solving or coping with them – is what the theology of presence requires of the Church.

The rural church and rural well-being

While acknowledging that personal experience of home may be difficult or distressing, the *concept* is associated with such words as security or safety, welcome and acceptance, belonging and being understood. All these are important to our well-being.

The Church can do much to ensure that they are, or become, the real experience of everyone in the local community—visitors (tourists or those who come on day trips to enjoy land- or water-based activities), those who choose to spend only part of their time as residents, and those for whom the area has always been home.

As the chorus of a hymn reminds us, a purpose of the church is to reveal God's love and acceptance of all in the welcome that is given to all who enter its doors:

All are welcome,
All are welcome,
All are welcome in this place.
(*Church Hymnary*, 2005)

All who come into the church building, for whatever reason, should find welcome and acceptance. The church, however, is not only present *within* the community but also present as *part* of it. Faith motivates us – and the teachings of Jesus help us – to identify appropriate ways to welcome, accept and meet the needs of all whom we meet, whether within or outwith the walls of the church.

Viewing the rural community as a home in which all are welcome is a helpful image when considering the specific role of the rural church.

Scripture teaches us that God is with us and welcomes us all. The Incarnation is an explanation of how God has made his home among us. Jesus, in the parable of the Prodigal Son (Luke 15.11–32), tells the story of a son being welcomed back into the family home to remind us of the inclusive love of God who welcomes everyone into his Kingdom.

This theological perspective reminds us that, within the safety of home, we receive challenge as well as acceptance. Both are necessary if we are to flourish. Home is a place in which we are nurtured and encouraged, where we learn to care as well as be cared for. It is a place where mistakes can be made without fear of retaliation and in which forgiveness is given. Welcome into such a place is no mere polite toleration of the stranger; it is, rather, the invitation to participate in and belong to the life of the community.

Having looked at the contribution that the presence of the church in a rural area can make to community well-being, we turn now to consider the potential benefits and risks of church attendance and of faith.

The rural church – enabling well-being through belonging?

Being accepted by others and experiencing a sense of belonging are recognized as protective factors for our mental health (Scottish Government, 2007, p. 18; Hothersall, Maas-Lowit and Golightley, 2008, p. 6), indicating that participation in Sunday worship or in activities organized by the church could be beneficial. Many of us would want to acknowledge such benefit in our own lives: suggesting that people might attend faith-based meetings in order to improve their mental health and well-being, however, raises some difficult questions. What is the significance of faith? What does attendance at a faith-based activity offer that is not found in other local groups or organizations? What can the church not provide that may be essential to mental health in particular circumstances? And is it possible for anyone ever to feel a real sense of belonging within the church if they do not share the faith of the church community? Such questions need careful consideration before belonging to the church can be said to benefit well-being.

It is important to be aware that simply opening the church doors and saying all are welcome here is not enough.

- Being made welcome can enable people to feel valued and accepted, but some churches may link belonging with confirmation or church membership, thus making newcomers or irregular attenders feel marginalized or excluded.
- A sense of belonging can give the confidence to develop new skills or to find a role and a purpose, all of which are recognized as beneficial to mental health (Scottish Executive, 2003, p. 5), but some church structures, or church leaders, discourage participation, thereby encouraging dependence or reinforcing any sense of inability or failure.
- Where attending church is common practice it can bring with it associated welcome and acceptance in the wider community, but in places where churchgoing is no longer the norm, any benefits from belonging to the church may be offset by the resulting separation from the wider community or from peer-group support.

As the Church, we need to be self-critical. One in four people will experience problems associated with mental illness at some stage in life (www.seemescotland.org.uk), a statistic indicating that within any congregation there will be several members who struggle with such problems. Yet few acknowledge this reality. The author notes that, throughout 20 years' mental health chaplaincy experience of giving talks at church meetings, never fewer than two people have approached her to speak of personal or family mental illness or distress. All said that, although relatives and neighbours were aware of their difficulties, they had been unable to talk about them with their Christian friends. Belonging, for these people, clearly did not provide the practical or prayerful support that they may have sought.

People whose experience, or current situation, puts their mental health at risk are often those least likely to attend church (Harris, 2008). As Christians, we must ask ourselves why this is so and do more to ensure, not only that the welcome extended really does welcome all, but also that our worship is accessible and meaningful to those unfamiliar with the traditions of the church.

Belonging to a community of faith may be beneficial: faith, too, can encourage well-being (Fisher, 2007, pp. 3–4; Rattray, 2002). The way belief is expressed, however, and how Christian teaching is interpreted and understood, affect the extent to which faith may, or may not, be beneficial to mental health and well-being (Harris, 2008; Murray, 2009).

The rural church – enabling well-being through faith

Faith enables the Church to care by providing both motivation and guidance. It can also sustain and keep hope alive as people struggle with loneliness or uncertainty: assurance of God's presence and love can enable well-being to be experienced, even in times of adversity or suffering.

The way in which faith is expressed, however, can confuse or cause distress. The ways in which the traditions of the Church and the words of the Bible are understood, both within and outwith the Church, can cause unnecessary suffering. Ensuring that hearers are aware that Bible stories rarely speak directly to present-day experience is an important aspect of pastoral care. Reflection is needed on the language of the Church and how it may be misunderstood.

There are, unfortunately, attitudes inherent in certain expressions of faith that are detrimental to mental health and well-being. There is, in pastoral care, the need to challenge attitudes or behaviour that is harmful to self or others. Such challenge, however, must be sensitive, and appropriate to the needs of each individual, and it should always be made clear that it is the behaviour, and not the person that is being criticized. People who lack the experience of love in their lives need to feel accepted for who they are, before they can appreciate that questioning their behaviour is intended as help. Those who, for whatever reason, believe themselves to be unworthy, require love and support, not criticism, if they are to be enabled to believe that they are worthy of *God*'s love. Where belief that suffering is caused by sin means that a church withholds support from individuals in distress, or opts out of its responsibility to establish a more just and caring society, people are being denied an opportunity to experience God's love for them. Where belief that faith alone can heal leads any church member to persuade anyone to stop taking medication, real harm is done, not only to the individual concerned but also to the credibility of the Church as a caring organization.

Faith should always motivate the Church to seek the well-being of everyone. Faith is belief in the God of love and of justice as revealed in the life and teaching of Jesus. It is also the outworking of such belief in the love and the justice that God asks us to seek for all people.

Pastoral care – care motivated by this faith – requires the Church not only to do what is just and show constant love but also to live in humble fellowship with God. Such relationship with God sustains us as we seek to encourage, or renew, hope in the lives of struggling individuals or communities. It enables the development of positive and mutually supportive relationships and helps people to discover, or rediscover, a sense of hope and of meaning and purpose in life. The Church should not be shy in speaking of this relationship with God: we work, however, to help everyone, whatever their views about our faith and whatever their belief. God loves all people and challenges those who trust in him to do the same.

Committed, faithful partnership

The presence of the rural church is significant primarily through its rootedness within, and commitment to, a particular rural community. Reflection, however, on rural issues in general and on rural mental health concerns in particular is also important and necessary. There follow, therefore, some suggestions for partnerships with organizations already working to improve rural wellbeing that highlight the potential value of partnership with the rural church.

1 Choose Life

Choose Life (www.chooselife.net) is the national strategy for the prevention of suicide in Scotland. It works both strategically, and through local area partnership support, to reduce the incidence of suicide in Scotland. Choose Life is based within NHS Health Scotland, the lead health-improvement organization and partner of the Scottish government.

The Choose Life programme operates a National Working Group focused on suicide prevention in remote and rural areas. This strategic group aims to identify the issues and needs of remote and rural communities, and to work together with other agencies and organizations to develop effective approaches to suicide prevention in these areas. Choose Life is implemented through consultation and partnerships with key organizations across Scotland and considers the involvement of faith communities, at local and at national level, to be an inherent part of its national strategy.

Choose Life also provides training to community groups. It offers training in intervention skills with people feeling suicidal as well as courses that raise awareness about issues related to suicide. Participation in such training offers not only the opportunity to learn but also to share information and experiences. Where congregation members take part in these courses they are able to contribute understandings from pastoral care and insights based on faith. Participation also gives the opportunity to develop helpful links with people in other caring agencies.

2 Care Farming

Care Farming creates 'partnership between land manager, service provider and client' (www.carefarmingscotland.org.uk). Those who come to work at a Care Farm discover, or rediscover, a sense of meaning and purpose as they learn new skills. They also benefit from fresh air, exercise and companionship, as they work alongside farm staff and fellow trainees.

Farmers benefit too as they share their skills and experience. Benefits may also be financial, as new uses are found for their land. Contact with service providers, as plans are made, and with trainees who come to the farm, mean that problems associated with isolation are reduced. Farmers, too, can rediscover a sense of purpose through developing their farm as a Care Farm.

This combination of caring for the land with caring for people is fundamental to the Christian understanding of creation and of our relationship with our Creator God. We need the land and must take care of it (MacDonald, 2005, especially pp. 12–33). Biblical writing about the care of the land focuses also on the care of the most vulnerable in any community: workers are encouraged to share their harvest with those who have no land of their own (Deuteronomy 24.19–21, 26.12).

Care Farming recognizes the interdependence of land and people and – through its bringing together people with various needs and skills, problems and capabilities – highlights the reality of our human interdependence. By working to encourage relationships between people with such wide-ranging experiences and the land on which all depend, Care Farming can be a sign of hope for the future of rural communities. The Church should, therefore, offer its resources and support.

3 Forestry Commission

The Forestry Commission is doing much to promote the benefits to well-being of woodland activities and to improve access to their forests (Forestry Commission Scotland, 2009).

Many who visit such areas for recreation or relaxation speak of feelings of awe and wonder. For some, such feelings contain an element of fear; woodlands, wide open spaces and rugged mountains are experienced as threatening. Nature is seen as in control, making people feel vulnerable or afraid.

Working together with Forestry Commission staff, the Church can help. Taking the time to listen and 'being there' with people as they speak of their fears, stresses and problems can contribute to the well-being they seek.

Where members of the rural church become involved in activities provided through organizations like the Forestry Commission, those who travel to rural areas, for whatever reason, can be encouraged to root their experience of the countryside within an understanding of all things as created by a loving Creator God.

4 Rural Support Networks

RSABI launched its new listening service, GATEPOST, in October 2010 (www.rsabi.org.uk). This telephone helpline offers a confidential listening and support service to Scotland's farming and land-based community. GATEPOST aims to encourage talking about concerns before they develop into significant problems. It therefore does not offer counselling but can make referrals to appropriate help when required.

By working together in partnership with rural support networks such as RSABI and the National Farmers Union Scotland (www.nfus.org.uk), the Church can contribute to the care of farmers and other rural workers.

Learning from the knowledge and expertise of those whose lives are spent working on the land, more sensitive and fitting pastoral care can be offered, and worship and liturgy made more meaningful to people whose lives are rooted in the land. Partnerships also enable biblical insights and theological reflection to be shared by the rural church, thereby adding a significant dimension to discussions about land use and planning for sustainability.

5 See Me

See Me (www.seemescotland.org.uk) is an anti-stigma campaign, working to reduce the amount of prejudice – a significant problem in rural areas (Philo *et al.*, 2004) – faced by people experiencing problems with their mental health. Users of the website are encouraged to contact See Me to report any inappropriate reporting in the media. Active use of this website by church members indicates, both to those who work to prevent prejudice and to those who suffer its abuse, the commitment of the Church to stand by and support in the face of injustice.

By increasing awareness of the harmful effects of prejudice to mental health and well-being, partnership with See Me can also enable congregations to become more conscious of the damage they themselves sometimes inflict, however unintentionally, through their responses to those who struggle with the symptoms of mental illness.

These and other local and national partnerships between the Church and other organizations enable the Church to become:

- more committed to the rural community in which its presence is rooted and to its well-being;
- more faithful to the people, by being there with and for each one;
- more faithful to the God of justice and love who requires those who worship him to do what is just, to show constant love, and to live in humble fellowship with God.

Conclusion

The committed and faithful presence of the rural church has much to contribute to the mental health and well-being of the rural community. Its very presence speaks of God: mere presence, however, is neither sign of hope nor proclamation of God's love for all people.

Presence that is faithful to God, who wants his love and his justice to be experienced by all people, is ready to offer the insights of faith and is willing to learn from the knowledge and experience of others. Sharing together in this way enables care and provision to be suited to the needs of local people. As needs are met and care received, love is shared and hope rekindled.

The faithful, committed and shared presence of the rural church can enable rural areas to become communities of well-being.

References

Antonovsky, A., 1987, *Unraveling the Mystery of Health: How People Manage Stress and Stay Well*, San Francisco: Jossey-Bass.

Campbell, Alastair V., 1987, *A Dictionary of Pastoral Care*, London: SPCK.

Choose Life, 2007, *Time to Talk, Time to Listen: Help and Support for Farmers, Farm Workers and their Families*. Leaflet containing contact details for organizations offering advice and support, produced by Grampian Choose Life Groups.

Church Hymnary, 2005, 4th edition, Norwich: Canterbury Press.

Church of Scotland, 1994, *Book of Common Order of the Church of Scotland*, Edinburgh: Saint Andrew Press.

Fisher, A., 2007, *Suicide in Remote and Rural Areas*, Report of Choose Life Stakeholder Event.

Forestry Commission Scotland, 2009, *Woods for Health*, Edinburgh: Forestry Commission Scotland.

Frankl, V.E., 1964, *Man's Search for Meaning*, London: Hodder and Stoughton.

Harris, F., 2008, *Religious Faith and Spirituality: A Critical Appraisal of the Evidence*. Presentation given at SIREN Seminar, Risk and protective factors for suicide and suicidal behaviour, Easter Road [Hibernian football team] Stadium, Edinburgh, 16 December 2008.

Hothersall, S., Maas-Lowit, M. and Golightley, M., 2008, *Social Work and Mental Health in Scotland*, Exeter: Learning Matters Ltd.

Levin, K.A. and Leyland, A.H., 2005, 'Urban/rural inequalities in suicide in Scotland, 1981–1999', *Social Science and Medicine* 60, pp. 2877–90.

MacDonald, I., 2005, *Land of the Living: Christian Reflections on the Countryside*, Texas: Virtualbookworm.com Publishing Inc.

Methodist Church, 1999, *Methodist Worship Book*, Peterborough: Methodist Publishing House.

Methodist Church, 2004, *Presence: A Workbook to Help Promote and Sustain an Effective Christian Presence in Villages*, London: Methodist Church.

Mowat, H., Stark, C., Swinton, J. and Mowat, D., 2006, *Religion and Suicide: An Exploratory Study of the Role of the Church in Deaths by Suicide in Highland, Scotland, Ltd*. Aberdeen: Mowat Research Ltd.

Murray, L., 2009, *Belonging or Believing? The Relevance of Faith to our Well-being*. Presentation to Choose Life National Remote and Rural Working Group, 30 July 2009.

NHS Education for Scotland, 2008, *The 10 Essential Shared Capabilities for Mental Health Practice: Learning Materials (Scotland)*, NHS Education for Scotland.

NHS Grampian [no date], *Promoting Mental Health – Raising Awareness*. Training material handout 2A.

Pattison, S., 1997, *Pastoral Care and Liberation Theology*, London: SPCK.

Philo, C., Parr, H. and Burns, N., 2004, 'Geographies of exclusion', *Mental Health Today*, May, pp. 20–3.

Platt, S., 2008, *Understanding and Building Resilience among at Risk Groups*. Presentation given at SIREN Seminar, Risk and protective factors for suicide and suicidal behaviour, Easter Road [Hibernian football team] Stadium, Edinburgh, 16 December 2008.

Rattray L., 2002, 'Significance of the chaplain within the mental health care team', *Psychiatric Bulletin* 26, pp. 190–1.

Scottish Executive, 2002, *Choose Life: A National Strategy and Action Plan to Prevent Suicide in Scotland*, Edinburgh: Scottish Executive.

Scottish Executive, 2003, *Building Community Well-being: An Exploration of Themes and Issues*. Project Report to the Scottish Executive prepared by the Scottish Development Centre for Mental Health.

Scottish Government, 2007, *Towards a Mentally Flourishing Scotland: The Future of Mental Health Improvement in Scotland 2008–2011*, Scottish Government.

Scottish Recovery Network, 2008, *Realising Recovery Learning Materials*, Scottish Recovery Network and NHS Education for Scotland.

See Me, 2008, *One in Four People in Scotland will Experience a Mental Health Problem at some Point in their Lives*, http://www.seemescotland.org.uk/.

Speck, P., 1988, *Being There: Pastoral Care in Times of Illness*, London: SPCK.

Stark, C., Hopkins, P., Gibbs, D., Rapson, T., Belbin, A. and Hay, A., 2004, 'Trends in suicide in Scotland 1981–99: age, method and geography', *BMC Public Health* 4.49, www.biomedcentral.com/1471-2458/4/49

Swinton, J., 2000, *Resurrecting the Person: Friendship and the Care of People with Mental Health Problems*, Nashville: Abingdon Press.

9

The trees of the field shall clap their hands: the metaphor of trees, woods and forests as symbols of creation, justice and hope

GRAHAM B. USHER

Trees, woods and forests are an important part of the makeup of the English countryside and are encountered in most terrain apart from the high peaks. Ours is a dynamic landscape that has changed throughout history. Perhaps 80% was originally forested. Following a pattern of gradual deforestation, with about 50% forest cover at the time the Romans arrived, this fell to 5% at the beginning of the twentieth century (Earl of Lindsay, 1999, p. 1). This was largely due to increasing agricultural development and the demand for wood, particularly to float a navy and then to fuel the industrial revolution, outstripping replanting and natural regeneration. The Forestry Commission was established in 1919 to create a strategic timber reserve, and since that point there has been a gradual recovery of forest cover to 1,128,000 hectares (Forestry Commission, 2009, p. 2), which is equivalent to 9% of the land cover.

To achieve this, the middle part of the twentieth century saw vast areas of our rural landscape planted with rows of conifers. This depressed many, including the walker and Lakeland writer Alfred Wainwright:

the transformation of Ennerdale from beautiful valley to a dense forest is now complete and is no cause of pride. Here trees are grown unnaturally and denied space and light so that the limbs wither and only a straight main stem develops. The aim is a thicket of living telegraph poles. This is battery farming, and because trees have life and dignity it has all the objections of battery farming. (Wainwright, 1971, p. 217)

This has now been reversed with deciduous species comprising 68% of the English forest landscape and coniferous 32%, and the former representing two thirds of the 4,300 hectares of new planting and re-stocking in the year to the end of March 2009 (Forestry Commission, 2009, pp. 4–5). In England the ownership of trees, woods and forests is divided between private owners (82%) and taxpayers through the management of the public forest estate by the Forestry Commission (18%) (percentages calculated from Forestry Commission, 2009 p. 2). Among private owners there is a growing charitable sector led by the Woodland Trust, which was formed in 1972 and now boasts a membership of over 300,000 supporting the management of more than 1,000 woodland sites covering 20,000 hectares in the UK (Woodland Trust, 2010).

Trees in biblical times were valuable economic resources, partly because of their scarcity. Their fruit provided food and this was an important consideration in whether an unproductive tree should be kept, Jesus himself making a theological point from a fruitless fig tree (Matthew 21.19–21). Oil, used for a whole variety of both secular and religious purposes, was extracted from the olive trees' fruit. Solomon on one occasion gave the servants of Hiram 20,000 baths full of olive oil (2 Chronicles 2.10). The trees themselves were the product of intensive husbandry skills, grafting material into older stock. Olive wood was used for carving and in Solomon's Temple it was the material chosen for the door posts and the ornate decorative cherubim. As well as being an important construction material, timber was used for fuel and to shelter livestock and humans (1 Kings 6.23, 31–34).

Likewise forestry contributes to our economy, providing an estimated £2 billion to the English economy (Forestry Commission, 2009, p. 15), employing 42,000 people in direct and primary wood processing business (Forestry Commission, 2009, p. 14), and recognized as contributing to the economic viability of many rural communities (Henwood and Pidgeon, 2001, p. 145). Over the last three decades, there has been an increasing cultural change within forestry, charted by Mather (2001), which has seen the rise of a post-industrial forest with a wider set of values. Forests are now seen as a resource for carbon sequestration, biodiversity and recreation, as well as contributing to less measurable social factors including health and spiritual well-being. Mather went on to note (2001, p. 249) that the role of the forest has changed 'from a place of production (of timber, largely destined for urban markets) towards a place of consumption of recreation and environment by a largely urban population'.

This change can be seen in the Labour Government's 2007 policy, *A Strategy for England's Trees, Woods and Forests* (Defra, 2007). This document set out the then Government's key priorities, with economic and market benefits sitting alongside climate change, the protection of biodiversity and landscapes and the cultural and amenity value that has the potential for the enhancement of the quality of life. Indeed, the value to the public of these ecological, cultural and amenity services was tested when the coalition government announced in a letter to Members of Parliament in October 2010 (Defra, 2010), that it intended to fundamentally reform the ownership of the public forest estate. The public consultation papers, launched in January 2011, proposed the leasing or selling off of the entire public forest estate, with safeguards put in place for heritage forests, public-access and the protection of rich or rare biodiverse sites. What began as rumblings of discontent from interest groups became a full scale public outcry and the consultation was abandoned three weeks later following the intervention of the Prime Minister and an embarrassing climbdown by the Secretary of State. In her House of Commons speech, Caroline Spelman said, 'If there is one clear message from this experience, it is that people cherish their forests and woodlands and the benefits they bring' (Defra, 2011a). An independent panel on forestry has been established, under the chairmanship of the Bishop of Liverpool, to advise on the future direction of forestry, including the increase of forest cover and options for enhancing public benefits (Defra, 2011b), and is due to report in 2012.

This chapter explores trees, woods and forests within the Christian tradition, and the use of metaphor and symbol in the biblical narrative, in order to explore where there might be areas that contribute to forest policy themes as well as providing a challenge to shape Christian engagement with forest policy in the future.

Stores of cultural values

In Hexham Abbey lies a tombstone attributed by some historians to be that of Elfwald, one-time King of Northumbria (who died in AD 788). Across its surface is chiselled a design of vine leaves and small clusters of fruit, emerging from two grotesque heads and culminating in a cross. This Tree of Life design, with its verdant cross, grew in popularity during the Middle Ages, signifying the crucifixion's complex story of atonement for all that had gone wrong in human sinfulness following the Fall. A much more elaborate representation of the Tree of Life can be seen in the mosaic east wall in the church of St Clement's in Rome, with each branch bearing exotic animals amid lush leaves. This biblical image appears in Genesis and Revelation, so is one of nostalgia when looking back, and hope of paradise regained when looking forward. In Genesis the Tree of Life offered the provision of life for Adam and Eve (Genesis 2.9). Drawn through and into the experience of the Tree of the Cross, we meet it again in the last chapter of Revelation as a symbol of God's benevolence, bringing a fruit in each season and leaves which will be the medicine of healing for the nations (Revelation 22.1–2). The Tree of Life represents balance within creation whereas the other tree of Genesis (though it is debated as to whether they are in fact separate trees), the Tree of Knowledge of Good and Evil, as its name implies, represents the polarities of life and therefore imbalance.

Trees, woods and forests play an important part in our cultural story and are often used as a metaphor to describe different forms of imbalance. We encounter this in fairy tales of Little Red Riding Hood set in a fearful place, to the folklore of yew trees (*Taxus baccata*) in churchyards symbolizing immortality and rowan trees (*Sorbus aucuparia*) warding off evil spirits. The greenmen carved into the ceiling bosses of churches still vomiting their hedgerow meal over our places of worship are an ancient fertility symbol Christianized to characterize God's forgiveness and redemption offered through Jesus (Caldecott, 1993, p. 133). In Bohemian legend the leaves of aspen (*Populus tremula*) still tremble, as its scientific name implies, due to its guilt of being the tree from which Judas Iscariot hung himself; elsewhere it is because it was the tree on which Jesus was crucified (Altman, 2000, p. 157). Maronite tradition holds that on the night of the Epiphany the Lord passes by at midnight to bless all creation and trees bow before him, but the reluctant fig tree is cursed. Many of these traditions, often relating to specific species of tree, have been collated in a lively genre of tree symbolism literature (for example, Altman, 2000; Caldecott, 1993; Hageneder, 2000 and 2001; Philpot, 1897).

Simon Schama, in his opus *Landscape and Memory* (Schama, 1995, pp. 185–242), charted how the powerful social myths and history of the woodland environment, as seen through the eyes of painters, preachers and poets, have entered the imagination both as places of awe and wonder as well as of savage brutality and danger. The Big Trees of the American west have been at the heart of American identity; the sequoias representing both freedom and a sacred quality, two attributes at the heart of the American understanding of themselves. Meanwhile the German understanding of forests had developed, Schama argued (1995, pp. 117–19), as representing the spirit of militarism, with the Nazis drawing forest scenes into their art and clearing human habitation from huge areas so as to provide hunting grounds. Research undertaken by Henwood and Pidgeon (1998) in Wales found that members of the public who took part in five community focus groups across the country viewed trees, woods and forests as having an integral cultural component within their national story, which was about an added value beyond their commercial and economic potential. They found also that for people brought up in rural areas, 'trees do signify "home", and as such comprise an integral part of their personal and community identity' (Hunter, Pidgeon and Henwood, 2001, p. 19).

The understanding of trees, woods and forests within English society is more subtle. Stories, other than those popularized by Walt Disney, are no longer being passed down from generation to generation, and rural folklore about the role of different types of timber and their properties for construction or fuel are being lost. How many children learn the weather forecast, 'oak before ash and you're in for a splash, ash before oak and you're in for a soak'? Traditional forestry skills have become marginal or interest-group activities, with parts of the countryside increasingly the playgrounds of consumption for suburbia. Forest environments are now regularly visited by 77% of the population over the age of 16 (Forestry Commission, 2009, p. 13).

Places of the sacred

'The Lord appeared to Abraham by the oaks of Mamre' (Genesis 18.1ff.). It was in that rare place of shade, thought to be Terebinth trees (*Pistacia terebinthus*), where spirits could be restored, that Abraham offered hospitality, realized a divine encounter with God and two angels, and heard a promise for his future and that of his, as yet unborn and unforeseen, descendants. This became recognized as a sacred space; the great oaks marking out hallowed territory as one man's story ran alongside and interwove with the history of those trees. Later Abraham would return to bury his wife (Genesis 23.17–20), placing her body in a cave in a field of trees (the first woodland burial). Being buried in that promised land was to become an important symbol of permanence. Later, the fig tree (*Ficus* sp.), with its many years of hard labour to establish, was to become a symbol for Israel of a settled life, the giving up of a nomadic existence for one of stability and hoped-for prosperity. Ingold (1993) has shown this to be true more generally of ancient trees which form part of long-established communities that have grown up alongside them.

People speak of entering into a sense of connectedness with creation when absorbed in an ancient woodland or in the presence of a specimen veteran tree. Ancient trees, with histories that link across generations, are seen as having a sense of wisdom. Some scholars believe this to be why the massive entrance pillars to Solomon's Temple were decorated with palm trees (Walker-Jones, 2009, p. 26). There are examples of ancient trees having taken on religious stories, such as the Fortingall Yew in Perthshire connected in folklore with a visit of Pontius Pilate to a nearby Roman encampment. Likewise, the Glastonbury Thorn is linked to Joseph of Arimathea, which grew amid great cultic reverence until the Puritans hacked it down (for a full account, and details of sacred trees in other traditions, see Caldecott, 1993). Other trees are the memory bank of local communities and the focus for events which then become immortalized, such as the story of how on Jubilee Day 1877 the vicar, two churchwardens and 95 Sunday School children squeezed inside the Copthorpe Oak at Wetherby and sang the National Anthem!

The Forestry Commission, recognizing the cultural heritage and interest in ancient trees, has established a policy and set of strategic objectives, under the title 'Keepers of Time', which aims to ensure that they are, 'adequately protected, sustainably managed in a wider landscape context, and are providing a wide range of social, environmental and economic benefits to society' (Defra and Forestry Commission, 2005, p. 9). Until recently simply regarded as scrub of little timber value, Mather (2001, p. 254) commented on the change in perception of these trees, now 'increasingly revered . . . and cherished for environmental reasons'. The Forestry Commission's strategy draws back from mentioning the spiritual value of these trees, referring instead to 'cultural heritage', which has been described by Tsouvalis (2000, p. 197) as containing 'symbols of identity that celebrate longevity of a culture grounded in a nature so fragile that it requires the utmost protection'. There is much in the Christian tradition about valuing age, wisdom and story that could contribute to this important work, seeing these veteran trees, already places of 'pilgrimage', as the saints of forestry.

In other cultures, sacred space, marked out and set aside by the individual or community, is often planted with trees which have been invested with mythical status. The native religions of West Africa frequently have their fetish shrines among sacred groves whereby 'members of the community identify a specific area in the landscape as a point of contact between the invisible and the human worlds, and establish a ritualized alliance with spiritual entities that dwell there' (Chouin, 2007, p. 179). There are sacred woods in contemporary Indian and Japanese cultures. The ancient Egyptians held the sycamore (*Acer* sp.) as having unique qualities, often planting it near tombs due to its manifestation with the goddesses Hut, Isis and Hathor, and the Greeks were drawn to the grove of oaks (*Quercus* sp.) at the Altis in Olympia, which was sacred to the god Zeus. Within the Christian tradition the grove of olive trees in the Garden of Gethsemane (meaning the place of the olive press) form the theatre for the story of Jesus' agony. These trees' descendents are still a place of pilgrimage, with the Church of All Nations next door being built as an architectural representation of that dark night of brooding waiting amid the trees.

From this idea of sacred groves, Luton and Bedford Councils of Faiths developed an initiative in 2006 to develop the concept of a 'faith woodland' to provide health, recreational and educational benefits. The Forestry Commission funded work and provided a site which, through an interfaith network, aimed to reach sectors of society who perceive themselves as excluded from woodland. Hand (2007) outlined how the project vision developed, was managed and delivered, describing (p. 8) that the consensus from the various participant faith groups was for a 'simple quiet area for contemplation, prayer and meditation', together with a labyrinth. The project tried to allow the woodland to speak for itself rather than be filled with pieces of art, interpretation and other objects, and was located some distance from the car park so that the journey to the clearing would in itself become a spiritual opportunity. The evaluation noted that there had been some tension between the management of the site by the Forestry Commission, with a primary focus on timber production and the conservation of a Site of Special Scientific Interest, and the social objectives that included community outreach, access and environmental awareness (Tabbush, 2008, p. 2). A balance needed to be struck between these contested needs.

There are other examples of trees, forests and woodlands developing a sacred quality, including the National Memorial Arboretum in Staffordshire, which is the 'living and lasting memorial to commemorate and celebrate those who gave their lives in the service of their country and all who have served and those who have suffered as a result of conflict'. It describes itself as a 'unique haven of peace, contemplation and hope for the future' (National Memorial Arboretum, 2010). The Whipsnade Tree Cathedral, a group of trees planted in a cruciform shape by friends of the landowner, who was killed in the First World War, in 'faith, hope and reconciliation' (National Trust, 2010), gained its inspiration from the nation's medieval cathedrals. The designers of these cathedrals are, in turn, thought to have gained their inspiration from sacred groves, recreating in stone pillars and ribbed vaulting the sense of walking amid huge towering trees that took one's imagination up into the canopy and so into the creativity of God. This re-imagining of the forest architecture of their cathedral led the Dean and Chapter of Exeter in 2008 to organize a series of workshops and poetry events to recognize the influence of timber and trees within the creation, design and song of their building.

We see the creation of today's sacred groves in the appeal of woodland burial sites, with the valuing of trees, woods and forests continuing in death. We have already recorded the woodland burial of Sara. Later in Genesis Deborah, Rebekah's nurse, also died and was buried under an oak at Bethel (Genesis 35.8), which was given the name Allon-bacuth, which translates from Hebrew as 'oak of weeping'. John Evelyn (1620–1706), in his 1662 lecture to the Royal Society, noting that Jesus was buried in a garden, commended the practice as:

> there are no places more fit to bury our dead in than our gardens and groves, or airy fields, where are beds may be decked and carpeted with verdant and fragrant flowers, trees and perennial plants, the most natural and instructive hieroglyphics of our expected resurrection and immortality. (Evelyn, 1662)

He was not impressed with the custom of burying people in churches, which he described as 'indecent, sordid and very prejudicial to health'. It is estimated that there are more than 200 natural burial sites, including meadows (Cranwell, 2010), which are mostly attached to existing local authority cemeteries, with the Church of England having a woodland burial site near Cambridge managed by the Arbory Trust on behalf of the Diocese of Ely. There is little in the literature about contemporary woodland burial places (see Scott, 2003) though there is a concern about the profusion of ornamental cherry trees (*Prunus* spp.) where the planting of native species is not a stipulated rule. The future thinning of these areas, when a single tree is planted over each grave, the choice of allowing the understorey vegetation to grow naturally or for it to be mown, and the profusion of grave paraphernalia, including wind chimes and windmills, are examples of where there is a need for sensitive planning and good ongoing maintenance.

Inge (2003, p. 113), in exploring shrines as places of pilgrimage sees them as places of memory (past), sacramental encounter giving us 'a glimpse of the consummation of all things in Christ' (present), and directing us to the new co-ordinates of time and place in Christ (future). This also holds true for sacred groves, which as a type of shrine are places that are a continued reminder of the covenant relationship between God, creation and humanity and so are places of sacrament. The Church of England, with its ancient graveyards and glebe land, could consider the planting of more areas with suitable native trees, as was done to celebrate the 125th anniversary of the creation of the Diocese of Newcastle. This type of project may attract local enthusiasm as the planting of Millennium Yew trees did in 2000. Not only would hallowed places be created, or places of creative life amid the dead, but also quality of life would be enhanced and a contribution made towards carbon sequestration and encouraging biodiversity.

Enablers for the quality of life

The need for fruit trees in the Middle East to be planted next to water channels so that their roots receive moisture, means that trees are a biblical metaphor for abundant living and wholeness 'leading to a righteous life' (Walker-Jones, 2009, p. 26). The Psalmist captures the essence of a person living within the law of God as being 'like trees planted by streams of water, which yield their fruit in its season, and their leaves do not wither' (Psalm 1.3), and that they become like specimen trees, well nurtured such as those in the Temple courts, which:

> flourish like the palm tree, and grow like a cedar in Lebanon. They are planted in the house of the Lord; they flourish in the courts of our God. In old age they still produce fruit; they are always green and full of sap. (Psalm 92.12–14 NRSV)

There is evidence (Tabbush and O'Brien, 2003; Forestry Commission Scotland, 2009) that having access to trees, woods and forests raises health through enhanced fitness and lowered pulse rates, and people with a view of woodland from hospital wards have been found to recover more quickly from surgery and are discharged earlier (Selman, 2003). MacNaghten and Urry (2000) explored how woods and forests relate to the human body, and while they found that different social groups react in different ways depending upon their needs and outlook, their respondents described the positive benefits of relaxation, refreshment, solitude, surprise, and re-forming of social relationships. They found (p. 171) that 'what many people desired was an unmediated relationship, in which they experience a profound engagement with oneself or others through a "raw" and unmediated nature', which is a recognition of the spiritual value of trees, woods and forests.

At the UN Rio Earth Summit in 1992 some attempt was made by the United Nations to outline the value and role of trees, woods and forests. The conference report concluded that 'forest resources and forest lands should be sustainably managed to meet the social, economic, ecological, cultural and spiritual needs of present and future generations' (United Nations, 1993, p. 481). The spiritual value of ecosystem services was later identified within the cultural attributes of the UN's Millennium Ecosystem Assessment (Millennium Ecosystem Assessment, 2005, p. 44). These are some of the few definitions that explicitly state the spiritual value of trees. The 'spiritual' sense is noted by many who work or spend time in woods and forests (Williams and Harvey, 2001, p. 249–51), and

Ashley (2007) conducted a literature review (p. 58) and research (pp. 62–5) supporting this. The major themes within the literature appear to be around landscapes having the capacity to evoke values that take one out of the self, so leading to enhanced purpose and meaning, an awareness of interrelationships within created matter, and a sense of oneness with nature. There is something about smelling a remnant ancient Scots pine (*Pinus sylvestris* sp) forest in the Cairngorms National Park, or being under the dappled canopy of the vibrant green beech (*Fagus sylvatica* sp), or kicking autumn leaves, that can lift mental spirits. This has been confirmed by research in Australia conducted by Williams *et al.* (2001, pp. 254–5), where their interviewees reported high levels of diminutive transcendence, described as a sense of awe and creaturehood, in forests where there were compelling elements of quality within the environment such as tall trees. Henwood *et al.* (1998, p. 25) found in their research that 'spiritual' experiences in woods and forests included feelings of being at peace in the solitude, of being comfortable in that space (existential well-being), and of altered states of awareness ('walked taller' or feeling 'really small'). Burgess and O'Brien (2001, pp. 4, 9), from their review of forestry social science research in the 1990s, concluded that there is a significant public view that forestry is concerned with moral uplift, rather than hedonistic consumption, and values simple sensory pleasures, contact with nature and naturalness, and spiritual feelings.

As woods and forests absorb sound there can be a greater sense of silence (depending on the volubility of immediate wildlife) and thus also of being more alone. In forestry literature this is more frequently referred to as tranquillity and is measured by there being an absence of unnatural noise such as traffic and aircraft and the absence of visual intrusions. The measure is also affected by the number of people present in a location and the age and structure of the forest to be able to absorb them. Compare the same area of open parkland and woodland, with the same density of people within each, and the woodland appears to be less populated. Bell (1999) shows how tranquillity can be mapped and how this can be used in forest design while also recognizing that trees can produce their own sound that can compete with or mask external noises.

Agreeing with research conducted by MacNaghten and Urry (2000, p. 176), Maitland (2008) found that silence heightens human senses. She describes being in a forest as a fearful experience because 'the silence of the forest is about secrets, about things that are hidden' (Maitland, 2008, p. 178). In this she is not quite as blunt as the seventeenth-century John Evelyn, who talks of humans feeling an 'awful and religious terror when placed in the centre of a thick wood' (Evelyn, 1662). The popular writer Bill Bryson (1998, p. 61) was no less critical:

So woods are spooky . . . there is something innately sinister about them, some effable thing that makes you sense an atmosphere of pregnant doom with every step and leaves you profoundly aware that you are out of your element and ought to keep your ears pricked.

To the paranoid Macbeth the march of Malcolm's army, under the guise of the wood of Birnam, was to reveal his mortal danger as the forest gave up its deadly secret. Others are more positive. Henry Thoreau, the transcendental radical philosopher (1817–62), gave his rationale for being drawn into, and living among the natural environment by writing: 'I went to the woods because I wished to live deliberately . . . I wanted to live deep and suck out the marrow of life' (Thoreau, 1854, pp. 90–1).

There appears to be a difference in much social research about attitudes to woods dependent on the previous experience and home backgrounds of interviewees. Burgess' (1995, p. 24) research about urban fringe woodlands noted many negative perceptions and only briefly mentioned more positive attributes, such as places of escape where peace and quiet could be found together with solitary contemplation and a closeness to nature. Possibly due to their focus groups having many more rural participants, work by Henwood and Pidgeon (1998) showed more positive themes, including 'the pleasure of being in woods, their perceived cleanliness in contrast to city life, "spiritual" feelings evoked by being in woodlands, and a sense of excitement, adventure, and curiosity at what might be found in woods' (Henwood and Pidgeon, 1998, p. 63). This curiosity links to childhood stories that speak of the hiddenness of the woods revealing delight, such as the nursery rhyme, 'If you go down to the woods today you're sure of a big surprise' and the tales of Robin Hood, who uses the woods to be countercultural and restore the balance of what he believed to be right from the greed of the despot. The forest 'leads the wanderer on' (Warner, 1989, p. 44), and Hamma, in a book of spiritual reflections, described how the 'forest calls me to discover who I am, to cultivate an inner and outer awareness' (Hamma, 2002, p. 82). All of this is familiar territory for the Christian understanding of the pilgrimage of faith with its times of familiarity and disconnectedness, knowing and unknowing.

Linked to this imagery is the role of trees, woods and forests as places of enlightenment. Moses heard God speaking from a burning bush (Exodus 3.2–6), Elijah sat down in despair by a broom tree in the wilderness and was met by an angel with fresh baking (1 Kings 19.4–5), Zacchaeus climbed up into his sycamore tree to glimpse salvation (Luke 19.2–4), Nathaniel was called from under his fig tree to a new way of living (John 1.48) and Augustine of Hippo reported that he flung himself down under a fig tree at the time of his conversion (Confessions 8.12). The experience changes all of these characters. Perhaps it is in entering into the rhythm of the seasons as buds burst into green life, and later in the year turn to other colours as their leaves are leached of nutrients, reminding us of the ongoing cycle of birth and death and rebirth. Hamma (2002, p. 85) interpreted this awareness as an entering into a rhythm of change, taking 'a moment's glimpse in a constant process'. Is it that to sit under a tree is to find occasion for praise because we are entering into a Sabbath rest or a *chronos* pause? Or is it that we are stripping away something of the complexity of our lives and learning, even for a moment, to walk humbly and gently on the earth, enjoying the sacrament of the present moment? Was this why St Bernard of Clairvaux (1090–1153) remarked, 'You will find something more in woods than in books. The trees and stone will teach you what you never learn from the masters' (Bernard of Clairvaux, Epistola 106, sect. 2)?

Forests can therefore be seen to be places of recreation that open up the human sense of well-being, or they can be places that are in some sense wild, inviting exploration or warning people off entering. McGrath (2001, p. 109) recognized these different ways of seeing nature and added a further two: nature as something in need of taming and control; and nature as a resource to be mined and used for humanity's benefit (which is the industrial model of forestry). He went on to argue that the Christian theologian sees nature as 'creation' (McGrath, 2001, p. 113). There is a tendency in some New Age movements to worship trees (pantheism – a view, not found in the Bible, that everything is God). Ramshaw (2002, p. 398) noted that we see a continuation of the imagery of the goddess as tree, representing Sophia in some passages of Wisdom literature (Sirach 24). There may well be a need to reinvest in an exploration of the panentheistic approach, whereby we see God manifest in all that lives.

The Deuteronomic laws about sieges contain the rule that trees around a town which is being besieged are not to be cut down. It is only possible to take food from them and cut down dead specimens (Deuteronomy 20.19–20). How much of this happened in practice is unknown. When trees are threatened with being cut down, particularly those seen as community or historical assets, there is often a public outcry, and if the destruction takes place there is a sense of community mourning. Olive branches are seen by all three monotheistic faiths as being symbols of peace; their destruction during the building of the partition wall within the West Bank has been a particular symbol of sadness and anger for Palestinian communities so reliant on their produce. A USPG sponsored worker, Ruth de Barros, has been a Christian voice campaigning against the destruction of the Amazon rainforest and has noted the effects of that destruction on the lives and well-being of local people. There have been periodic phases of direct action whereby tree dwellers and huggers campaigned against development by literally chaining themselves to trunks or living within the canopy. There is a clear linkage here with the Christian tradition of protest and a hunger for justice which seeks to value creation and allow the voiceless to be heard. The trees that these people are trying to protect are seen as being 'not just individual entities of ethical, aesthetic, or spiritual note, but symbols of wider nature and the landscape' (Jones and Cloke,

2002, p. 38) which is under threat and no longer valued. Worth (2006) studied the values that people held towards the logging of native forests in three local government areas of Western Australia and found that while religious affiliation had declined over a period of 30 years, there had been an increase in an acknowledgement of the spiritual value of these forests with a corresponding rise in opposition to logging within them.

Walsh, Karsh and Ansell (1994) argue that we should engage with trees in the Martin Buber prism of I–Thou (Buber, 1937), seeing trees as responsive subjects and possessing agency, so that they 'do not merely react, but act on and interact with us, other creatures, and we would contend, God'. This I–Thou ethic and relationship works with the metaphorical language of trees in the Bible, and Walsh, Karsh and Ansell (1994) remark that:

> to say that trees praise, sing, clap, and rejoice is to say that trees, as trees, in their whole physical, chemical, spatial, biotic functioning can fully respond to their Creator when that functioning is uninhibited and free. To say that trees groan is to say that trees experience and respond to conditions of human abuse or neglect that inhabits and closes down their responsiveness. In this way metaphors of praising and groaning enable us to 'hear' what the trees have to 'say'.

To hear the groaning, they suggest, is to be invited to participate in that groaning and to look to ways to alleviate the suffering. As humanity responds, the groaning might then change to become as if the trees are clapping their hands and rejoicing in a celebration of creation. Recognizing the fact that woods and forests play an important part in the quality of people's lives, the Community Forest Programme, which aimed to create well-wooded countryside around towns and cities to provide a better environment in which people can work, live and spend their leisure time, was launched jointly by the Forestry Commission and the Countryside Commission in 1987. This bringing of the rural into the urban landscape has been shown by Collins and Stewart Roper (1999) to demonstrate that trees can play a part in the environmental regeneration of towns and cities, and contribute to wider non-market benefits of forestry, such as recreation, house prices, health enhancement and carbon sequestration, in economic models to justify public purse expenditure. Of the 14 ambitious objectives (Collins and Stewart Roper, 1999, p. 315) for community woodlands set in 1990, none of them directly mention a spiritual dimension; the closest is 'to increase opportunities for sport and recreation, including artistic and cultural events, and access'. However, there is a strong emphasis upon social inclusion and participation; examples of kingdom values about all people contributing to self-determination and upholding issues of justice. (For a review of social justice issues in forestry see Milbourne, Kitchen and Stanley, 2006.) Mather (2001, p. 262) sees the 'social construction of the forest as the antithesis of the urban as well as the epitome of the natural'. In trying to create a little bit of rural, or even a sense of Eden, for urban dwellers, so the Tree of Life story is taken, as it is in the Bible, from the garden to the city. Yet O'Brien, Foot and Doick (2007, p. 150) found that, 'the evaluation of monetary benefit [of community woods] does not adequately reflect the wider benefit that can be achieved' and noted that further work is required to develop 'a toolbox of wider indicators of success, including non-monetary, quantitative and qualitative criteria'.

Reducers of climate change

Trees, woods and forests, by constantly locking up carbon through the process of photosynthesis and storing it as biomass in their trunks, branches, leaves, roots and in the humus in the soil beneath them, remove carbon dioxide from the atmosphere. By planting a new forest, carbon is soaked up as the trees grow until a point when the forest reaches maturity, when the amount of sequestration equals decomposition and the scales of carbon change are equal. At this point the forest is acting as an immense carbon reservoir. Globally this reservoir is decreasing by about 13 million hectares every year, though the forest area in Europe grew by 13 million hectares (roughly the size of Greece) between 1990 and 2005 (Forestry Commission, 2007, p. 2).

The Tree of Life in the book of Revelation is described as having leaves which will be the medicine of healing for the nations (Revelation 22.1–2). Could trees be part of the medicine of healing as we face up to our global concerns about climate change and our ability to mitigate its effects and adapt to its inevitable changes? Trees are mentioned eight times in the creation story and are seen as a vital life force (Genesis 1.11–13), and they could go some way in capturing carbon and being used as a fuel supply as they emit less carbon than fossil fuels. This is especially true when trees are planted on soils poor in organic material, as more carbon can be released from carbon-rich soils such as peat, than the tree is sequestrating for much of its life. In order to secure the potential carbon storage we will need to protect what we already have, be prepared to see a changed and afforested landscape, and recognize that climate change may result in the need to plant different species which are more adapted to increased temperatures and not placed under the stress which can lead to a greater susceptibility to harmful insects and diseases.

In the medieval tradition the Tree of Life was also the Tree of the Cross, and the symbolism was drawn as a tree rooted in the earth and with its canopy in the heavens. Eaton (2006, p. 2) remarks that 'through the tree of his cross [Jesus] bears the eternal fruit of God, the sheltering, healing and blessing of all creation'. Again, this could be a fruitful metaphor, pointing us to the fact that through the degradation and brokenness of the Tree of the Cross there was the hope and expectation, again seen in medieval tradition, that on the day of Resurrection the tree would blossom again, refusing to despair. Simon Schama (1995, p. 219) includes a twelfth-century legend where:

[Adam] nine hundred and thirty-two years old and (understandably) ailing, sends his son Seth to fetch a seed from one of the Edenic trees. Returning, the son drops the seed in Father Adam's mouth, from which it sprouts into sacred history. It supplies a length for Noah's ark (a first redemption), the rod of Moses, a beam in Solomon's temple, a plank in Joseph's workshop, and finally the structure of the Cross itself.

The metaphor might stretch to trees being part of the ongoing salvation of the earth, reminding us of humanity's interrelationship and interdependence with God and earth; saving us from destroying ourselves through our own sins against the created environment. Atkinson (2008, p. 69), an Anglican bishop, commented that:

> Creation also becomes the context for the drama of redemption through which God's healing and recreating love does not abandon the world which has 'fallen' and gone astray, but in which God keeps faith with his people and constantly holds out visions of hope.

So the Tree of Life, which Warner explored in art, continues, as she put it, to grow 'as a symbol of hope, of future, of fullness . . . it points to another world, a beyond which is or will be different' (Warner, 1989, p. 44).

Conclusion

John Muir (1838–1914), the Scottish émigré who captured people's imagination for protecting wilderness places, resulting in the first National Parks in the United States, wrote, 'I could distinctly hear the varying tones of individual trees – Spruce and Fir, and Pine, and leafless Oak. Each was expressing itself in its own way – singing its own song, and making its own particular gestures' (Austin, 1987, p. 29). While this may be a somewhat romantic view, it does look to make a greater connection, largely lost from western culture, between humanity and creation. Trees, woods and forests draw humanity to see and experience the gift of the divine in the ordinary, and Christian communities have a role in making the connections between their cultural stories and spirituality from which emerges a sense of justice to safeguard the protection of trees around us. Without them we lose hope, both for ourselves and the future of our planet, vital as trees, woods and forests are in carbon sequestration and the protection of the natural environment. This sense of trees, woods and forests leading to a greater understanding and awareness of creation, justice and hope emphasizes that churches should encourage communities, and international partner churches, to see our connection to, and dependence on the natural world, and to get involved by seeking to value, plant and manage woodland well.

References

Altman, N., 2000, *Sacred Trees*, New York: Sterling.

Ashley, P., 2007, 'Toward an Understanding and Definition of Wilderness Spirituality', *Australian Geographer* 38, pp. 53–69.

Atkinson, D., 2008, *Renewing the Face of the Earth: A Theological and Pastoral Response to Climate Change*, Norwich: Canterbury Press.

Austin, R.,1987, *Baptized into Wilderness: A Christian Perspective on John Muir*, Atlanta: John Knox Press.

Bell, S., 1999, *Tranquillity Mapping as an Aid to Forest Planning*, Edinburgh: Forestry Commission.

Bryson, B., 1998, *A Walk in the Woods: Rediscovering America on the Appalachian Trail*, London: Black Swan.

Buber, M., 1970, *I and Thou,* trans. Walter Kaufmann, New York: Charles Scribner's Sons.

Burgess, J., 1995, *Growing in Confidence: Understanding Peoples' Perceptions of Urban Fringe Woodlands*, Cheltenham: Countryside Commission.

Burgess, J. and O'Brien, L., 2001, 'Trees, woods and forests: An exploration of Personal and Collective Values', in L. O'Brien and J. Claridge (eds), *Trees are Company: Social Science Research into Woodlands and the Natural Environment*, Edinburgh: Forestry Commission, pp. 5–10.

Caldecott, M., 1993, *Myths of the Sacred Tree*, Vermont: Destiny Books.

Chouin, G., 2007, 'Archaeological Perspectives on Sacred Groves in Ghana', in M.J. Sheridan and C. Nyamweru (eds), *African Sacred Groves: Ecological Dynamics and Social Change*, Ohio: Ohio University Press, pp. 178–94.

Collins, J. and Stewart Roper, C.,1999, 'Development of Community Forest Policy in England: Delivering Public Benefits on the Urban Fringe', in C. Stewart Roper and A. Park (eds), *The Living Forest: Non-market Benefits of Forestry*, London, The Stationery Office, pp. 313–19.

Cranwell, B., 'Laid to Rest – in Woodland', *Church Times*, 1.1.2010, p. 12.

Department for Environment, Food and Rural Affairs and Forestry Commission, 2005, *Keepers of Time: A Statement of Policy for England's Ancient and Native Woodland*, Bristol and Cambridge: Defra and Forestry Commission.

Department for Environment, Food and Rural Affairs, 2007, *A Strategy for England's Trees, Woods and Forests*, London: Defra.

Department for Environment, Food and Rural Affairs, 2010, www.defra. gov.uk/news/2010/10/29/forestry/

Department for Environment, Food and Rural Affairs, 2011a, www.defra. gov.uk/news/2011/02/17/futureforestry/

Department for Environment, Food and Rural Affairs, 2011b, www. archive.defra.gov.uk/rural/forestry/documents/forestry-panel-tor.pdf

Eaton, J., 2006, *Psalms for Life: Hearing and Praying the Book of Psalms*, London: SPCK.

Evelyn, J., 1662, *Silva or a Discourse of Forest-Trees and the Propagation of Timber in his Majesty's Dominions Together with an Historical Account of the Sacredness and use of Standing Groves*, York: Royal Society.

Forestry Commission, 2007, *Forests and Climate Change*, Edinburgh: Forestry Commission.

Forestry Commission, 2009, *Forestry Facts and Figures 2009*, Edinburgh: Forestry Commission.

Forestry Commission Scotland, 2009, *Woods for Health*, Edinburgh: Forestry Commission.

Hageneder, F., 2000, *The Spirit of Trees: Science, Symbiosis and Inspiration*, Edinburgh: Floris Books.

Hageneder, F., 2001, *The Heritage of Trees: History, Culture and Symbolism*, Edinburgh: Floris Books.

Hamma, R.M., 2002, *Earth's Echo: Sacred Encounters with Nature*, Notre Dame: Sorin Books.

Hand, K., 2007, *Faith Woodlands December 2006 – March 2007 The First Phase*, Forestry Commission England, www.forestry.gov.uk/pdf/ fce-faith-in-the-woodlands.pdf/$FILE/fce-faith-in-the-woodlands.pdf

Henwood, K. and Pidgeon, N.,1998, *The Place of Forestry in Modern Welsh Culture and Life: Report to the Forestry Commission*, Bangor: University of Wales.

Henwood, K. and Pidgeon, N., 2001, 'Talk about Woods and Trees: Threat of Urbanization, Stability and Biodiversity', *Journal of Environmental Psychology* 21, pp. 125–47.

Hunter, S., Pidgeon, N. and Henwood, K. (2001), 'Forests, People and place: How individuals and communities perceive and relate to trees, woodland and forests in a Welsh Context', in L. O'Brien and J. Claridge (eds), *Trees are Company: Social Science Research into Woodlands and the Natural Environment*, Edinburgh: Forestry Commission, pp. 15–21.

Inge, J., 2003, *A Christian Theology of Place*, Aldershot: Ashgate.

Ingold, T., 1993, 'The Temporality of the Landscape', *World Archaeology* 25, pp. 152–74.

Jones, O. and Cloke, P., 2002, *Tree Cultures: The Place of Trees and Trees in Their Place*, Oxford: Berg.

McGrath, A., 2001, *A Scientific Theology*, Vol. 1, *Nature*, London: T. & T. Clark.

MacNaghten, P. and Urry, J., 2000, 'Bodies in the Woods', *Body and Society* 6, pp. 166–82.

Maitland, S., 2008, *A Book of Silence*, London: Granta.

Mather, A.S., 2001, 'Forests of consumption: Postproductivism, Post-materialism and the Postindustrial Forest', *Environment and Planning C: Government and Policy* 19, pp. 249–68.

Milbourne, P., Kitchen, L. and Stanley K., 2006, 'Social Forestry: Exploring Social Contexts of Forests and Forestry in Rural Areas', in P. Cloke, T. Marsden and P. Mooney, *Handbook of Rural Studies*, London: Sage, pp. 230–42.

Millennium Ecosystem Assessment, 2005, *Ecosystems and Human Well-being: Synthesis*, Washington, DC: Island Press.

National Memorial Arboretum, 2010, www.thenma.org.uk/the-nma/about-the-nma/who-we-are.aspx

National Trust, 2010, www.nationaltrust.org.uk/main/w-whipsnade treecathedral

O'Brien, L., Foot, K. and Doick, K.K., 2007, 'Evaluating the benefits of community greenspace creation on brownfield land', *Quarterly Journal of Forestry* 101, pp. 145–51.

Philpot, J.H., 1987, *The Sacred Tree in Religion and Myth*, London: Macmillan and Co.

Ramshaw, G., 2002, *Treasures Old and New: Images in the Lectionary*, Minneapolis: Fortress Press.

Schama, S., 1995, *Landscape and Memory*, London: HarperCollins.

Scott, S., 2003, 'Woodland Burial Grounds: A case study', *Quarterly Journal of Forestry* 97, pp. 35–43.

Selman, P., 2003, 'Putting a Value on Woodland: Framework for the Future', *Quarterly Journal of Forestry* 97, pp. 193–8.

Tabbush, P.M., 2008, 'Maulden Faith Woodland: An investigation', Unpublished report to the Forestry Commission.

Tabbush, P.M. and O'Brien, L., 2003, *Health and Well-being: Trees, Woodlands and Natural Spaces*, Forestry Commission: Edinburgh.

Thoreau, H.D., 1854, *Walden*, Princeton: Princeton University Press.

The Earl of Lindsay, 1999, 'Opening address', in C. Stewart Roper and A. Park (eds), *The Living Forest: Non-Market Benefits of Forestry*, London, The Stationery Office, pp. 1–3.

Tsouvalis, J., 2000, *A Critical Geography of Britain's State Forests*, Oxford: Oxford University Press.

United Nations (1993), *Report of the United Nations Conference on Environment and Development, Rio de Janeiro, 3–14 June 1992. Volume 1: Resolutions Adopted by the Conference* New York: United Nations.

Walker-Jones, A., 2009, *The Green Psalter: Resources for an Ecological Spirituality*, Minneapolis: Fortress Press.

Walsh, B.J., Karsh, M.B. and Ansell, N., 1994, 'Trees, Forestry, and the Responsiveness of Creation', *Cross Currents*, 44, pp. 149–63.

Wainwright, A., 1971, *A Third Lakeland Sketchbook*, Kentmere: Marshall.

Warner, M., 1989, 'Signs of the Fifth Element', in J. Drew and R. Malbert (eds), *The Tree of Life: New Images of an Ancient Symbol*, London: The South Bank Centre, pp. 7–47.

Williams, K. and Harvey, D., 2001, 'Transcendent Experience in Forest Environments', *Journal of Environmental Psychology* 21, pp. 249–60.

Woodland Trust, 2010, www.woodlandtrust.org.uk/en/about-us/Pages/about-us.aspx

Worth, D., 2006, 'Our new cathedrals: Spirituality and old-growth forests in Western Australia', *Journal of Multidisciplinary International Studies* 3, pp. 1–15.

10

Spirituality and the countryside: a rural perspective on Christian formation and the Big Society

TIM GIBSON

The rural church can nurture a distinctive spirituality that is grounded in its worshipping life and encourages participation in the local community. The Christian narrative, embodied in the life of the church, provides a distinctive spirituality in which regard for others is held to be of central importance. This framework is given expression through worship, especially the Eucharist. Such a Christian-specific construal of rural spirituality has clear common ground with elements of the Coalition Government's hopes for a 'Big Society'.

When David Cameron talks about empowering local communities, and encouraging voluntarism and philanthropy, there is something missing. The problem is that Cameron and his fellow enthusiasts for the Big Society cannot give a reason *why* people should want to contribute more fully to the life of their community. Indeed, the idea that citizens might become more altruistic in their conduct, which lies at the heart of the Big Society rhetoric, ignores the fact of 'the subjective turn'. This is where people are more interested in themselves than in other people, which is supposedly a characteristic of our late-modern society (Heelas and Woodhead, 2005, p. 2). So the Coalition Government's notion of the Big Society is out of step with contemporary culture, which seems to be more about individualism and self-interest than other-regard and philanthropy.

The idea of the Big Society seems to lack a foundational narrative. Politicians cannot explain why people should be motivated to act in the ways they are being encouraged to, and their rhetoric is therefore rather unpersuasive. Part of the problem is that the Big Society does not have an anthropology; that is to say, a view about what is the essence of being human. Neither does it have an awareness of people's spirituality, which often lies at the heart of their relations with others.

Christian theology can fill the gap. It has a sustained anthropology, which views humans as created in the image of God who is the Trinity, and therefore humans are inherently relational beings. It understands that spirituality has both an individual and a corporate dimension. Individual, because one's spiritual life is sustained on a personal level through prayerful encounters with the risen Lord, and corporate, because the worshipping life of a Christian is communal. Christian spirituality provides a way of thinking about personal formation which shows that participation in community is at the heart of our call to be fully human. In other words, Christian spirituality offers a deeper narrative concerning community than the secular narrative of the Big Society. The church in the countryside and government have the potential to work together to build the sorts of vibrant communities of which the Big Society speaks.

If what is said about the rural church could just as easily be said about churches in other contexts – urban, suburban – it is by no means accidental. Although theology is inherently contextual, akin as Mike Higton reminds us to the performance of a piece of music where no two performances are ever the same (Higton, 2008, p. 47), it nonetheless consists in truths that apply universally. Just as the notes of a manuscript remain the same wherever the violinist stands to perform, so the essence of our faith is constant regardless of where we are called to live it.

The focus for this chapter, however, is rural. Statements about the interplay between church and society are therefore addressed principally to the church in the countryside and its concerns are central. This chapter outlines the concept of the Big Society and considers the contribution rural church members make to their local communities using the research by Coventry University published as *Faith in Rural Communities* (2006).

The Big Society explored

The political rhetoric

The idea of the Big Society now seems to be nothing new. David Cameron's Conservative Party spoke about it long before it formed a Coalition Government with the Liberal Democrats in May 2010. Cameron used the concept in his pitch to be leader of the Tories, in 2005, and has subsequently expanded it so that it might become the legacy of his period as Prime Minster (speech by David Cameron at the launch of the Big Society programme, 18 May 2010 (Cameron, 2010a)).

At the heart of the Big Society is the idea that government might be reduced in order that people will make a more active contribution to the lives of their local communities. Cameron speaks of the Government fostering 'a culture of philanthropy, voluntarism and social action' (speech by David Cameron in Liverpool, 19 July 2010 (Cameron, 2010b)). The Big Society will involve community members working with one another in order that their communities flourish. People will help one another out, rather than relying on the State for support and they will have the right to take over the running of services that have hitherto been run by public bodies. They will be empowered to save services that are under threat by undertaking to manage them themselves and they will be encouraged to volunteer, to contribute to society in ways that they have not done before because, so the rhetoric goes, 'we are all in it together' (Cameron, 2010b).

As a contributor to the *Daily Telegraph's* website noted, much of what Cameron and his colleagues talk about in relation to the Big Society is what used to be called 'community' (discussion on Toby Young's *Telegraph* Blog, 'The Big Society – Not Balls After All', 26 October 2010). Yet Cameron himself notes that such an idea is outmoded and out of touch with contemporary mores. The Prime Minister attributes this to the damage done to society by the growth in the State witnessed during the Labour Government of 1997–2010 (speech by David Cameron on 'The Big Society', 10 November 2009 (Cameron, 2009)). He says that rather than promoting social solidarity, as socialism claims to, the interventionism of the Blair and Brown years led to a cultural attitude of selfishness and individualism.

Whether Cameron's analysis is accurate or not is debateable but there is an inconsistency in his rhetoric: on the one hand he dreams of a society whose members are principally concerned with the good of one another, and the flourishing of society writ large, and on the other hand he sees that society is currently characterized by an attitude of self-interest and individualism. So how does he hope that the Big Society will ever take root in such shallow soil?

Red Toryism

The lack of a foundational narrative for the Big Society is regrettable because much of its content is sound. Few would argue that a society in which people look out for one another, help each other out and contribute to social organizations such as the Scouts and local committees is undesirable. Yet, as Robert Putman noted of America in his seminal *Bowling Alone* (2000), and which is certainly true of the UK as well, fewer people are motivated to act in these ways. Empirically, the level of support currently received by social institutions is low and participation in society is something that people do minimally – in so far as they have to in order to earn a living, or educate their families.

Such is the state of affairs in UK society identified by Phillip Blond in *Red Tory* (2010). Blond is widely credited as being David Cameron's 'Philosopher King' – the architect of the Conservative Party's commitment to the Big Society. In *Red Tory*, Blond states that Britain is 'broken' because people are motivated by individualistic concerns and have no sense of their orientation to a wider community of persons whose flourishing should be a proper concern. Blond is a theologian and philosopher by background, much influenced by Alasdair MacIntyre, and his understanding of the state of British society certainly echoes the memorable 'disquieting suggestion' MacIntyre

makes at the start of *After Virtue* (MacIntyre, 1985, pp. 1–5).
MacIntyre imagines a world of systemic fragmentation, where ideas
are disconnected from the narratives that give them meaning, and
where moral decision making is undertaken by individuals without
any wider reference point than their own concerns. In such a world,
community has little or no role – humans are taken to exist as if in a
vacuum and therefore to act without recourse to society in general.

In arguing that British society bears these hallmarks Blond ap-
portions equal blame to the two political parties that have held
power in the last 30 years. Margaret Thatcher's Conservatism was
certainly predicated upon individualistic assumptions. Thatcherism
created a culture in which self-interest, if not selfishness, was taken
to be essential to economic growth and social stability. Blairism,
because it was not so different from Thatcherism, might be said to
have augmented this culture.

Likewise the interventionism that many would say is characteristic of Gordon Brown's influence, first as Chancellor and then as
Prime Minister. By giving more and more power to the State, Blond
argues, the Labour Government disempowered people so that they
became accustomed to acceding to the centre rather than taking
responsibility for their own well-being and for the well-being of the
communities in which they lived (Blond, 2010, pp. 71ff.).

Whatever the aetiology of our current crisis, Blond's point is that
it needs fixing. He claims that a higher doctrine of community is the
answer through what he terms an 'associative society':

> The revival of an associative society . . . would bring with it a
> revival of those flourishing relationships that make up a society,
> and which both empower and protect the individual from the
> arbitrary sway of external power. For a free society demands an
> account of the common good that is cultivated organically from
> within rather than imposed arbitrarily from without, and it is this
> that trumps both the extreme individualism and the statist au-
> thoritarianism of liberalism. Once the common good is restored
> as the associative expression of commonly shared moral and so-
> cial belief, then the very first question to be asked is not 'how do
> I protect myself from everybody else?', nor 'how do I ensure my

own sensory happiness and cosy comfort?', but rather '*how do we look out for the needs of the other?*' (Blond, 2010, pp. 153–4, author's italics)

Blond does not discourse at much length about the precise philosophical basis of the 'associative society' of which he writes. We can assume from his discussion of it that it is broadly Aristotelian in character (Blond, 2010, pp. 160, 173), and this would certainly chime with his enthusiasm for MacIntyre's project. However, despite his background as a theologian and a few passing references to Christian and, specifically, Anglican and Catholic moral teaching (Blond, 2010, p. 141), he does not engage with the most obvious narrative of all in support of his own approach, which is the Christian narrative of human beings made in the image of a Trinitarian God whose very being is relational.

There is something of a lacuna in Blond's reflections concerning the narrative that undergirds his vision of an associative society. While it is self-evident that the Christian narrative is not the *only* one that could provide a basis for a society ordered around altruism rather than egoism, it is certainly the case that the Christian narrative provides *one* foundational narrative for such a view. It might thus be fairly said that those who have a political interest in the idea of an associative, or 'Big' society, would do well to consider the role of the Church in helping to build it.

Churchgoing and social activism

A call for optimism

Rural Christians have more grounds for optimism about the state of our society and the motivations of human beings than most. In rural areas especially, church people make a profound contribution to community life. Moreover, the 'broken' society of which Blond writes and Cameron claims he is trying to address might not seem to be so much in evidence in rural areas as it is elsewhere. There is certainly a perception that residents of rural areas enjoy stronger bonds of mutuality and reciprocity with their neighbours. As a 1999 Countryside

Agency report stated: 'The perceived strength of the community is one the most prized features of rural life – an asset that is largely seen to be lost in urban areas' (Countryside Agency, 1999, p. 24).

We might say that the pessimism of the view of society seen in *Red Tory* is coloured by an urban-centric view of the nation. Attempts to build community life in a rural context would hit the ground running because it is not necessary to persuade people of the good of social activism in the first place. Such a commitment is already enshrined in the local culture.

The Archbishops' Commission on Rural Areas (ACORA), which produced *Faith in the Countryside* (1990), encountered many vibrant rural communities (ACORA, 1990, p. 18). More recently, the Commission for Rural Communities' 2008 *State of the Countryside* report noted that many rural dwellers enjoy a better quality of life than their urban counterparts (Commission for Rural Communities, 2008, p. 17), and a key feature of this is stronger communal bonds between residents.

Even so, it is not sufficient to say that community participation will get off the ground in a rural context simply because there is a perceived commitment to such participation in these areas. *Faith in the Countryside* also identified the danger of romanticizing life in the countryside (ACORA, 1990, p. 3), and similar concerns have been expressed by Alan Smith in his recent *God-Shaped Mission* (Smith, 2008, p. 3). As successive *State of the Countryside* reports remind us, evidence of the breakdown of society can be witnessed as much in the countryside as it can in the city. Therefore, although the church in the countryside has reasons to feel optimistic about the opportunity to foster community in rural areas, such optimism needs to be tempered by a healthy dose of realism. There is work to be done if rural communities are really to flourish in the manner envisaged by Cameron and Blond – and the Church can be a key agent in helping to effect such flourishing.

Churchgoing and rural community

Churchgoers make a significant contribution to life in rural communities. *Faith in Rural Communities* (2006) showed that empirical support was provided for an intuition shared by many that: 'people who attend church regularly make a significant contribution to community vibrancy' (Farnell, Hopkinson, Jarvis, Martineau and Ricketts Hein, 2006, pp. 6–7). Based on their research, the report's authors agreed that rural churchgoers are more likely than non-churchgoers to undertake tasks such as caring for the elderly, visiting the sick and offering help with childcare; to participate in the activities of community organizations like Parent Teacher Associations, the Women's Institute and Age Concern; and to be involved in voluntary activities in the wider community – National Park committees, sports clubs and the like (Farnell *et al.*, 2006).

In short, *Faith in Rural Communities* revealed that there is significant engagement in community life among rural churchgoers. Participation in the worshipping life of the church, it seems, encourages people to participate in the wider life of their local community and become involved in activities that contribute to the well-being of their fellow residents. This insight is borne out in the researchers' findings concerning the motivations of the respondents for their commitment to community. *Faith in Rural Communities* reports that the people surveyed spoke of five broad types of motivation:

- Involvement in community life flows from life as a person of faith – regular prayer and worship gives rise to right living.
- Involvement in community life is a 'practical and visible out-working of faith'.
- Involvement in community life falls to churchgoers because no one else is willing to do it.
- It is the Church's role to 'make things happen' in the community, and the church's members must therefore play their part in this.
- A blending of the previous different types of motivation (Farnell *et al.*, 2006, pp. 44–5).

Each type of motivation speaks of the distinctive witness of the church and its members as agents of community vibrancy in rural areas. Churchgoers contribute to the life of their communities because they see it as something that flows naturally from their participation in the worshipping life of the church. Some cannot speak any more precisely about their reasons for acting other than to say that they are simply a part of what it means to be a Christian.

Robin Gill has conducted research into the impact of churchgoing on moral attitudes and found that it makes a difference to how people view the world. Thus, he states, 'Those who go regularly to church appear to be more honest and altruistic in their attitudes than other people' (Gill, 1999, p. 178). Such an assertion is supported by the findings of Farnell *et al.*, and we might use their research to make a further claim: that rural churchgoers in particular play an important role in building community in the areas where they live.

Some Christian commentators have expressed frustration that the contribution of church members to rural communities is not recognized by public bodies, as the church has too often been 'overlooked and undervalued' by the Government and other interested parties (Archbishops' Council, 2006, pp. 1, 8). It is my contention that, whether or not this has been the case historically, the current Government should take the opportunity to build a constructive relationship with the rural church since it is a key agent in building flourishing communities in the countryside and can thus help to realize the Big Society. What is more, as I shall now discuss, the church provides a deep narrative for the kind of community engagement envisaged by proponents of an associative society, that is a *reason* to engage in community life as well as prompting such engagement among its members.

Christian spirituality

Christianity and community

There is a clear communal dimension to Christian life. Discipleship consists in regular participation in corporate acts of worship as well as engagement in other practices – bring and buys, jumble sales, harvest suppers – that bring us into close contact with other people.

At the centre of this is the Eucharist, which gives best expression to the corporate character of discipleship and feeds a spirituality in which the good of the other is of central concern.

The Eucharist is what philosophers might term a 'theory-laden practice'. That means it is a practice through which participants come to discern a sense of what matters in the Christian tradition. The eucharistic liturgy contains the narrative of Christian faith – of a God who creates, a world that falls, a saviour who reconciles us to God, and a Spirit that sustains us while we await our full redemption at the promised end. Regular participation in the Eucharist is therefore a means of becoming oriented to the story that Christians tell about themselves and about their place in the world.

More than that, the Eucharist is a practice through which the body of Christ is formed. In sharing bread and wine Christians are reminded that they are brothers and sisters in Christ and that this means they are bound to one another, to love one another and live as friends with their fellow creatures. As Tim Gorringe observes when writing about the Eucharist as a formational practice for Christian disciples:

> The situation of being 'in Adam', which did not end in AD 35 or thereabouts, but describes an ongoing human situation, is that of relationships of dominion, hierarchy, division and the attempt to solve problems through law and violence. The situation of being 'in Christ' is that situation where there is 'no Jew or Greek, slave or free, male or female' – where, in other words, our status as friends under God is recognized. (Gorringe, 1997, pp. 30–1)

The Eucharist is a means by which the corporate dimension of Christian spirituality is nurtured, therefore. This is important because spirituality is a term often taken to denote individualism and the satisfying of one's own spiritual cravings (Heelas and Woodhead, 2005, p. 2). For the Christian, spiritual life is about more than inward contemplation which alone might very well result in a highly individualistic spirituality. In worship Christians focus their attention on God, who is entirely other, and they also come together with fellow disciples and are bound to them through liturgical acts that remind them of the communal character of the Christian life.

More than that, through its eucharistic life the church is formed as a community of mutuality and reciprocity. Because the climactic moment of the eucharistic act comes at the end, when congregants are sent out into the world to love it and serve it, the disciple's fundamental orientation is to the life of the communities in which they are called to live their faith (Radcliffe, 2008, p. 208; Gorringe, 1997, p. 67).

That such an insight is borne out by the research in *Faith in Rural Communities* and by Robin Gill in *Churchgoing and Christian Ethics* is surely no surprise. For we would expect that if participation in worship is the means by which Christians come to discern their place in the world as people of faith, then this will help them to form habits that are imbued with values that are important in the Christian tradition. Thus members of the worshipping community of the rural church would see their participation in the life of the communities of which they are a part as an expression of the distinctive spirituality that is nurtured through their participation in the church's practices.

The Eucharist and Christian spirituality

Great significance is attached to the Eucharist as a liturgical act, and by participation in it Christian disciples come, to quote Stanley Hauerwas and Sam Wells, 'to take the right things for granted' (Hauerwas and Wells, 2004, p. 25). In emphasizing the role of the Eucharist in forming disciples to have a particular orientation towards altruism, which is a key part of Christian spirituality, the significance of other acts of Christian worship or the wider practices of the Church in helping to sustain such an outlook are not denigrated. There is a clear sense in which the participant in a Book of Common Prayer Matins service is also oriented to the narrative of Christian faith, since the liturgy of such a service is structured around that same story of creation, fall, reconciliation and redemption. Similarly, Fresh Expressions can be profoundly formational for worshippers and help form the same dispositions of character mentioned earlier.

The church's eucharistic life is given expression in ways that transcend the celebration of the Eucharist as a liturgical act, that is, the church lives its Eucharist in these other activities. It also lives its Eucharist beyond worship, so that we might properly understand the exercise of hospitality by church members to the wider community as being eucharistic. We might discern that a church which opens its doors to local school children is being properly eucharistic, as is a church which sets aside an area of its churchyard so that local residents might come and spend time wondering at the beauty of creation.

At the heart of these activities is the regular celebration of the Eucharist that is central to the corporate life of the body of Christ. There is something about this particular act, given to us by Jesus (1 Corinthians 11.23–6), that is the essence of a life of faith. It is what prompts us to engage in all those other practices and it is what brings life to our other acts of worship. It is what animates us to work for the good of our local communities and it is what lies behind our desire to fling open the church doors and welcome all comers into our hospitable presence. Without the Eucharist lying at the heart of our community life these other activities would be found to be lacking.

The Eucharist: some recommendations

However, even though the rural church, through its eucharistic life, is fundamentally oriented to serve the wider community of which its members are a part, there is a problem. Regular celebration of the Eucharist is under threat in many rural locations where clergy are stretched over larger areas and where lay-led services are becoming more common. If the rural church's eucharistic life involves opening its doors to the wider community and engaging with the lives of non-churchgoers who live in them, there will be difficulties with the fact that many residents will not be able to participate in the Eucharist regularly due to a lack of priests to celebrate it, or because they have not been confirmed. In response to these concerns, two recommendations to church authorities are made:

1 That flexibility be granted in the use of Communion by extension.

2 That baptized congregants should be able to receive the eucharistic elements prior to confirmation, as part of the church's hospitality to the wider community.

Communion by extension

Extended Communion is the practice of using eucharistic elements that have been consecrated by a priest at a previous service perhaps in a different location. The service of extended Communion is then led by a licensed lay person or deacon. *Faith in the Countryside* recognized that for many churches extended Communion represents the only means of church members receiving Holy Communion frequently (ACORA, 1990, p. 190). The report urged the House of Bishops to review its discussion of the practice with a particular focus on rural areas where priests are in short supply. The Commission's urging led the House of Bishops to stipulate that extended Communion could be allowed with the permission of the diocesan bishop.

Many bishops have given such permission, but I believe that it would serve the rural church better if permission were not specific to each diocese. The Church of England should consider making Communion by extension possible in every diocese by removing decision making about the practice from the hands of diocesan bishops. This would consistently safeguard the eucharistic life of churches where there is no priest to celebrate regularly. In this way, the corporate life of the Church is sustained through a nationwide commitment to making eucharistic worship as frequent as possible.

Confirmation and the Eucharist

Many rural residents are baptized even though they do not attend church on a regular basis, but fewer have been confirmed. Similarly, many children are excluded from receiving the Eucharist because they are not yet confirmed, and many will not seek confirmation, sometimes because there are insufficient numbers in the community to join a class of preparation. Both sets of circumstances are problematic for a church that sees its eucharistic life as a commitment to fostering community in the local area. When there are community members who may be put off from attending church, and who are anyway prohibited from participating fully in its worshipping life by rules about who can and cannot receive the Eucharist, there seems to be an argument to change the rules.

The issue of who may or may not be admitted to Holy Communion has long been a concern of commentators on the rural church. It is by no means an uncontroversial issue in wider theological discussions. St Augustine, for example, wrestled with the idea that children should be confirmed before they could receive the elements, arguing that there can be 'no halfway house between the unbaptized and the communicant' (Howells and Littler, 2007, p. 14). As with Communion by extension, the Church of England's official position gives decision-making authority concerning baptized children and the Eucharist to diocesan bishops, while stating that baptized adults may only receive the elements if they have decided to seek confirmation (see the Church of England regulations concerning admittance to the Eucharist).

I recommend that the policy of rural churches, of whatever denomination, should be to admit baptized congregants of any age to the Eucharist on the basis that this will enable more members of the wider community to participate fully in the church's worshipping life, and will therefore help the rural church to build community in its local area. Such openness will also enable more people to be oriented to the Christian narrative that undergirds the Eucharist and should therefore further contribute to the vibrancy of rural communities. Baptism should remain a precondition of admittance to the Eucharist, in spite of the suggestion made by Gorringe that participation in the Eucharist might even come before baptism (Gorringe, 1997, p. 24). Without some orientation to the story that undergirds Holy Communion the participant will not be formed by the practice. Thus, when the House of Bishops of the Church of England states of the Eucharist that it 'unites creation and redemption, life and liturgy, porch and altar' (House of Bishops, 2001, p. 5), we learn something of the need to belong to the community which celebrates it in order to understand its story. Baptism is a sign of such belonging, a means by which we are oriented to the foundational narrative. With such orientation comes a right to participate fully in the Church's eucharistic life.

The Church, the Government, and the Big Society

The Church's role in the wider community

I have argued in this chapter that the Church's eucharistic life is given expression in the contributions made by church members to the life of their wider communities. I have expressed this idea by reference to a distinctive Christian spirituality, in which the personal dimension is held together with a corporate spirituality derived from the communal character of Christian worship, and eucharistic worship in particular. I have argued that churchgoing Christians can and do make a profound contribution to community vibrancy in rural areas and that the Church has the potential to play an important role in helping the Government to realize its ambitions for an associative society, predicated on voluntarism, philanthropy and social action.

It is important to be clear that saying that the Church can be an agent in the realization of the Big Society does not mean that its motivations are political. It is because its members are fundamentally oriented to contribute to the lives of their communities that it can help to build those that bear the hallmarks of which Cameron and his colleagues speak in relation to the Big Society. The Church would be making such a contribution to society even if it was not politically fashionable to do so – because that is its fundamental (eucharistic) orientation. Even if the political mood were to change, the Church's witness in rural areas, and the work of its members in building community, remains. However, if the rural Church is to make such a contribution to community vibrancy, it is important that its leaders are fully committed to the wider community of which their churches are a part. It will not do for priests and ministers to focus on the narrow concerns of the church community alone. They must be engaged in the wider life around them and be willing to open their churches to non-churchgoers and involve themselves in initiatives that build community, even if there is no clear benefit to the church in so doing. Indeed, they might need to be willing to put 'churchy' concerns to one side in order to focus their energies on the wider community and to prioritize these concerns as part of their role in helping the church to live its eucharistic life. They will certainly need to be willing to free the time of the members of their congregations in order to enable them to participate more fully in community life. For example, relieving them from the PCC in order that they can serve as a school governor, or reducing the demands of the cleaning rota so that people have more time to run errands for neighbours.

What matters is that people appointed to work in rural churches have a genuine commitment to participating in the life of the wider community, and openness to working with non-churchgoers. I recommend that such a commitment be made a standard item on job specifications for appointments in rural churches.

Conclusion

As has been noted, the Christian tradition has a deep narrative concerning the importance of community, and the church's members have a practical commitment to building vibrant communities, both of which help the Government to realize its hopes for a Big Society. The government should recognize the potential contribution made by the rural church to its communities and proactively seek opportunities for collaboration. Such a commitment should be enshrined in the Big Society policy framework, in order that the role of the rural church is formally recognized. Second, the Government's openness to working with rural churches should be supported by a financial commitment to support church projects that contribute to community vibrancy. The Government has undertaken to set up a Big Society Bank, using funds from dormant bank and building society accounts (Cabinet Office, 2010). It should consider ring-fencing some of these funds for projects involving rural churches.

If the Government is serious about realizing the kind of associative communities that lie at the heart of the Big Society rhetoric, the rural church will be a key partner in helping such a vision come true in the countryside.

References

Archbishops' Commission on Rural Areas, 1990, *Faith in the Countryside*, Worthing: Churchman Publishing.

Archbishops' Council, 2006, *Seeds in Holy Ground: A Future for the Rural Church?* A background briefing from the Mission and Public Affairs Council, London: Church House Publishing.

Blond, P., 2010, *Red Tory: How the Left and Right have Broken Britain and How we can fix it*, London: Faber & Faber.

Cameron, David, 2009, *Big Society Speech*, 10 November 2009, www.conservatives.com/News/Speeches/2009/11/David_Cameron_The_Big_Society.aspx

Cameron, David, 2010a, *Speeches at Launch of Big Society Programme*, 18 May 2010, www.number10.gov.uk/news/speeches-and-transcripts/2010/05/pm-and-deputy-pms-speeches-at-big-society-launch-50283

Cameron, David, 2010b, *Big Society Speech*, Liverpool, 19 July 2010, www.number10.gov.uk/news/speeches-and-transcripts/2010/07/big-society-speech-53572

Cabinet Office, 2010, *Building the Big Society*, London: Cabinet Office, www.cabinetoffice.gov.uk/media/407789/building-big-society.pdf

Church of England regulations concerning admittance to the Eucharist, www.cofe.anglican.org/lifeevents/baptismconfirm/sectionc.html

Commission for Rural Communities, 2008, *State of the Countryside*, Cheltenham: Commission for Rural Communities.

Countryside Agency, 1999, *Living in the Countryside: The Needs and Aspirations of Rural Populations*, London: Countryside Agency.

Farnell, R., Hopkinson, J., Jarvis, D., Martineau, J. and Ricketts Hein, J., 2006, *Faith in Rural Communities*, Stoneleigh: ACORA Publishing.

Gill, Robin, 1999, *Churchgoing and Christian Ethics*, Cambridge: Cambridge University Press.

Gorringe, T., 1997, *The Sign of Love: Reflections on the Eucharist*, London: SPCK.

Hauerwas, S. and Wells, S., 2004, *The Blackwell Companion to Christian Ethics*, Oxford: Blackwell.

Heelas, P. and Woodhead, L., 2005, *The Spiritual Revolution: Why Religion is Giving Way to Spirituality*, Oxford: Blackwell.

Higton, M., 2008, *Christian Doctrine*, London: SCM Press.

House of Bishops of the Church of England, 2001, *The Eucharist: Sacrament of Unity*, London: Church House Publishing.

Howells, A. and Littler, K., 2007, 'Children and Communion: Listening to Churchwardens in Rural and Urban Wales', *Rural Theology*, Vol. 5, Part 1.

MacIntyre, A., 1985, *After Virtue: A Study in Moral Theory*, London: Duckworth.

Putnam, R., 2000, *Bowling Alone*, New York: Simon & Schuster.

Radcliffe, T., 2008, *Why Go To Church?* London: Continuum.

Smith, A., 2008, *God-Shaped Mission*, Norwich: Canterbury Press.

Young, Toby, 'Blog on Big Society', *Daily Telegraph*, 26 October 2010, http://blogs.telegraph.co.uk/news/tobyyoung/100060971/the–big–society–%E2%80%93–not–balls–after–all/

11

The contribution of church tourism to the rural economy

JEREMY MARTINEAU

Tourism is the world's largest industry by category. It is estimated that over 1.36 million people in the UK work in tourism-related employment (Deloitte, 2010, p. 18). Spending by overseas visitors to England in 2010 was over £14.5 billion (Office for National Statistics, 2010, p. 20). Deloitte's forecast for 2010 was that the visitor economy would grow at an above average rate compared to other sectors, reaching perhaps 3.5% p.a. (Deloitte, 2010, p. 54).

The gathering of uniform data on tourism in an increasingly devolved group of four countries like the UK is becoming more difficult. Some data are gathered from the whole of the UK; others from member countries; yet others from individual regions. There is little coherent strategy in data collection even in bodies like Visit Britain, the Westminster Government's agency. A further difficulty is that the Government has shown little interest in identifying 'rural' as a distinct descriptor, so finding data relating to the rural economy apart from agricultural data is a challenge. A third difficulty is created by the absence of much data on church tourism, particularly any economic data. So the contribution of church tourism to the rural economy is almost impossible to measure quantitatively, but is nonetheless important. As many rural churches struggle for survival, the potential to further their mission to visitors as well as residents needs to be appreciated and considered by those who will decide their future. The future for many rural churches is to have a multi-functional role in their local community. Their contribution in relation to tourism can help with that.

This chapter will begin by examining the wider picture of tourism before looking more specifically at its role in the UK rural economy. It will then focus on the Church's contribution, first by defining some terms about visitors, tourists and pilgrims. Then, using data from a large research project of 2001, it will look at what visitors seem to want. Before concluding with some recommendations, it will look at some examples of what has been achieved in church tourism.

International travel, whether for business or pleasure, is today commonplace even in times of recession. The widely accepted definition of tourism is the temporary short-term movement of people to destinations outside places where they normally live and work, and their activities during their stay at these destinations.

It is a fact that, with increasing wealth and time to spare, people want to go and see other places, especially those that can be reached in a couple of hours. It is said that when the bicycle was invented, some clergy warned against the moral dangers offered with the opportunity for young men to visit strange places to meet girls without the oversight of parents. *Plus ça change*. For the purposes of this chapter, tourism includes international travel, package holidays, domestic holidays, day trips and visiting friends and relatives (VFR). The spending of money is like the oil of an engine: as the oil circulates, the whole machine is lubricated. The more people spend their money the more benefit is spread. Tourism is favoured in developing countries as a way of bringing the wealth of richer nations to the benefit of poorer ones. In the UK some rural areas have also become dependent on tourism as an employer and a bringer of wealth. It is beyond the scope of this chapter to discuss the ethical questions raised by tourism – the level of pay and the casual or seasonal nature of employment, the impact on local economies and the issue of ownership of rural tourism businesses.

Tourism and the rural economy

The rural economy, particularly in Scotland and Wales, is more dependent on tourism than the urban economy, with a greater proportion of people employed in this sector. England is little different:

35 of the top 50 English council areas that are heavily dependent on tourism are rural. They range from West Somerset's 26% to Ryedale's 11.6% of businesses being visitor-related (Deloitte, 2008, Fig. 5.3, p. 25). Such businesses will be the obvious ones of accommodation, food providers and attractions, but also include secondary businesses that service the primary providers. Then there are third-tier businesses including all shops, taxi firms, leisure centres, post offices and garages. For many of these the spending by visitors may form a significant proportion of annual income. Indeed, for some areas the tourism industry is all-pervasive, and if visitor numbers and spending are down, everyone feels the strain. Some of these third-tier businesses do not operate when the tourist season is closed. A local church whose theology is one of engagement with the whole life of the locality will therefore find it relatively straightforward to work in partnership with those whose livelihood depends on visitors.

In too many places there is unnecessary and damaging competition rather than co-operation between the various tourism-related businesses. A project developed by the Arthur Rank Centre, Hidden Britain, helps a community present a coherent welcome to would-be visitors. The church can be a catalyst to bring that about. This was the case in the first Hidden Britain location, the village of Dent on the Cumbria and Yorkshire border, which started in late 2001. The vicar saw Hidden Britain as a way of helping the community develop economically following the foot and mouth outbreak of 2001, and the church now houses an unstaffed visitor centre.

Such a collaborative approach is particularly appropriate to small rural communities who may need to cluster their tourism businesses to ensure there is enough critical mass to attract a visitor who might be planning a short break through the internet. There needs to be just enough choice of accommodation and places to eat, with activities, organized or informal, to help the internet surfer stop and decide to make that place their next destination. A core aim of Hidden Britain is to help the visitor enjoy a locality in depth and reduce the need to spend time driving around a larger area. Contact with the local culture is an important ingredient.

Local councils are also promoters of rural tourism, but their perspective is understandably distorted by the need to be neutral and so they are unlikely to promote one area or settlement over others as a destination. There is no one-size-fits-all structure for the promotion of tourism and there is much competition between the promotional bodies. One result is that attractions are often presented regionally or nationally in a thematic way, such as music, sports events or white-water rafting, horse-riding, etc., rather than as specific locations. The internet surfer still has to decide where to make a booking. This thematic approach does not help the individual rural community improve its visitor numbers and manage its own tourism.

Rural tourism suffers as a concept as there seems to be a shortage of agreed elements for analysis. Some studies include only farm-based or countryside activities, others include any tourism business that is located in a designated rural location. The definition of rural is a further cause of obfuscation. This chapter accepts the destination definition used by the annual UK Tourism Survey that invites visitors to indicate out of four categories whether they visited: the countryside or village, small town, the seaside, city or town.

Economic benefit

The favoured calculator of economic benefit from visitors is a sophisticated spreadsheet package designed by David James and called STEAM, the Scarborough Tourism Economic Activity Monitor (James, 2004). Most of the data used in this chapter derive from this method, which is good at showing trends but is not intended to support claims by any one business sector of its contribution to the economy. Caution should be used in how economic benefits are claimed. However, it is vital that reliable data is gathered on visitor numbers to churches for a different reason. The numbers give churches credibility to the tourism business community so that there will be a more positive approach to working in partnership with church tourism.

In 2007 Wales was host to under than one million overseas visitors, but in that year visitors from elsewhere in the UK numbered

8.9 million and they spent £1.4 billion or an average of £43.60 per night stayed (UK Tourism Statistics, 2009, p. 8). Spending per night in England (£52 per night) and Scotland (£60 per night) is significantly higher than in Wales (UK Tourism Statistics, 2009, p. 7). How do the Scots manage to persuade visitors to part with more money than do the Welsh? Day trippers in or to Wales account for 41% of all tourism spending there, and those from the UK who stay overnight spend a further 40%. So while international tourism is significant throughout the UK, our home market has the lion's share. This has implications for church tourism that will be discussed later.

That spending in Wales is lower than in England or Scotland may be accounted for by the fact that the enjoyment of the country-side invites those whose pleasure comes, not from spending lots of money, such as in business tourism, but from those healthy activities of walking, cycling, horse-riding and enjoying the beauty of creation. Wales has majored its tourism promotion on the enjoyment of the outdoors. There may be an issue for churches to consider how they fit with this theme of enjoying the natural environment.

Contribution from agriculture

It is important to inject a cautionary note here about the interdependence of rural tourism and agriculture. Agriculture is being asked to provide a complex of perhaps competing products – wholesome food, energy, space for waste disposal, landscape, leisure and adventure experience, a pleasant environment for visitors as well as safeguarding wildlife habitat for flora and fauna. Tensions between tourism and agricultural businesses persist. Agriculture and tourism need each other to sustain the rural economy.

The spend by visitors to UK countryside locations in 2008 totalled £3.5 billion. Within UK farming, 16% of farms that have diversified, with business activity additional to the farming, have developed a business in providing accommodation, sport and recreation opportunities for visitors. Farm tourist accommodation is worth £10 million to those farms (Defra 2010, Table 4, p. 7). According to Andy Woodward, CEO of Farm Stay UK (2009), a co-operative of farm accommodation providers, a good number of early members providing B&B have withdrawn but three times as many have joined as self-catering providers. This may indicate not only a change in what holiday makers want but also a change in willingness of the farm family to provide labour-intensive service.

How much is it worth?

Visiting friends and relations (VFR) is important for the UK as a whole: 43 million trips were made in the UK in 2008. The average length of stay is 2.9 nights, with an average spend of £100. Some 55 million UK holidays were taken by UK residents in 2008, staying an average of 3.7 nights, spending around £212. Of all overnight trips in 2008 made by UK residents, 24% were to rural locations, 19% to seaside and 24% to small towns (UK Tourism Statistics, 2009, p. 24). Of those who took a holiday of more than two nights, 22% went to the countryside and 33% to the seaside. For longer holidays of seven nights or more, 25% went to the countryside and 49% to the seaside (UK Tourism Statistics, 2009, p. 34).

The impact of these UK data on the wider economy is illustrated by data for Pembrokeshire. In that county over 14,000 full-time-equivalent (fte) jobs are in tourism and over £500 million was spent by 4.2 million visitors in 2008 who stayed an average of 3.3 nights. Of these 43% were from Wales (Pembrokeshire County Council, 2009).

Attractions

Day visitors are predictably mostly UK residents, although there may be some day trips by those from over the Channel or Irish Sea. In 2008 there were 870 million day trips, with spending totalling over £37 billion. Only 16% of such trips were to the countryside. Data does not reveal how many visits were made to rural churches, but of the total trips, 55% included a visit to a church, cathedral or abbey (UK Tourism Statistics, 2009, p. 44). Such visits were the most popular (29%) among over-65-year-olds. Nearly half of those making day trips decide within the week before, and a further 35% go on the spur of the moment, which possibly reflects how the

British respond to our uncertain weather (UK Tourism Statistics, 2009, p. 50). For nearly half, the attractive setting and somewhere good to eat are important factors, with novelty important for 34% and peace and quiet for 30%. Just over half of visitors did not consciously use any information garnered from elsewhere to plan their visit. They just went on instinct, and a further 23% were advised by friends and family only (UK Tourism Statistics, 2009, p. 53). This point re-emerges later.

Donovan D. Rypkema, of Heritage Strategies International in the USA, speaking at a National Trust conference in London in May 2009, encouraged Government to look to Norway for inspiration. Norway allocated 9% of its spending to get out of its economic depression on developing, maintaining and improving its heritage sector. France and Hong Kong also saw the role of heritage, including churches, as both an employer of skilled workers and as important to rebuild civic pride and reinvigorate local economies (Rypkema, 2009). In 1984 Max Hanna, of the English Tourism Council, conducted a most thorough research project with a questionnaire to every Church of England incumbent, and reported that in the recession of the late 1970s visitor numbers to churches increased by 1% while those to museums and secular heritage sites decreased by between 12% and 15% (Hanna, 1984, p. 21).

As churches begin to take the opportunities to engage with visitors, church councils need to understand the motivations and intentions of those they seek to attract. The novelty, peace and quiet, and positive welcome which churches can offer may be just what visitors are looking for.

Tourists, visitors and pilgrims

Human beings have always been on the move. The movements considered under the description of tourism are purposeful and focused, and generally assume a return home. Religious faith continues to be a significant motivator in human behaviour and most religions encourage a spiritually motivated journey as a regular or occasional activity. Even going to church can be seen as a focused and deliberate journey; going on retreat may be less frequent and over a greater distance.

Pilgrimage suggests a long journey to a place that is imbued with special holiness, although the journey itself may be a mix of spiritual and physical adventure. Chaucer's *Canterbury Tales* were of people on a pilgrimage, from Southwark to Canterbury, a journey then of a few days. For Christians, the Holy Land or Rome have been the favourite destinations for pilgrimage over many centuries. Shorter journeys, but still challenging and risky, were to many other special places, such as St David's in Pembrokeshire or Santiago de Compostela in Spain. The latter is currently being heavily promoted by the Spanish Tourist Board. Other faiths also encourage or even require pilgrimage as a spiritual discipline, particularly the Islamic Hajj to Mecca. Even non-religious organizations tend to use the concept of pilgrimage to their special places, such as the tomb of Lenin, or a particular football stadium.

It is believed that tourists were first so named by Thomas Cook, who arranged day trips for citizens of Leicester in the nineteenth century. The *Shorter Oxford English Dictionary* (1973) has 1800 as the date when the word 'tourism' was first used. John Byng in his *Rides Round Britain*, which he made between 1782 and 1793, is plainly describing his adventures as those of a tourist (Byng, 1996). Tourists may come by the coach load, on tours that confuse the participant so that it is difficult for some of them to know what day it is and where they are. Bewilderment can be seen on their faces as they pile off the coach into yet another new place to be consumed. Tourism is now the world's single largest business activity, encompassing such a wide range of activities, not all of them wholesome, that there is a move in some sectors to promote a more friendly, hospitable word. Those associated with church tourism have for some time preferred to speak about 'visitors'. They come in smaller doses and may be made more welcome!

Whether they be pilgrims, tourists or visitors, will they find the church locked, or open, welcoming and well presented? People may carry images in their head about the behaviour and responsiveness of the different categories of those who come. Do tourists set out to capture a place on camera? Do visitors spend longer and are they more thoughtful, while pilgrims seek a place to pray? Many church tourism discussions have focused on how to turn tourists into pilgrims, clearly revealing that pilgrims are assumed to be more likely to be responsive to a Christian message than tourists. Are those on holiday visitors, pilgrims or tourists? They may be staying for a week and take the opportunity to join the congregation for worship. As few of our rural churches have the benefit of anyone on welcoming duty other than at times of worship, it is clear that church buildings have to be helped to speak for themselves of the faith which they enshrine and reveal.

Pilgrims may be described as people wanting a heightened spiritual experience, both by the making of the journey and by the arrival at a special or sacred place. For some the motive may be an atonement for sin, with the effort of the journey being the price to pay. It used to be said that two pilgrimages to St David's were worth one to Rome. Those with responsibility for churches need to be alert to a mix of spiritual rewards that may be sought by visitors as well as pilgrims.

The work of the St David's diocesan tourism group has shown that the significant draw of the Cathedral in the far corner of Pembrokeshire even has an impact on neighbouring counties. New pilgrimage trails and other important churches and places on these routes have developed their relationship with tourists. One is St Dogmael's, where the coach house of the former rectory has been leased at a peppercorn rent to a new trust which has opened a visitor centre adjacent to the parish church and the ruined Abbey. It employs 13 people. Visitor numbers were 35,000 in the first year (2008) and estimated to be 50,000 in 2009. Local businesses report that they are feeling the benefit of this venture, which is now expanding to include important churches to the south, especially St Brynach's at Nevern with its Ogham stones.

Tourists to pilgrims

Just east of Snowdonia and about 15 miles from Bala is a remote and ancient church and shrine in Pennant Melangell (www.st-melangell.org.uk). Michael Keulemans (2004) studied this sacred place and the visitors to it, wanting to find out if tourists can become pilgrims by the experience they have. The guardian to the shrine estimates 15,000 visitors a year. Keulemans observed that most visitors spent 20–60 minutes in this tiny church, even on fine days. Some 107 completed a questionnaire that was available for several weeks in the spring of 2004. He found that 37% of those visitors who used his questionnaire attended church once a year or less. More than three out of four visitors said a private prayer, 60% lit a candle and 57% meditated. He calculated that among non-churchgoers 34% expressed a heightened interest in the Christian faith and 32% an increased interest in the church. The mission potential of an open and well presented church is clear.

Not all places of worship can weave the wonder that this church plainly achieves. It is clear that there is much to be done by churches that focus primarily on their resident population to widen their appeal to those who come from near and far. Andrew Duff suggests that:

> While fewer people attend church services regularly today, more are visiting churches outside formal service times. This reflects, in part, a growing interest in cultural heritage and in family history, but also a more individualistic approach to spirituality. (Duff, 2009)

Revenue generated by visitors to faith buildings

One region has estimated the total value of faith-based tourism at nearly £150 million, of which £10 million is income direct to the faith buildings visited (Yorkshire and Humber Faiths Forum, 2009, p. 35). This includes York Minster, so it is not possible to determine from this the benefit to the rural economy alone.

The Historic Houses Association claims to generate £1.6 billion to the wider economy. Church tourism contributes possibly four times as much as historic houses because there are many times more churches than historic houses, even allowing for an overstated claim of benefit (Cooper, 2004, pp. 55–6). The presence of so many religious buildings may help account for the data from Visit Britain's report from the International Passenger Survey of September 2010, that of the 29.9 million overseas visitors in

2009, 6.4 million visited a religious building; more than castles and historic houses (Visit Britain, 2010, p. 6). The North West Multi Faith Tourism Project claims that the 697,114 faith visitors in that region contribute £8.4 million per annum to the regional economy (North West Regional Development Agency, 2005, pp. 23–4).

There is little data collected by church authorities on the financial benefits directly accruing to the churches visited. Hanna estimated £2 million income to churches in England in 1982. In that year 48% of income reported from 56 churches was in sales of books and souvenirs 44% from donations and 8% from catering and fees for brass rubbing (Hanna, 1984, p. 24).

In 2008 the Church in Wales surveyed 584 churches and reported an average income from visitors of £400 per church (Glanville, 2009). The most visited place of worship in Wales is St David's Cathedral, which receives over 250,000 visitors contributing just over £200,000 in net income to the Cathedral alone. This is the fourth most visited free attraction in Wales. In contrast, the church in Fishguard dedicated to St Mary receives about £100 a month in visitor donations. The Church of St Pancras at Widecombe in the Moor is promoted by the Dartmoor National Park as the 'Cathedral of the Moor'. No visitor numbers are recorded either by the Park, the National Trust or the church authorities. What is known is the financial benefit to the church itself. In 2009 just over £13,000 was left in donations and a further £4,000 was profit from the sale of books and cards. The four local businesses, pub, shops and café employ over 50 people. The loss or closure of the church (which is not under consideration) would seriously damage the local economy. The church council is clear that, without visitor income, they could not maintain the building or meet their ministry share.

How do the secular tourism authorities view church tourism?

Churches are like the countryside. They are part of the background, the photograph that tells the viewer that this is a village or rural scene. A report by Deloitte, *The Economic Contribution of the Visitor Economy* (2010), does acknowledge historic churches under the heading 'arts and culture' as part of the UK's offer to visitors, but the visual images in the report do not include a place of worship. The recent report from the Rural Cultural Forum makes no reference to churches or other faith buildings (Rural Cultural Forum, 2010). Because churches seem to be taken for granted their contribution has not been fully analysed in respect of how visitors might enjoy them. Even one of the basic textbooks on rural tourism in 1981 failed to mention churches, managing only to refer to stained-glass workshops (Robert and Hall, 1981). There is much work to be done to raise the profile of churches in the consciousness of tourism bodies, and prove that there is something special and of quality that can be provided.

A short questionnaire was sent in 2009 to every Tourist Information Centre and Local Authority in Wales, 63 in all, asking a number of questions about: how they saw the significance of church tourism; its contribution to the local economy; whether an open church provided a link into and information about the local community; whether it provided a good venue for arts and music for visitors to enjoy; and whether churches should be eligible for grant aid to support this work.

Of the 38 respondents:

- 36 agreed that it was important that churches were open for visitors
- 25 saw them as making an important contribution to the local economy
- 30 agreed that they offered visitors an understanding of the local community
- 32 that they offered a point of contact with the local community
- 31 that they offered a point of contact with local culture and history
- 34 that they provided a good venue for the arts and music
- 28 saw them offering information about what's on in the community

- 27 agreed that they should be eligible for grant aid for their contribution to the economy
- only half had any experience of working with churches in the promotion of tourism.

Respondents were invited to add their own comments on any aspect of church tourism. There was general regret at the resistance that some churches reveal at being open for visitors. Also respondents identified that there was a reluctance to share information about special events that could interest visitors, such as displays and concerts, and acknowledgement that some churches had no interest in being connected into their local community. There was recognition of the paucity of volunteers.

On the positive side there was a desire to see training for those volunteers in how to deal with visitors; a recognition that burial grounds are an untapped resource, particularly of interest to those exploring family history; and there was a general willingness to liaise with churches that wish to take a proper part in being an attraction to visitors. There was recognition that church visiting was a secondary rather than a primary activity. This shows that there is strong encouragement for churches to form partnerships with other tourism businesses and promoters. Duff recommended to destination managers that:

> Church tourism can also help to spread visitor activity beyond the obvious 'honeypot' attractions, and there is potential for churches and their stories to play a part in the strengthening of secondary visitor destinations, building upon aspects of history, community and sense of place. (Duff, 2009)

Most local authorities in Wales now have programmes of support or greater involvement with faith groups in the promotion of tourism. This is a significant improvement from Max Hanna's report in 1984, where he found that of 2,626 open Anglican churches in England only 11% had any contact with a Tourist Information Centre. Although it may be true that many day visitors to the countryside take advice only from friends and family on where to go, those on longer trips and overseas visitors do use Tourist Information Centres (TICs) as important points for information and advice. Churches would be well advised to alert their TIC, even if it is in a nearby town, when the church is open and what visitors can expect to see or experience in the case of special events. TIC staff may be amenable to being inducted by way of a tour of open churches in the area in the quieter months, so that they are better informed.

West Lindsey District Council in Lincolnshire has a long history of co-operation with the Diocese of Lincoln. There has been an annual Churches Festival for over ten years. The participating churches now pay £25 each to be part of this programme. This has led to an increase in participating churches to 86 in 2010. The data in Table 11.1 are drawn from the last three years of the festival for which data is available. The festival runs over two weekends in May.

A majority of visitors were female and most visitors come from within the West Lindsey district. Most heard about the festival from friends rather than through the promotion through the TICs, presumably because it was already well-known and promoted in the area. It does not therefore seem to have succeeded in generating significant spending into the area by visitors coming from elsewhere.

Ceredigion County Council in Wales has identified faith tourism as one of six strands that it is working on as part of the special attractions of the area. It is one of the coastal counties facing the Irish Sea and is nearly all small rural communities, with only three places having a population larger than 2,000. It has an uphill task as of the 41 Anglican churches responding to a short diocesan questionnaire in 2009, only 11 claimed to be open during daytime. The most

	Churches	Visitors	Via TIC	£ raised
2007	89	6,529	16%	9,300
2008	84	6,172	11%	11,570
2009	82	8,200	24%	14,695

Table 11.1: West Lindsey Festival.

active participants have been a cluster of Unitarian chapels who are able to celebrate the 'birth of democracy' by virtue of their close ties with the founders of the Constitution of the United States of America.

An example of quick thinking and an ability to think creatively comes from Leicestershire, where the Rural Partnership of Leicester County Council offered a grant to the Diocese of Leicester if they could spend the £5,000 within a few months. The diocesan tourism group employed a researcher to identify ten popular tourism attractions in the county with a church nearby, so that visitors could also visit the church. www.treasuresunlocked.co.uk has been well received and is linked to the county tourism website.

Attitudes and expectations of visitors

One priest has stated that he doesn't visit churches when on holiday, not because he was not interested or wanted a break from them, but because he did not expect them to be open. This is a very big problem indeed. Visitors want to get in, but are unable to with the door locked in their face. The Ecclesiastical Insurance Company verbally encourages churches to remain open during daytime.

For the church to be open is as much a theological as a spiritual or economic statement. God has welcomed us with open arms of love and grace. Our response will include being open-hearted to strangers; our open churches express that love which is appreciated by those who come through the doors. If a church is locked it gives a message of rejection, of absence and alienation that is counter to the core message of the gospel.

The vicar of one church in rural Cheshire studied the link between the number of signatures in the visitors' book and the number of prayer requests. He calculated that 14% of visitors left prayer requests. The ratio of visitors who sign the visitors' book is generally calculated at 10% of those who come through the door. People who live locally may still sign the visitors' book, seeing themselves as visitors. Over 70% of those signing that church's visitors' book recorded their appreciation of the tranquillity of the place. This is no surprise and reflects the data from the UK Tourism Statistics that peace and quiet is a motivation for 30% of all day visitors to rural areas (Brown, 2004).

The potential for faith tourism is discussed in a paper from tourism consultants on behalf of North West Faith Tourism (Connor & Co, 2003, pp. 31–2). They identified distinctive groups to whom open churches might appeal:

- regular church attenders
- faith professionals from the UK and overseas
- attendees from the UK and overseas at faith conferences
- educational visits
- community and church groups within the UK
- cultural tourists
- pilgrims and genealogists from the UK and overseas
- rural explorers – note the steady increase in walking and cycling
- stressed souls.

The report recognized that faith tourism is but a part of a visitor experience, and not the primary motive for making a visit to an area.

Ten years ago the National Churches Tourism Group (now the Churches Tourism Association) carried out a survey with the help of 164 member churches. Visitors to these churches completed a questionnaire on their origin, distance travelled, church allegiance, method of travel, size of party, reason for visiting, expectation and experience of their visit to the church. *Rural Visitors* (Francis and Martineau, 2001) sets out the findings from over 12,000 respondents. The most of important of these are:

- even local people may think of themselves as visitors if they are not members of the congregation
- nearly 70% wanted to use the church as a place of prayer even though only 56% were regular church attenders
- nearly three out of four would like to have a free guide-sheet while 54% expected to be able to buy one
- 44% would like to find information about what else to do in the area
- 40% wanted to learn about local events.

These last two show something of the potential for the church to be a signpost to the rest of the community. A church which recognizes its mission to be involved in the life of the secular community will welcome opportunities to demonstrate the incarnational nature of the Christian gospel. Links to other places of interest are likely to be replicated and appreciated. Such links can pave the way for other opportunities to share in building the strength of the community.

Regional projects

When General Synod passed a Private Member's motion in July 2008 encouraging dioceses to, among other relevant activities, form a churches tourism group, it also asked the Archbishops' Council to report before July 2010. That report to Synod contains this cry from Canon John Brown, chair of the Churches Tourism Association: 'I find it astonishing that some diocesan bishops and other clergy and laity fail to appreciate the fundamental part played by church buildings in the Church's mission' (Archbishops' Council, 2010, p. 5).

The failure that is referred to is not reversed by the detail in the report to Synod, with most dioceses being able to provide only an hour or two a week to tourism in someone's already over-committed working time. In contrast, the Diocese of Oxford is commended for its bold approach in committing £30,000 a year for three years in contracting with a commercial tourism company with the expectation that the income generated will provide for a continuing programme of work (Archbishops' Council, 2010). Other less well-resourced dioceses might consider sharing to achieve a similar approach. The lesson of the benefits from partnership working has yet to be learned across the churches.

There are a growing number of good-quality church-based tourism projects, often involving the wider community. A church in Somerset has created a set of leaflets on local walks. There are many examples of church trails, a notable one being Saints and Stones in Pembrokeshire (www.saintsandstones.co.uk). This project has created a network of 52 churches on the pilgrimage routes to St David's. The trails are well signposted through the brown tourist signage provided by the local authority.

Rotherham and South Yorkshire

Heritage Inspired has to date generated over £800,000 into the economy of South Yorkshire by presenting a large number of faith buildings to the visiting public (Heritage Inspired, 2009). This project has been successful for two main reasons: the commitment, continuity and competence of the core staff, and the flow of funding which has sustained the project over several years. Too often short-term funding does not allow sufficient momentum to be built up to ensure long-term sustainability. The original vision to employ a development officer in 1998 to present the three churches in Rotherham to visitors has led to Lottery funding from 2007, both to continue that work and to develop the range of cultural and artistic events across the region (www.heritageinspired. org.uk). It has been so successful that the Heritage Lottery Fund has invited the project to extend its know-how over other parts of Yorkshire.

Go West

There are 50 ancient churches along the 74 miles of the River Teme. The Teme Valley Heritage Quest (www.temevalley.org.uk) in Worcestershire and Herefordshire has developed an imaginative approach by using a professional storyteller to open up history to children through a 'Seeing Stone'. These listening posts have been set up in six village churches. There has been no estimate of the economic benefit, but estimates of visitor numbers would suggest that the financial payback to the area has been considerable.

The Open Church Network – Wrexham

This project has involved 16 churches in the rural parts of Wrexham County Borough in North East Wales. The churches have been enhanced by improved facilities and attractions funded by Leader+ and other European funds. External signage and internal displays have helped with visibility to visitors. Visitor numbers have increased over the four years of the project from 13,000 to over 30,000 a year, generating over £1.6 million of income to the rural economy (Open Church Network, 2009). This project was a real partnership between willing church volunteers, the project officers and funders. The churches in these villages are now seen as a real asset by the local authority, both to the local economy and to local civic pride (www.openchurchnetwork.co.uk).

Examining the experience of these short case studies a set of principles can be discerned:

- be ambitious, and draw in other churches and other bodies to enable work in partnership so that external funds might be available
- work in partnership so that the message of the church can be heard outside the church's walls
- successful projects are probably best built on the skills of lay people
- ensure that a count of visitor numbers is taken to be able to argue the case for the importance of church tourism.

Eileen McLean, Vicar of Bamburgh, visited 100 churches all over England and reflected in her sabbatical report (McLean, 2006), on many aspects of what churches are doing well or badly. She commented that only 13 of the 100 had any statement on what Christians believe today. Some 25 had:

> erected notices beside key artefacts to explain more fully the use of fonts, altars . . . and the meaning of Baptism, Communion . . . Some of these are done beautifully, perhaps with illustrations of biblical parallels and photos of contemporary practice . . . but so few seem to have asked themselves that question 'who is this for and what can they be expected to know?'

How can the benefits of church tourism be spread widely to more churches? The opportunities to help the church building itself speak about faith lie in the hands of those who so easily take the building for granted or even resent the work involved in maintaining it. The very furniture and layout as well as its fine features can speak movingly of God, who is the inspiration for artists, craftsmen as well as musicians, flower arrangers and churchwardens.

The Anglican Church in one town is a member of the local Chamber of Trade and Tourism. The congregation was asked to send out to friends and relations the new leaflet promoting the area. It was the most successful member in distributing that leaflet. Word of mouth is one of the best ways of sharing information, and church congregations are a hidden resource. Church networks offer a great opportunity to share information about each other's places. Alliances can be formed with accommodation providers so that churches and guest houses, for example, know about and promote each other.

Conclusions

The age profile of visitors to churches reflects that of church attenders. Churches would do well to explore how their buildings can engage more closely with the current interest in spirituality which is less connected with traditional religion.

Churches are playing a growing and important part in the rural economy by improving its engagement with visitors and developing this in imaginative ways for a society that is losing contact with Christian tradition. There is need for a greater sharing of experience in how to share the Christian faith with visitors.

It is vital for the purposes of building the church's contribution to gather data on visitor numbers and to work more closely with TICs and other tourism promotional organizations. Secular tourism organizations welcome the involvement of churches as adding value and attraction to an area. While support and encouragement from clergy is important, this work is usually better led by lay people using the many skills that often lie dormant in congregations.

References

Archbishops' Council, 2010, *A Report Back on Progress since the Passing of the Private Members Motion on Church Tourism at the July 2008 Synod in York*, GS Misc. 954, London: Archbishops' Council.

Brown, A., 2004, 'Visit and pray: the experience of visitors to Great Budworth Church, Cheshire', MA assignment for the Centre for Studies in Rural Ministry, unpublished.

Byng, J. (ed. J. Adamson), 1996 edition, *Rides Round Britain*, London: Folio Society.

Connor & Co., 2003, 'North West Faith Tourism Scoping Study, Final Report', unpublished.

Cooper, T., 2004, *How Do We Keep Our Parish Churches?* London: The Ecclesiological Society.

Deloitte, 2008, *The Economic Case for the Visitor Economy: Final Report*, London: Deloitte.

Deloitte, 2001, *The Economic Contribution of the Visitor Economy*, London: Deloitte.

Defra, 2010, *Farm Diversification in England: Results from the Farm Business Survey 2008–9*, London: Defra.

Duff, A., 2009, 'Unlocking the Potential of Church Tourism', *Tourism Insights*.

Francis, L. and Martineau, J., 2001, *Rural Visitors*, ACORA: Stoneleigh Park.

Glanville, A., 2009, 'Report on Church Tourism to the Church in Wales Bench of Bishops'.

Hanna, M., 1984, *English Churches and Visitors*, London: English Tourism Council.

Heritage Inspired, 2009, 'Report to Heritage Lottery Fund', unpublished.

James, D., 2004, 'Scarborough Tourism Economic Activity Monitor', unpublished.

Keulemans, M., 2004, 'Pennant Melangell: A Case Study in Sacred Place and Pilgrimage', unpublished MA assignment.

McLean, E., 2006, *Churches and Visitors*, www.churchestourism.info

North West Regional Development Agency, 2005, *Faith in England's North West: Economic Impact Assessment*, Warrington: North West Regional Development Agency.

Office for National Statistics, 2010, *Quarterly Travel and Tourism: Quarter 4, 2010*, London: Office for National Statistics.

Office for National Statistics, 1999, *UK Balance of Payments 1998*, London: Office for National Statistics.

Open Church Network, 2009, 'Presentation to Church Tourism Network for Wales', CTNW, unpublished.

Pembrokeshire County Council, 2009, *STEAM Report 2009*, Haverfordwest: Pembrokeshire County Council.

Robert, L. and Hall, D., 1981, *Rural Tourism and Recreation*, Wallingford: CABI.

Rural Cultural Forum, 2010, *Creative Rural Communities: Proposal for a Rural Cultural Strategy*, www.ruralculture.org.uk/

Rypkema, D.D., 2009, *The Role of Heritage Conservation in a Sustainable Economy*, London: National Trust Conference.

Shorter Oxford English Dictionary, 1973, Oxford: Clarendon Press.

UK Tourism Statistics, 2009, *The UK Tourist 2009*, London: Visit England.

Woodward, A., 2009, *Today's Opportunities in Farm Tourism*, Stoneleigh Park: Farm Stay UK.

Visit Britain, 2010, *Foresight*, Issue 83, September 2010, London: Visit Britain.

Visit England, 2011, *Inbound Tourism to England Factsheet*, London: Visit England, www.visitengland.org/Images/Inbound%20Factsheet%202 02010%20-%2013.05.11_Layout%201_tcm30-26357.pdf

Yorkshire and Humber Faiths Forum, 2009, *Economic Impact Assessment of Faith Communities in Yorkshire and the Humber*, Yorkshire and Humber Faiths Forum, www.yorkshirefutures.com/articles/economic-impact-assessment-faith-communities-yorkshire-and-humber

12

Marks of mission: the spread of the gospel through the occasional offices in a small rural village

ANNE RICHARDS

This chapter uses three particular case studies of a baptism, a wedding and a funeral which took place in the same small rural community to illustrate how the five marks of mission can be served by the provision of the occasional offices. It will be argued that mission theology and mission studies often overlook the dynamics of such events, and miss small details of human interaction which in fact have important effects and wide consequences which are also mission opportunities. Mission is often understood strategically and in terms of guided processes such as church planting or basic Christian courses such as Alpha. There are also good resources for engaging with people outside the Church and for event-based evangelism. However, certain sorts of mission potentials are particularly, even uniquely, strong in rural areas and these can be overlooked and even ignored because of the small numbers involved. It will further be argued that it is the small village community which often best illustrates such mission outcomes and benefits, but which is paid scant attention by the Church at large. The reasons for this refusal to take the missional impact of rural churches seriously will be examined.

In addition to analysis of the social interactions and beneficial effects of the occasional offices, it will also be necessary to discuss how changes to the structure of village life and loss of facilities to the community in recent years affect its mission impact and its faith-supported structure. It will also be shown how the report *Faith in the Countryside* raised questions about mission in rural areas which are illustrated and answered by an interrogation of rural Christian faith and life.

The village – setting the scene

Sotton (names and identities have been changed throughout) is today a small village of approximately 300 people living in just under 100 houses in a deeply rural area. The village has a medieval foundation and some of the local families can trace their roots back to Tudor times.

A small, narrow and winding road passes through the village and exits over a single-track bridge over a river. The unlit road on the way in has many hidden corners and is famous for vehicles ending up in the adjoining fields on dark nights. It is also supposed to be haunted. After any period of heavy rain the bridge floods and the road becomes impassable, although animals and tractors can ford it. The village road connects to two larger rural roads linking other villages and market towns. In one direction a main route connects eventually to a motorway, in the other to a university town. Sotton is not on a main route to anywhere, which means that the only traffic using the road are locals going in or out. In that sense, the road around the village itself is considered very safe and 'strangers' are unusual. That said, it was for a while a useful dumping ground for stolen objects discarded by thieves, such as empty wallets or handbags, which were often retrieved by Mickey (see below) and handed to the local police.

Sotton has a small Anglican church of ancient medieval foundation, a village hall and a pub, but no shops, health-care facilities, schools or public transport. In that sense it is very isolated. Its main connection to the outside world is through the team ministry of which it is a part, through the schools in neighbouring towns and villages to which its children travel and to the university town which is the major source of shops and employment. There are two small farms adjoining the village.

The village has always had some exceptionally wealthy people living in it, who own a series of secluded, large houses, some thatched and some set back very far from the road and difficult to find. It also has some much poorer villagers who live in a small lane of social housing on the outskirts. There are a few families with children but many of the villagers are elderly, having retired to Sotton.

The village has an interesting social structure with two or three principal families 'ruling' Sotton's affairs and vying for attention, some academics who work in the university town, some professionals who undertake the long commute to London and are mainly around at weekends, and other local working people who have teaching or hospital jobs in the outlying small towns. There is also a set of local families who have lived in the village for generations and who work locally, principally in a small machinery workshop or on the farms.

Sotton is part of a team ministry with 12 rural churches served by four clergy, spread over a large geographical area. Other churches in the team are also small village churches, though the team rector's principal church is the largest and the most well attended. Services take place in most churches each Sunday, although three of the churches provide a gathered congregation which rotates around their buildings. If there is a fifth Sunday in the month there is a team service. The vicar of Sotton lives outside the village and is also responsible for other churches in the team. This generates a familiar rural problem for the parish priest, who is supposed to know everything that is going on in the village by telepathy. The numbers in church at the main family service on a Sunday in Sotton vary from three to 20 people. Another group come to Evensong. The church is packed out at Christmas and Harvest by people who go 'regularly' – once a year.

On the face of it, Sotton does not look much like a bustling hive of mission activity. It is too isolated, too insular, too small and ill-equipped to put energy into events, outreach, or faith-sharing exercises. Yet for all that the village makes converts, builds up faith, sustains worship and faith continuity and engages in mission in unusual and perhaps surprising ways. Its spiritual activity is not at all detectable by the usual tools of mission audit. From the outside, using the kinds of measuring devices the Church of England uses to gauge success, it probably appears to be gently mouldering away. Yet it can be argued that seen from the inside, with an eye for mission, the village is responding to the empowering work of the Holy Spirit in an unusual and creative fashion.

In order to demonstrate this, three specific instances of the occasional offices which have taken place in the village will be examined, reading these events against the five marks of mission to show that Sotton, despite its small eclectic congregation and community, builds up Christian life in remarkable ways.

What are the marks of mission?

The five marks of mission, developed by the Anglican Consultative Council[1] and widely adopted now by churches, demonstrate how complex and varied the concept of mission is. The five marks are not a programme or template for how mission works, but facets of a mission enterprise which involves the whole Church and which both interpenetrate and complement each other. As generally accepted by the Church of England, these 'marks' are:

- To proclaim the Good News of the Kingdom.
- To teach, baptize and nurture new believers.
- To respond to human need by loving service.
- To seek to transform the unjust structures of society.
- To strive to safeguard the integrity of creation and sustain and renew the life of the earth.

Many of these marks have been demonstrated in church life by large events and movements, programmes and processes. These are worthy causes and make substantial contributions to the Church's life and profile. However, this has sometimes led people to believe that small villages in isolated rural areas are somehow cut off from frontline evangelism and have little to contribute to the wider mission of the Church other than the struggle for survival. However, in Sotton, despite a tiny congregation and a constant concern about the fabric of the building, the lives of Christians through the particular environment nurtured by the village's life has had the capacity to build, grow and sustain Christian community. This has been done in ways which not only enhance the impetus of the five marks of mission but which do so in unplanned, even unconscious ways, which also create kingdom values and loving community. Part of the problem is that the five marks make no overt mention of *worship*, so that sometimes there seems to be an unintended demarcation between the worship of God in church and the sharing and living the gospel that goes on outside it. In the stories which follow it is evident in each that although the occasional offices can sometimes end up below the radar of missional impact, such events and the worship they embody fuels and drives the witness of Christians out into the community in ways which enrich and nurture the lives of others.

Baptizing Edward – proclamation, teaching and nurturing new believers

Edward was the second child of Vicky and Stephen, a couple living in one of the largest houses, with tennis courts and extensive grounds. Vicky was a churchgoer and brought her children to church most Sundays, but Stephen, who worked long hours in London and was often away on business, did not feel connected to church and did not attend. Vicky joined a baptism preparation group which included other parents from the team churches, and Stephen came along to those meetings when he was back early enough.

As the date of the baptism grew nearer there was a renewed interest in the village because children were so far and few between, and so a baptism was quite a novelty event. More and more people began to wonder about it, some with the hope that there would be a big party but others enquiring about what the baptism preparation meetings were about. Although Vicky was 'the churchy one', people also just as eagerly asked Stephen about the forthcoming baptism and, as a result, Stephen began to feel more included in village life.

On the day of the baptism Stephen's father arrived in a gold Rolls Royce which was parked in the lane next to the church and created a huge stir in itself, with many of the younger people coming out to look at it and admire it, including some from the outlying villages who had been alerted by friends. This phenomenon led even more people to come and see what was happening, so that by the time of the service a crowd of people, in addition to Vicky's and Stephen's family, were coming into the church.

Edward was baptized in the family's christening gown, which had been worn by several generations of the family's babies. The parish priest made a comment about this during the service and afterwards made the ancient baptismal records available so that local people could look through and find *their* ancestors. A number of the villagers had generations of ancestors who had been baptized in the church, so this caused quite a stir of interest and discussion. After this, there was a gathering at Vicky's and Stephen's house for a party, where Stephen's father thanked the community and the parishioners for their welcome, interest and hospitality and gave the parish priest a large donation for the work of the church.

At the next Parochial Church Council (PCC) meeting it was decided that part of the donation should be given to a women's group in the village to establish a sewing circle. The money would pay for canvas, wool and silks so that the sewing circle could produce new tapestry kneelers, a heavy door curtain to keep out punishing draughts and other furnishings for the church. A small fee was paid to a sewing expert who came to teach beginners embroidery skills, and because it was free the sewing circle began then to attract more and more people into the group, many of whom were not church-goers. The group began with eight people and swelled to 20, ten of whom came from outside the village. Five of those people came from other Christian denominations and were delighted to make other Christian friends.

The interest in the baptismal records also led to the formation of a history society, with volunteers transcribing some of the handwritten records to make them more accessible and to protect the originals. This led to a group of enthusiasts coming together focused on the church, and talks from the university genealogy society on how to trace a family tree. This was interesting because it gave greater prominence to some local families who had felt rather eclipsed by wealthy incomers, but who were able to talk about the history and heritage of the village and its church as belonging to them and as stakeholders for its future.

The story of the baptism with its gold Rolls Royce, party and donation, continued to circulate until it reached almost mythic status. One result of this was that people stopped Stephen whenever they saw him to talk about it and to say that they remembered the baptism as a marvellous event. A year after Edward was baptized, the parish priest visited the family with a card and to say prayers in their home. Stephen said then that he felt he would like to become more committed in order to support his wife and sons in their Christian life and because he had enjoyed baptism preparation. He therefore decided that the next step would be for him to be confirmed. After this Stephen became a full-time member of the church community, despite his long hours in the city, taking a full role in the PCC and becoming churchwarden.

What is interesting about this story is how mission outworking resulted from a single sacramental event. For many clergy baptism becomes routine when baptisms take place often, but in a tiny village with few children this baptism became not only special but a catalyst for renewed interest in the church and what it had to offer. What is especially noticeable is that the baptism preparation process, although taking place elsewhere, fed back into the community so that both Vicky and Stephen were sharing their faith after they had had the chance to explore it with other parents. This means that preparation for the sacraments can equip people not only to understand and respond to the occasional offices, but also equip them for evangelism and faith-sharing in a meaningful way. In this case the process of teaching and nurture became the occasion for proclamation, *both* through the 'committed' church person and the enquiring and uncertain agnostic. This process in turn tied them more firmly into the village community and enabled that community to share in their public witness of the Christian life they wanted for their child.

While the baptism preparation and its news energized more people in the community over the period before the baptism, it is also noticeable that something as mundane as a christening gown could open up a link to another kind of important witness: the history of the place and the generations of worshippers who had proclaimed their faith there. The link between the gravestones in the church-yard, the names in the baptismal register and the local families de-scended from those ancestors confirmed a sense of the church as the centre and pillar of the village community. It also emphasized it as a living centre of Christian faith here and now, building on the traditions and Christian heritage of those who had lived in the village in generations past. When the history society became estab-lished it focused a good deal of energy on those who had died in war, with the result that more or less the whole village turned out on Remembrance Day and became involved in the procession from the war memorial to the church. Remembrance Day also thereafter became one of the special days when the 'regulars' turned out once a year.

If the simplicity of the family christening gown was one catalyst for focus on the church and its history, something as extraordinary as a gold Rolls Royce, never before seen and unlikely to be seen again, also drew people into the event. Just as wedding couples often choose vintage cars or 'special' forms of transport, so people were attracted by the idea that something 'special' was going on and wanted to be part of it. From the initial event, with its opportunity for both hospitality and giving, two new church/community soci-eties were formed extending the links and bonds between church-goers and non-churchgoing villagers. As *Faith in the Countryside* commented:

> in the village, evangelism takes place through personal and family relationships rather than through crowded rallies. Furthermore, the character of the evangelist is as important as either the mes-sage or its presentation. In the village one is known and 'no se-crets are hid'. Therefore integrity is the key, together with a slow, gradual 'softly, softly' approach. (p. 266)

This observation is particularly apposite in understanding the mis-sion importance of Edward's baptism since it is possible to see the baptism in the scriptural sense of preparing the way of the Lord. The focus in baptism preparation often tends to be on making sure the parents understand what they are asking for their child, teaching them about the promises and what they mean and preparing them for the sacramental event itself. What happens after that tends to be oriented to the duties of parents and godparents in bringing up the child in faith. What can be easily overlooked is the *mission* focus of baptism in the sense that the Baptist meant in calling people to begin to change their lives (Mark 1.1–5). In this case baptism was a preparatory experience for the parent, tilling the soil of his own spirituality and sowing a seed which needed time to mature and grow. The baptism of his child prepared Stephen for the Lord's entrance into his life. Moreover, it was also surely a factor in his spiritual growth, that he was urged by the community to share his experiences of the journey and so became an evangelist, not out of immediate conviction but by being on a journey. This too is often overlooked in an understanding of mission. Effective evangelists do not always have to have the conviction and passion of those secure in faith. People struggling in discipleship, like the disciples themselves, trying to work out who Jesus is for *them,* also have much to offer in terms of proclamation and witness.

Faith in the Countryside also remarked that: 'The challenge of evangelism is how to develop the faith of those whose response is behavioural and not yet worshipful' (p. 243). A final significant factor in this continuing nurture of the family was the action of remembering the baptism anniversary and the use of a simple home liturgy to offer prayers and thanksgiving for the child and the family. This was also mission activity, nurturing the family in faith and exploring faith together over time, so allowing Stephen the space to reflect on his experiences and to come to a decision. While the role of the parish priest was important in allowing Stephen the opportunity to ask for further help to become integrated into the church, the role of the villagers, churchgoers and non-churchgoers alike, was also important, keeping the memory of the baptism event alive, asking after the child and providing positive feedback about the experience. The nurturing of Stephen as a new believer, as well as his child, was therefore instrumental in helping him make a commitment to being an active participant in the church.

Marrying Jane and Nicky – loving service

Jane and Nicky were both farm workers and well known in the village. Both came from families with a history of genetic disorders and both had moderate learning difficulties. Jane's brother Robbie was particularly disabled and unable to communicate, but the families were much loved by the villagers. Although Jane was bullied at school and taunted about her brother, within the village community the family was accepted, understood and cared for. This was perhaps because there was a high level of illness, disability and difficulty among many of the elderly in the village, including Charles, a quadriplegic who, with his wife, made his home available for many village events. This meant that villagers were used to people who had to struggle with wheelchairs or who were reliant on others, and so Jane and Nicky were not considered unusual and Robbie was not subject to 'Does he take sugar?' attitudes, even though they regularly experienced this outside the village.

Faith in the Countryside noted:

> The division between Church and Community is necessarily blurred. The difficult question is how one can live an openly Christian life in a way that does not alienate those who do not share the faith, but attracts through interest into commitment to Christ. (p. 243)

This question is addressed by the response shown by both congregation and community as they committed themselves to the couple's wedding. When Jane and Nicky announced their engagement and forthcoming marriage in the local church the event was quickly gossiped around the village. Jane and Nicky and their families had very little money so the farm owner, their employer, mobilized friends and neighbours in the community to help out. Shortly after the engagement was announced the marriage turned into a village event that was planned for and celebrated for months by church and community working together.

Jane's dress was made by the sewing circle from some rolls of white satin that were donated by Sasha, a set designer for the BBC who lived locally. The church crèche organizers decided to recruit their usual children (about three in total) to help with 'the wedding' preparation, but since three was not enough, non-churchgoing children were also invited to come along and be part of the wedding preparation, and events were organized in the village hall. Some of the older children sewed beads and sequins on the dress and veil and went to all Jane's fittings, while smaller children made confetti, keepsakes and place cards. Inevitably, the non-churchgoing children also wanted to come to the wedding to see the fruits of their labours.

The organist sat with Jane and Robbie singing through various hymns until Jane felt able to choose hymns that Robbie liked and would not shout at when he heard them. They chose 'All things bright and beautiful' and 'Lord of all Hopefulness'. The flowers, food and drink for the party afterwards, a room in the village hall, donations from the local pub, parking and all the small details were taken care of by villagers in consultation with the family. The local thatcher, responsible usually for mending and restoring roofs on expensive houses, made a number of thatched decorations for the porch of the church. The farmer's son, Donald, even decided to surprise the couple by flying his microlite with a celebratory banner around the village on the day. Jane's family had no telephone, so messages were often carried by dog walkers carrying information and requests back and forth. The two existing bell ringers living in the village asked around for more ringers to help them ring the complete set of six bells for the event, tempted by the offer of free drinks in the pub afterwards.

The only hitch in the proceedings, which had involved the co-operation of just about everybody in the village, was that on the day Robbie, who had become especially attached to a new pet goldfish, roundly refused to leave the house without it. In the end Robbie arrived in the church, complete with goldfish in a bowl, and the parish priest was able to mention it in his wedding sermon and invite the family to help Robbie bring the fish up for a blessing.

Again this single event had a number of outcomes which were significant to the idea of mission as loving service. For example, the wedding photographer, a local man who had a shop in the university city, put some pictures in his shop window of the smiling couple with Robbie in his wheelchair (with their permission), and later reported that he had had a number of enquiries from families with disabled family members, not only about photography, but about managing family events for people with disabilities in particular. Those families had only ever seen pictures of perfect couples standing in idyllic settings before, and the photographs of real people coming from less than perfect lives celebrating their happiness as a family made a deep impression. The wedding planners in the village responded by putting together a list of items to think about when organizing events, to make sure people with disabilities were properly included, and later wrote a recipe book which was sold throughout the team ministry area in aid of a disabilities charity.

Jane's and Nicky's wedding was particularly fruitful in bringing church and community together. The way in which the loving service was administered was particularly important in making this a truly mission-oriented event. In particular the integrity and dignity of the couple and their families was nurtured, not through any conscious sense of how they should be treated but emerging naturally from their role and status in the small rural community. They were fully involved and consulted and continually placed at the centre of 'the wedding', and more than once Jane commented that she was 'Princess Di' in the village. On the day they were the proper centre and focus of the marriage ceremony, and so many villagers attended that most had to stand outside. Yet the community involvement brought many people into church to see the culmination of their effort and energy working together.

When Jesus attended the wedding in Cana (John 2.1–11), he came as a guest and performed an extraordinary miracle, a sign of God's power so that God might be glorified. When his mother alerts him to a problem with the hospitality ('they have no wine'), he combines a powerful sign with both service and bounty. His attention is not on the couple but on the whole wedding party, who will be disappointed when the wine runs out. He did not draw attention to himself or even attempt to change or run the show, merely advising the servants to draw the water which, when it was tasted by the steward, became the best wine of the party. The way that this piece of scripture works itself out shows that God's power is evident through the co-operation and outworking of community. Mary saw what was needed and asked Jesus to help, the servants obeyed, the steward tasted the wine, drew the bridegroom's attention to the wonderful gift, and through this interplay of roles and relationships God was glorified. But the bridegroom and bride were still the focus of the event and Jesus remained a guest. It can be argued that this is at the heart of all mission as loving service: through having Jesus present and underpinning human endeavour, the community can be uplifted in such as way as to glorify God more effectively. It is possible to see this process deeply at work in Jane's and Nicky's wedding as their boss noticed what they needed, villagers took on roles to make the couple happy and effected a transformation that glorified God through the celebration of the marriage. Moreover, just as Jesus' sign confirmed the disciples' faith, so the closeness of the community and its relationship to the church spread beyond the village into the lives of other families in the surrounding area and the university city. Loving service therefore also tells its story and evangelizes others.

Mickey's funeral – to challenge unjust structures, care of creation

Mickey was a widow who was one of the village's longest established residents. She had been a military officer's wife, but on his death was left more or less penniless. Because she was extremely proud, others in the village contrived to make sure she was cared for by inviting her for meals most days of the week. In a village which enjoyed dinner-party culture and a great deal of mutual hospitality, this was reasonably easy to arrange. Mickey knew quite well that they were doing this, but still went for the meals, always bringing something to the table like warm rolls or flowers from her garden. She liked to be active and outdoors so she had taken it upon herself to go round the entire village every day picking up litter, becoming the scourge of anyone seen littering and occasionally rescuing any animals or birds she found injured, which she would then take home and nurse. This led to many people bringing her animals to see if she could help until she was more or less a one-woman animal hospital for frogs, ducks and baby birds. This meant that Mickey was extremely well known in the village and became its official, if eccentric, spokesperson. She was fiercely protective of the village and its inhabitants, including Jane and Nicky, and was not above 'sorting people out' when she felt the village was under threat or its inhabitants were out of line. She campaigned tirelessly against the loss of the small local post office and shop until, despite her best efforts, it closed, then she ran the village newsletter with another elderly lady and posted all the copies herself. When the village realized that one of the houses for sale had been bought by a gay couple (literally the only gays in the village), there was some shock and muttering from some of the older residents who didn't know how to cope with the incomers and their lifestyle. Mickey made it very clear to Cal and David that she could not understand or condone their lifestyle ('I'm *far* too old to understand this sort of caper'), but she took it upon herself to champion the couple to the village, bringing them with her to her dinner invitations, stamping on gossip, berating anybody she heard making a joke or crude remark and bringing them to church.

Mickey faithfully came to church every Sunday and to every church event, although she would not participate in the service by reading or leading prayers and she would not take communion. She was a lover of the Book of Common Prayer and constantly moaned about 'modern' services. However, she was excellent at bringing people with her into church and getting them to be part of the service. Cal was soon actively engaged in making the church run smoothly on Sunday as well as organizing drinks after church for the congregation. Mickey was also instrumental in getting Ben, a lecturer at the university and a dedicated non-believer, not only into the church but also to change his mind about religion. She simply put on her most eccentric manner and nagged him until he agreed to go with her and have a look. Once there, he found he enjoyed the worship, especially Evensong, and so he stayed. From then on they came together and sat together: 'the sinner and the atheist' as she put it.

Mickey was always seen around the village on her bike, since she did not own a car and had to cycle eight miles to the next village if she wanted to shop for herself. When Mickey fell ill she tried to continue to manage, but without a bus service or available medical care she had to go into hospital in a town 12 miles away, where it was discovered she was suffering from an advanced cancer. For a while friends from the village made trips to see her and the parish priest took her communion (which she received), but the village itself began to suffer without the familiarity of her active energy. Eventually it was agreed that it would be best for all if Mickey came home, and people rallied round to provide her with round-the-clock care. The Macmillan nurses who also came to look after her were quickly accepted into the community and they too came to church to pray for her. Eventually Mickey returned to the hospital when it became impossible to manage her pain, but still everyone came to see her. After a final visit from the parish priest, she asked a friend to go outside and shut the door and not let anyone in for half an hour. When the friend returned with Ben to see her, Mickey had died.

Mickey's death threw the whole village community into grief and mourning and there was much discussion about how such a life could be celebrated. The problem was that while the community wanted to give thanks for all she had done for the village she had loved so passionately, there was also the matter of acknowledging the loss not only of a loved and respected person, but of one of the church's and community's energizers, the 'soul' of the village as the parish priest put it. In the days that followed her death the community seemed to continue in a kind of shock at her passing, and with people avoiding her empty cottage. The matter was solved by having a funeral and a memorial which included both church and community. The funeral service in church was small and quiet at her own request, but the wake in the village hall was

attended not only by her friends and neighbours and a throng of
villagers but also by people who arrived with animals – dogs, cats,
even a hedgehog – that Mickey had helped with. The parish priest
said prayers here too, and people told their favourite stories about
life with her. While the wake was in progress the church was left
open for people to sit quietly if they wanted to, light a candle, or
shed a tear in peace. At the next PCC meeting, however, it was
agreed that the best tribute to Mickey would be to continue with
her work – making sure there were volunteers to care for the cleanliness and appearance of the village and that people knew who to
contact if they had an injured animal.

Faith in the Countryside asked: 'how does organized religion
touch and help seekers who are not attracted enough to test it for
themselves? A seeker in a small rural church cannot test the service
without being obvious' (p. 245). Mickey answered that question by
not only witnessing to others but accompanying them when they
responded to her energetic evangelism. She was not an 'orthodox'
Christian herself, but this also made her an attractive person to be
with and easier for people like Ben to come into church services
without being overly obvious. Mickey also witnessed to a care and
love for the creation in her care for the appearance of the village
and her care for its animals and birds. Although she was elderly
and poor she nonetheless had a profound effect on the community through her visibility and her energy, and this was apparent
from the intense emotion of the whole community at her funeral.
As *Faith in the Countryside* observed:

> indeed, while the Gospel is deeply personal, it is never individualis-
> tic. It recognizes both the interrelatedness of all humanity and also
> the corporateness of human society which is as much in need of
> redemption and liberation as is the individual person. (p. 264)

This was the arena in which Mickey excelled. In many ways she
was a prophetic figure, often saying uncomfortable, even outra-
geous, things such as lecturing an adult dinner-party group, including Cal and David, on the importance of sexual faithfulness and
the dangers of AIDS, and prophetic actions such as putting a set

of plastic can holders on a fence post with a stern note about the dangers to ducks.

The funeral, in this case, was also a particularly important event for the village and one which it was necessary to get right. The community had to be given space to mourn its loss without turning the dead person into a saint, or leaving things to collapse with her passing. One of the most important aspects of the funeral and its aftermath was to identify and continue the mission legacy that Mickey left behind her, a process which was started in the celebration of her life in the village hall among the people and animals whose lives she had touched. There is a delicate balance between closure and continuity which it can be easy to misunderstand, tipping people either into over-idealization or a sense of ennui because the dead person is not there to make things happen.

We can learn more of this from the actions of Jesus after the death of John the Baptist. In Mark (1.14–15) Jesus responds by picking up John's message and making sure it is not lost. There is continuity of the gospel demand to make known what God wants for his people. In Matthew, Jesus is seen withdrawing to a quiet place presumably to digest this news, pray and consider its implications for his own mission and ministry. But when the people hear the news of John's death, they seek out Jesus and he responds to their needs, curing the sick and feeding them in another miracle (Matthew 14.13–21; Luke 9.10–17). In Luke, this response to the death of a prophetic personality to whom people had looked to defy the authorities and show them how to live, leads to a clearer understanding for the disciples that Jesus is the Messiah of God (Luke 9.18–20). There are therefore powerful missiological possibilities in the response to death, and these were seen in the aftermath of Mickey's death: continuity with her good work, response to the physical and emotional needs of the community and an understanding that she created spaces in which Jesus could be seen more clearly.

Conclusion

Occasional offices in rural churches provide narratives which can generate powerful mission opportunities. Clergy can facilitate, provide direction and root the congregation in worship, but rural laity can carry the gospel everywhere. People do what they do best: inspiring, remembering, repeating, celebrating, creating kingdom pictures for others to inhabit. Mission is much more inclusive in the rural church than it is often given credit for, and depends on deeper readings of surface information that can easily be dismissed. For example, when people in the next village along from Sotton heard the story of the Rolls Royce in the lane, they first saw it as an expression of arrogance and snobbishness from the rich village down the road. In similar fashion the blessing of the goldfish might be superficially seen as a means of pandering to a disabled child to stop him disrupting the service, and Mickey might be seen as an eccentric old lady who made a life out of campaigning for hopeless causes because she was one herself. It takes a much more personal and pastoral engagement with the Christian lives of people in rural areas to see how closely they live the gospel narrative and how this works itself out in the people they touch. As *Faith in the Countryside* says:

> For the rural Church these opposites are expressed as the gathered church, a light to shine out for the gospel; and alternatively as a community church, the salt within the whole life of the parish. It may often be more appropriate to use another analogy used by Jesus: the faithful as the leaven in the lump. (p. 257)

In these three stories of a baptism, a wedding and a funeral, it is possible to see the Isaiah vision quoted by Jesus at the beginning of his ministry being implemented (Isaiah 61.1–2; 58.6 in Luke 4.18–19). The poor can be raised up and the needy supported; those imprisoned or oppressed by work, wealth, 'difference' or disability can be released into community and friendship. These actions of raising up and releasing people as neighbours and friends is a particular potential of small rural communities and has tremendous mission potential for nurturing faith and making spaces for that faith to be expressed and to grow.

Why doesn't the Church at large make more of the mission potential of rural churches? It is perhaps because many rural narratives of church life are seen as problematic (and many of them *are* problematic). These are narratives of survival, maintenance, tiny numbers, elderly congregations, 'basic' services, deployment issues and financial constraints; yet we talk of 'successful' mission in terms of growth and flourishing leading to church planting, large numbers of committed Christians forming outreach groups, churches attractive to mixed congregations and young people, a variety of services and events reaching out to different communities and financial growth and backing for evangelism. A problem then arises when we believe our own myths: if a church does not have these markers of 'success' and opportunity then it cannot be a missionary church. Yet this is to forget that *God*'s mission is at work everywhere and the fact of continued, faithful worship and Christian life, irrespective of numbers or other constraints, is meaningful in every context. Not all fruits look the same, but we have become accustomed to seeing a particular kind of outcome as mission fruit and overlooking fruits which continue to be formed and nurtured in the rural context. For *God*, all such fruit is part of the harvest.

Today, Stephen is still active in the village church and his latest child was recently baptized. Jane and Nicky also have children who come to the church crèche. Amanda makes sure any litter is collected from the hedgerows and Ben still comes to Evensong. Christmas and Harvest are packed out with regulars, who come once a year. From the outside Sotton is a tiny, struggling congregation; inside it is thriving.

Reference

Archbishops' Commission on Rural Areas, 1990, *Faith in the Countryside*, Worthing: Churchman Publishing.

Note

1 For more information see: www.anglicancommunion.org/ministry/mission/fivemarks.cfm

Index